CULLEN BUNN

JUAN DOE

DARK ARK

VOLUME

1

RYANE HILL

DAVE SHARPE

DARK

ARK

VOLUME 1

FORTY NIGHTS

CULLEN BUNN creator & writer

JUAN DOE artist

RYANE HILL letterer issues #1-3, #5

DAVE SHARPE letterer issue #4

JUAN DOE front & original series covers

ANDY CLARKE w/ DAN BROWN, JUAN DOE, ELLIOT FERNANDEZ, PHIL HESTER w/ ERIC GAPSTUR & MIKE SPICER, NAT JONES, PATRICK OLLIFFE, MIKE ROOTH, BEN TEMPLESMITH, ALESSANDRO VITTI, LARRY WATTS variant covers

COREY BREEN book designer

JOHN J. HILL logo designer

MIKE MARTS editor

AFTERSHOCK

MIKE MARTS - Editor-in-Chief • JOE PRUETT - Publisher/ Chief Creative Officer • LEE KRAMER - President
JAWAD QURESHI - SVP, Investor Relations • JON KRAMER - Chief Executive Officer • MIKE ZAGARI - SVP, Brand
JAY BEHLING - Chief Financial Officer • STEPHAN NILSON - Publishing Operations Manager
LISA Y. WU - Retailer/Fan Relations Manager • ASHLEY WYATT - Publishing Assistant

AfterShock Trade Dress and Interior Design by JOHN J. HILL • AfterShock Logo Design by COMICRAFT
Original series production (issues 1-5) by CHARLES PRITCHETT • Proofreading by DOCTOR Z.
Publicity: contact AARON MARION (aaron@publichausagency.com) & RYAN CROY (ryan@publichausagency.com)
Special thanks to CHRIS LA TORRE, SVEN LARSEN, TEDDY LEO, LISA MOODY & KIM PAGNOTTA

DARK ARK VOL.1: FORTY NIGHTS Published by AfterShock Comics, LLC, 15300 Ventura Boulevard Suite 507, Sherman Oaks, CA 91403.

Originally published as Dark Ark #1-5. PRINTED IN KOREA.
Second Printing: February 2019. 10 9 8 7 6 5 4 3 2

AFTERSHOCKCOMICS.COM Follow us on social media

INTRODUCTION

This is a book I never imagined actually writing.

I think every writer has a handful of amusing ideas that they're always turning over in their head, more for their own enjoyment than anything else. These are absurd little ideas with weird hooks and oft-ridiculous titles. Among mine are "Werewolves on the Moon", and "Attack of the Attacking Sharks", and "Think Tank" (which is a story about the Creature from the Black Lagoon...only the Creature is the world's greatest detective). These aren't stories that I ever intended to be anything more than jokes I tell myself every now and then.

DARK ARK started out the same way.

I mean, no one is going to publish such a strange concept with such a ridiculous (and straight-to-the-point) title.

No one would be CRAZY enough to try.

Except that AfterShock WAS crazy enough.

They became interested in the story based on a very short pitch I had put together. It only gave the bare bones of the idea. "You know how Noah put all the animals on an Ark and rode out the flood? Well, what if there was another Ark, and it was full of all the monsters of the world?" There might have been more to it than that, but not much.

So, when we started talking about the idea in more detail, I had an important decision to make. Until that point, DARK ARK was sort of a goofy, funny little story I kept to myself. But if I was going to write it—I mean REALLY write it—did I want to do something more with it?

In the end, I decided to take the story a little more seriously and to explore some of the darker aspects of the monsters...and of the humans who tended them. If I was going to tell the tale, then I was going to pour as much heart and soul and tragedy and horror and monstrousness and humanity into it as possible. Sure, I kept some of the more absurd aspects of the story. The idea of unicorns being on the wrong Ark always amused me. But even the ridiculous aspects of the story would play out across a grim backdrop.

In short, DARK ARK is no longer a joke.

Except for when it is.

I'm glad I pushed the story into a different direction than was originally intended. If this is your first time reading about Shrae, Khalee, Orin, Janris, Kruul, Nex and all the others, I hope you enjoy the ride.

But AfterShock was still crazy to greenlight this story.

CULLEN BUNN
February 2018

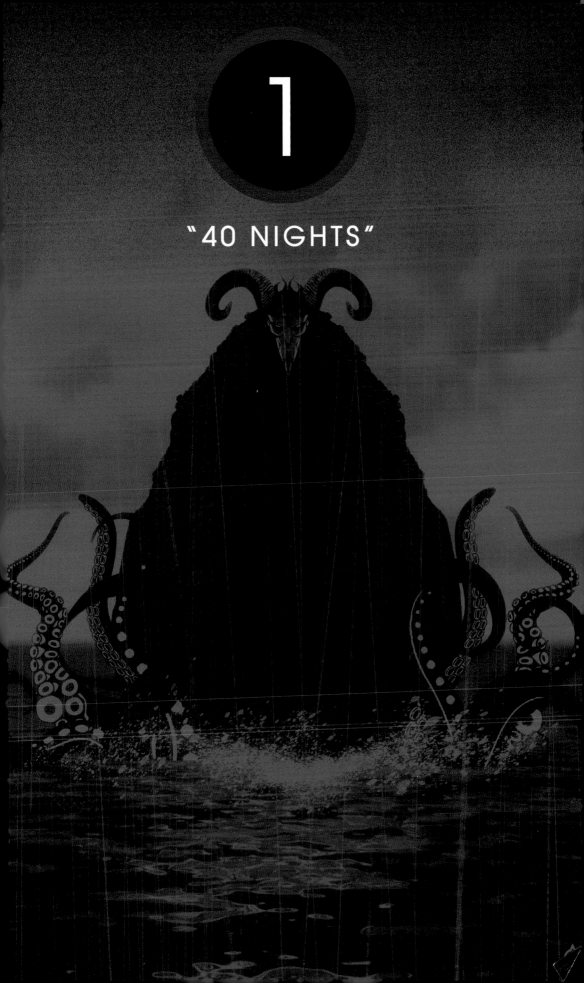

1

"40 NIGHTS"

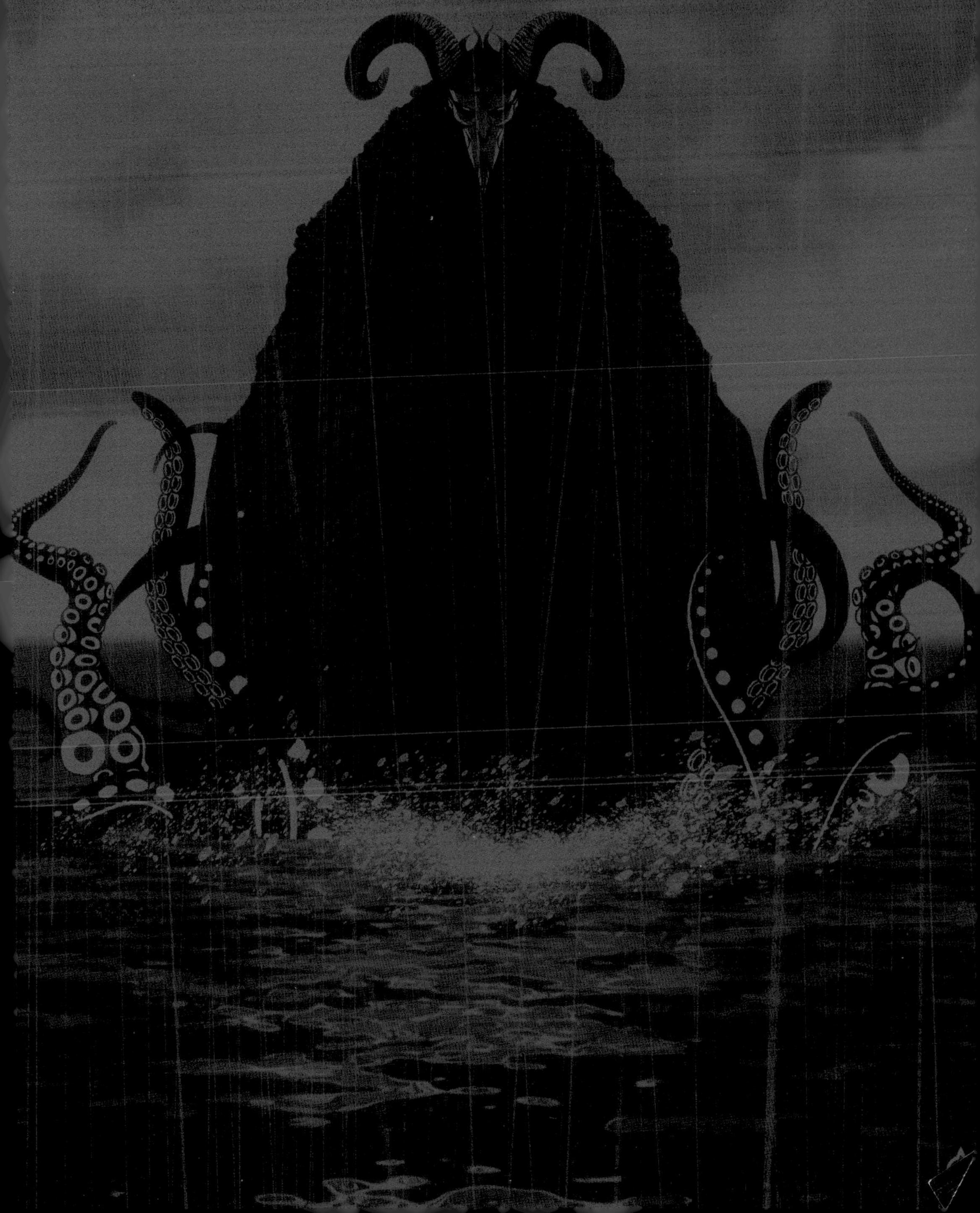

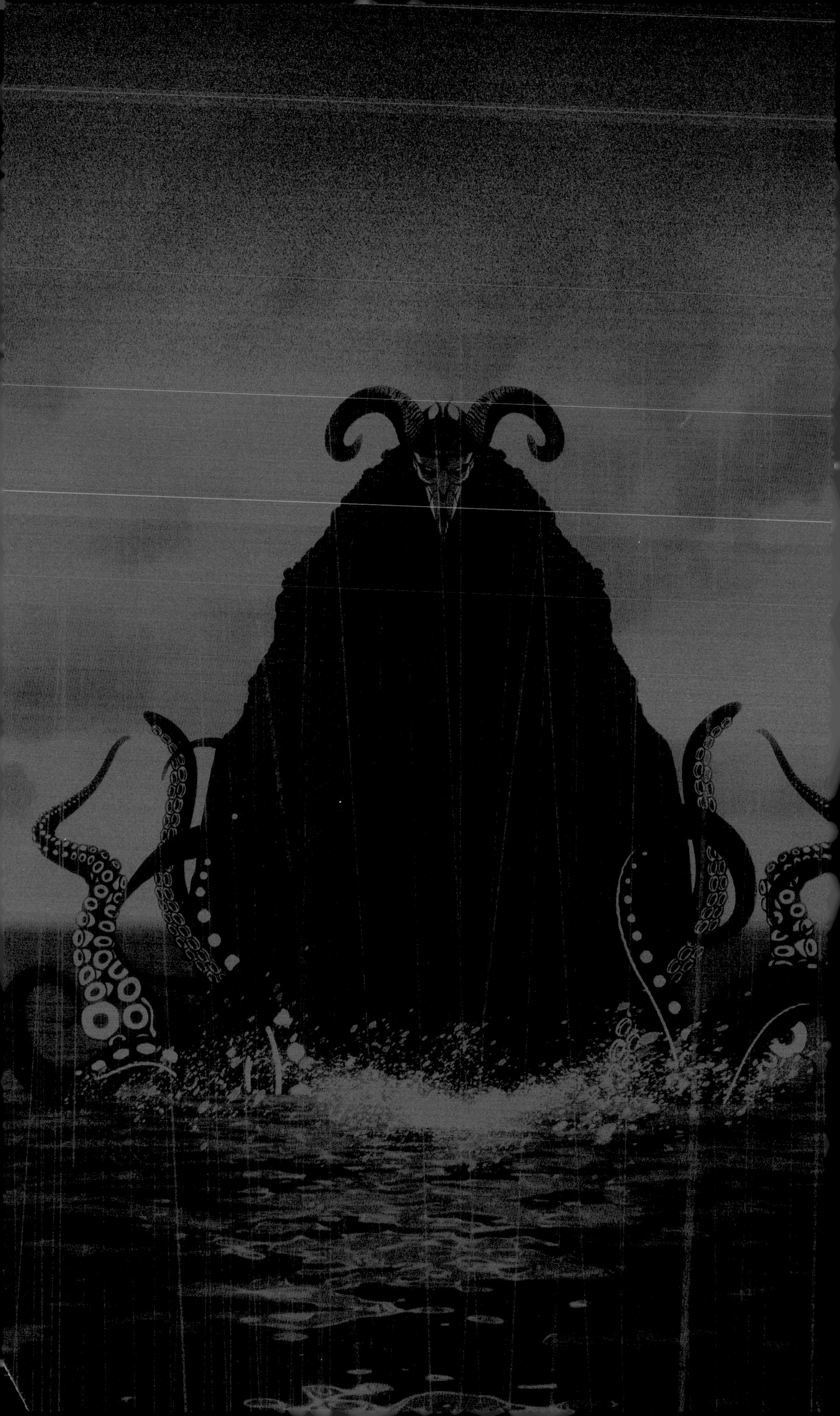

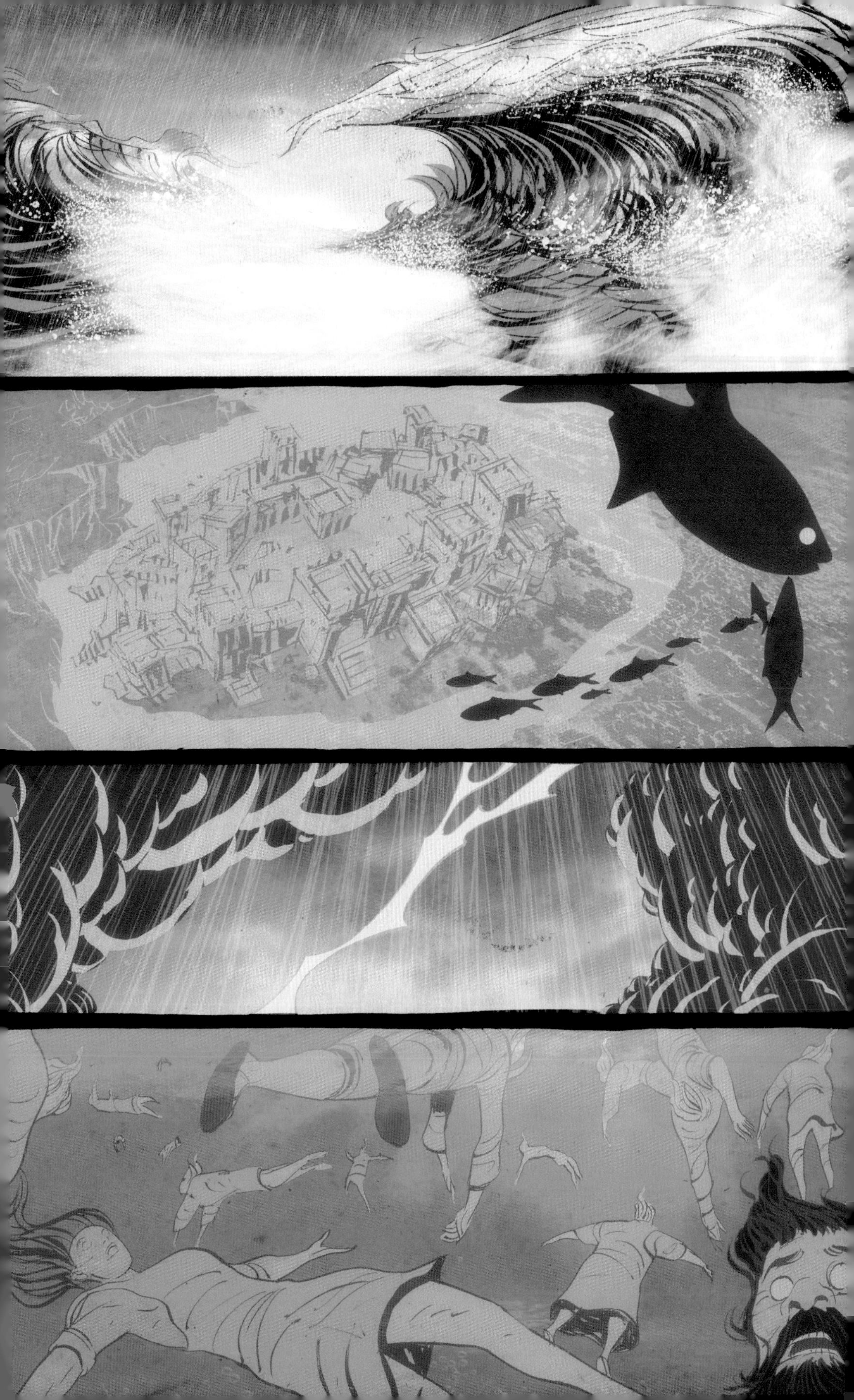

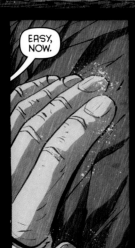

EASY, NOW.

NOTHING FOR YOU TO FEAR.

JUST THE RAIN.

IT PLAYS TRICKS ON *ALL* OF US.

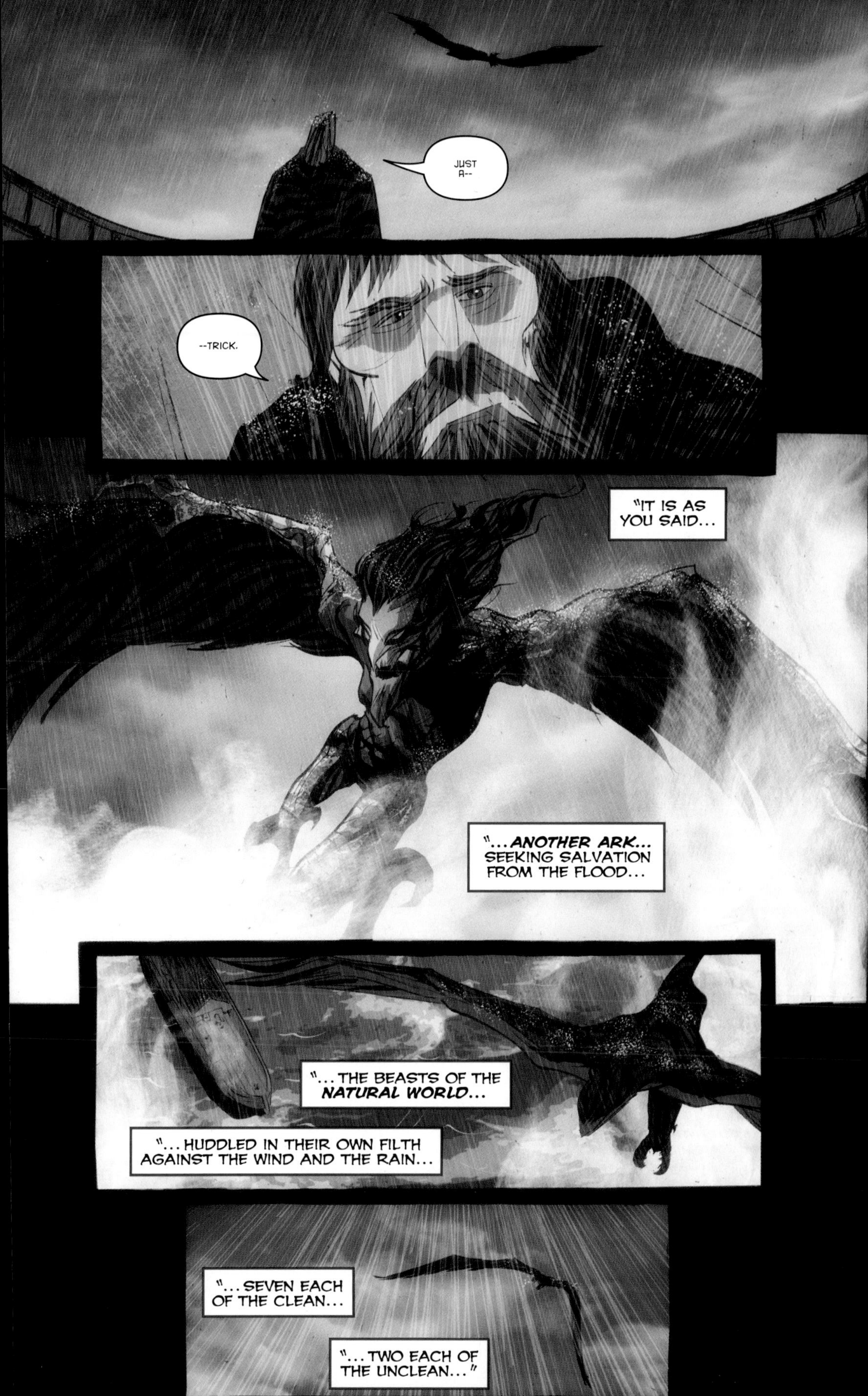
JUST A--
--TRICK.
"IT IS AS YOU SAID...
"...ANOTHER ARK... SEEKING SALVATION FROM THE FLOOD...
"...THE BEASTS OF THE NATURAL WORLD...
"...HUDDLED IN THEIR OWN FILTH AGAINST THE WIND AND THE RAIN...
"...SEVEN EACH OF THE CLEAN...
"...TWO EACH OF THE UNCLEAN..."

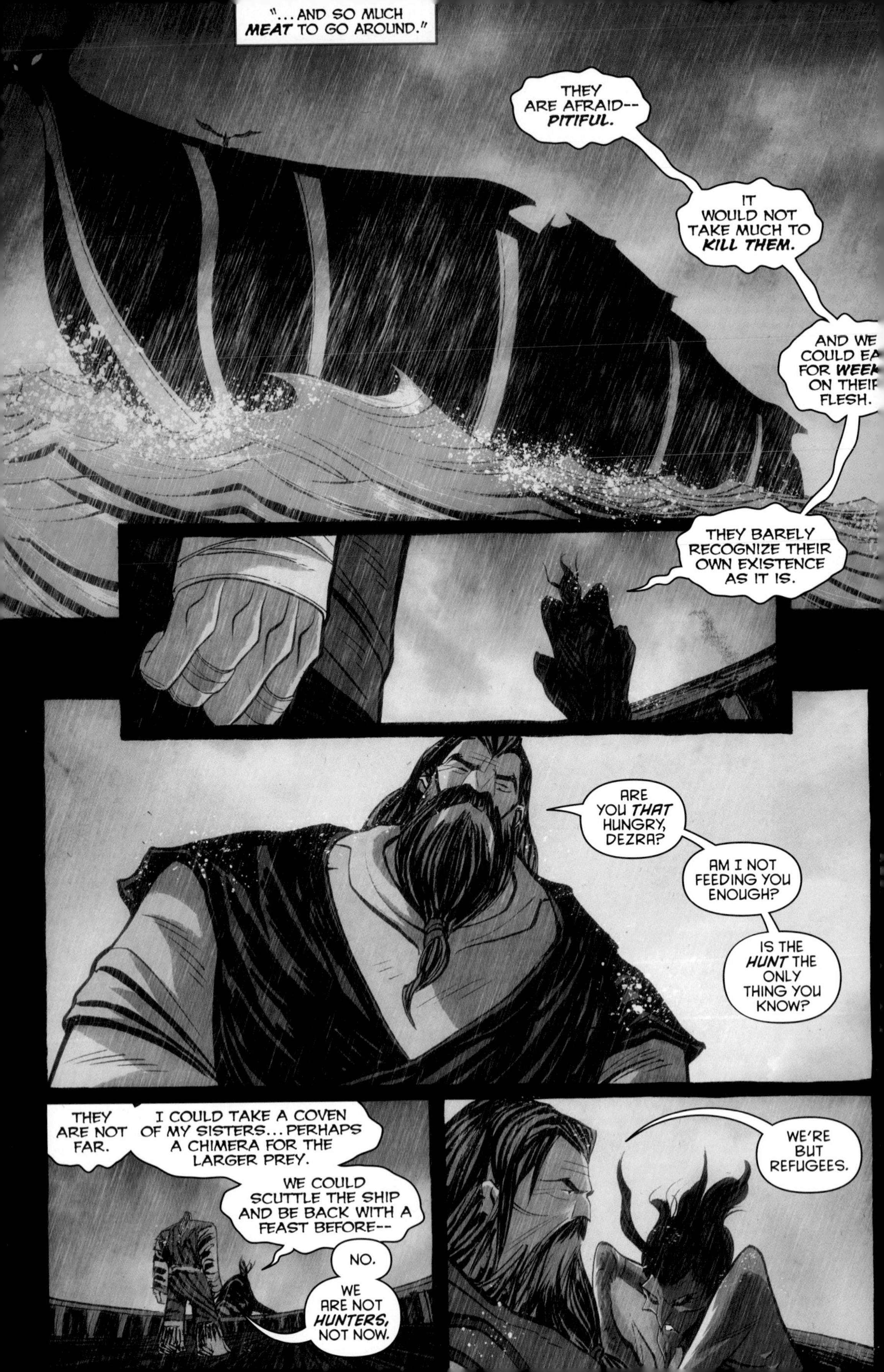
"... AND SO MUCH MEAT TO GO AROUND."
THEY ARE AFRAID-- PITIFUL.
IT WOULD NOT TAKE MUCH TO KILL THEM.
AND WE COULD EA FOR WEEK ON THEIR FLESH.
THEY BARELY RECOGNIZE THEIR OWN EXISTENCE AS IT IS.
ARE YOU THAT HUNGRY, DEZRA?
AM I NOT FEEDING YOU ENOUGH?
IS THE HUNT THE ONLY THING YOU KNOW?
THEY ARE NOT FAR.
I COULD TAKE A COVEN OF MY SISTERS... PERHAPS A CHIMERA FOR THE LARGER PREY.
WE COULD SCUTTLE THE SHIP AND BE BACK WITH A FEAST BEFORE--
NO.
WE ARE NOT HUNTERS, NOT NOW.
WE'RE BUT REFUGEES.

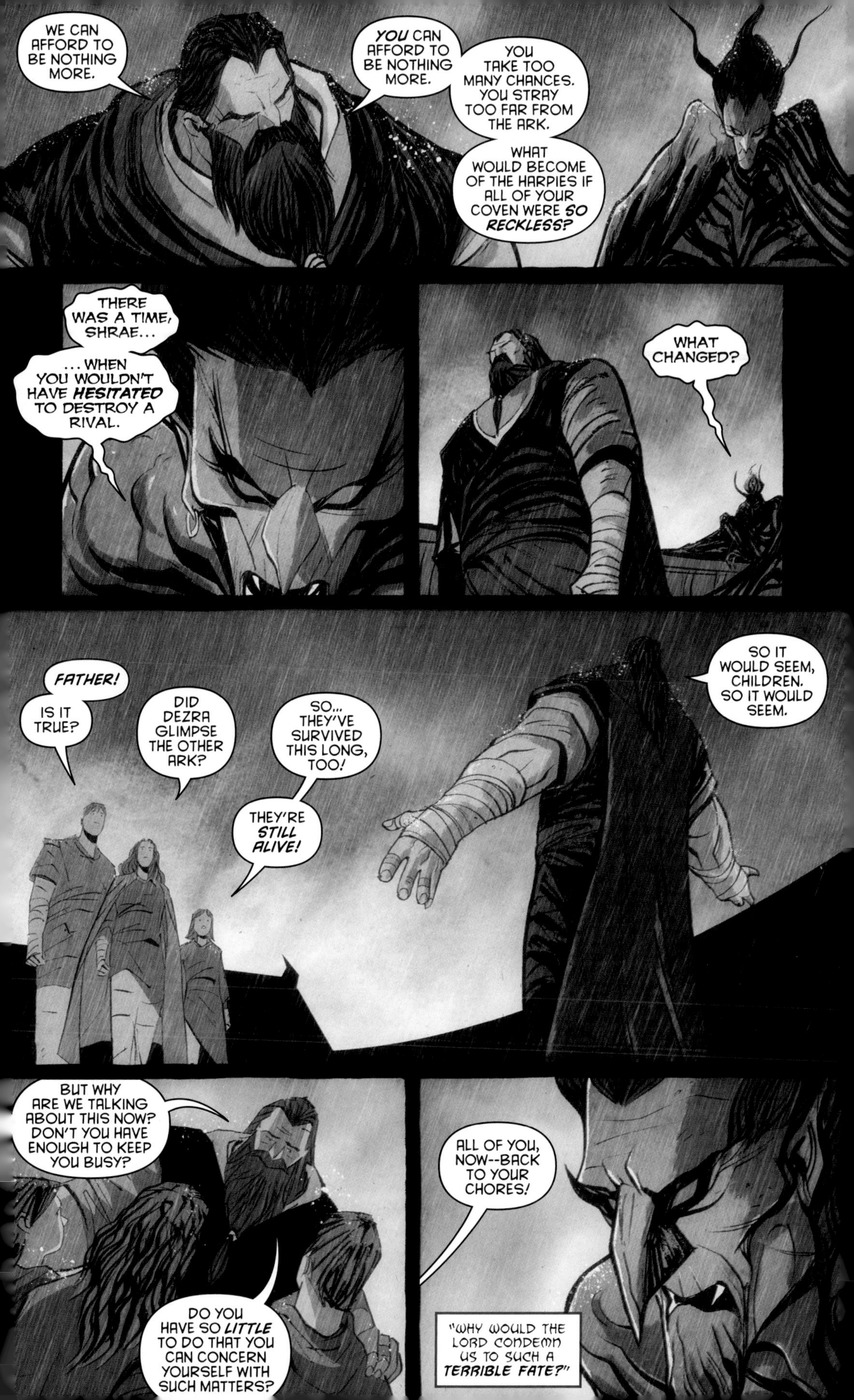
WE CAN AFFORD TO BE NOTHING MORE.
YOU CAN AFFORD TO BE NOTHING MORE.
YOU TAKE TOO MANY CHANCES. YOU STRAY TOO FAR FROM THE ARK.
WHAT WOULD BECOME OF THE HARPIES IF ALL OF YOUR COVEN WERE *SO RECKLESS?*
THERE WAS A TIME, SHRAE...
...WHEN YOU WOULDN'T HAVE *HESITATED* TO DESTROY A RIVAL.
WHAT CHANGED?
FATHER!
IS IT TRUE?
DID DEZRA GLIMPSE THE OTHER ARK?
SO... THEY'VE SURVIVED THIS LONG, TOO!
THEY'RE *STILL ALIVE!*
SO IT WOULD SEEM, CHILDREN. SO IT WOULD SEEM.
BUT WHY ARE WE TALKING ABOUT THIS NOW? DON'T YOU HAVE ENOUGH TO KEEP YOU BUSY?
DO YOU HAVE SO *LITTLE* TO DO THAT YOU CAN CONCERN YOURSELF WITH SUCH MATTERS?
ALL OF YOU, NOW--BACK TO YOUR CHORES!
"WHY WOULD THE LORD CONDEMN US TO SUCH A *TERRIBLE FATE?*"

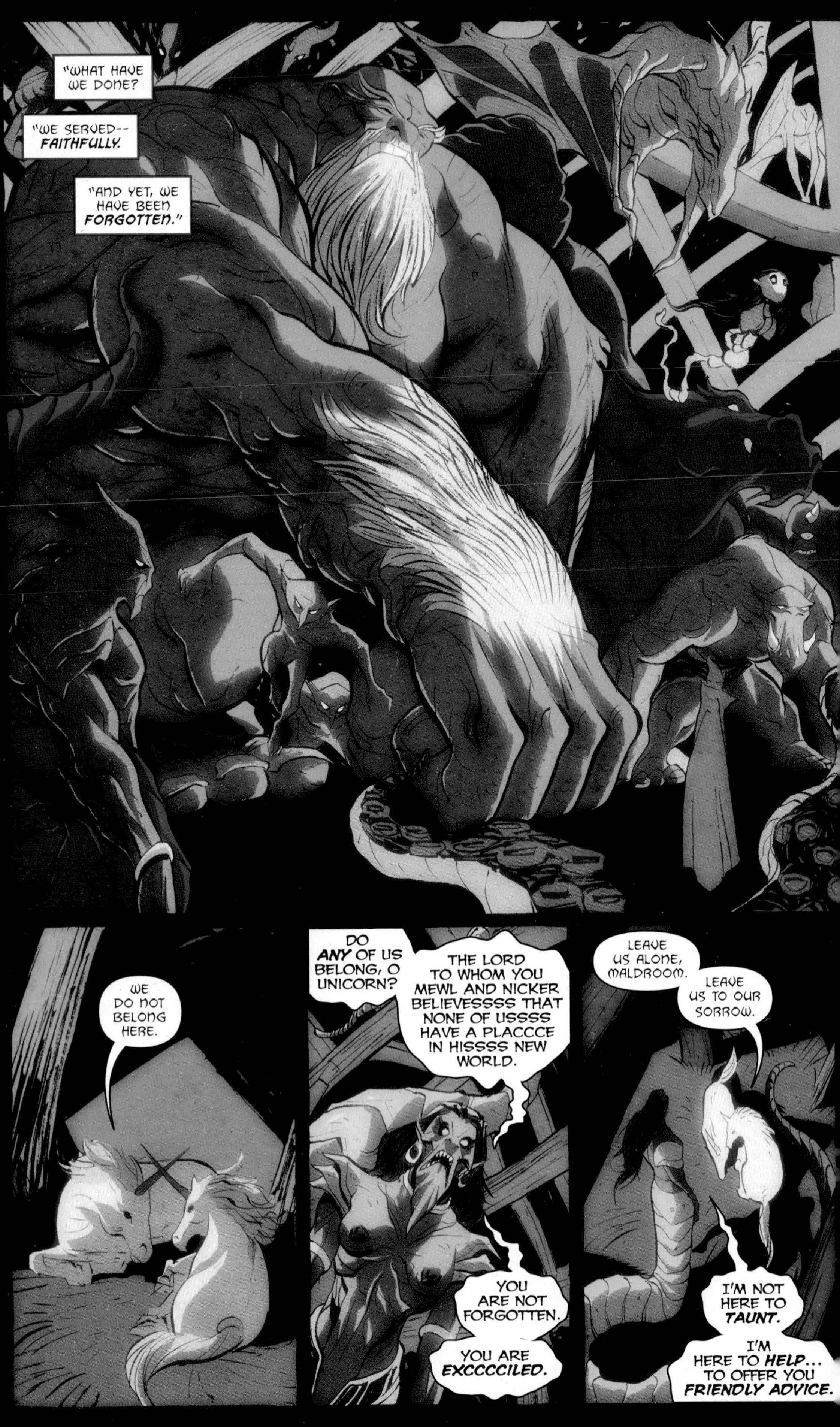
"WHAT HAVE WE DONE?
"WE SERVED-- FAITHFULLY.
"AND YET, WE HAVE BEEN FORGOTTEN."
WE DO NOT BELONG HERE.
DO ANY OF US BELONG, O UNICORN?
THE LORD TO WHOM YOU MEWL AND NICKER BELIEVESSSS THAT NONE OF USSSS HAVE A PLACCCE IN HISSSS NEW WORLD.
YOU ARE NOT FORGOTTEN.
YOU ARE EXCCCCILED.
LEAVE US ALONE, MALDROOM.
LEAVE US TO OUR SORROW.
I'M NOT HERE TO TAUNT.
I'M HERE TO HELP... TO OFFER YOU FRIENDLY ADVICE.

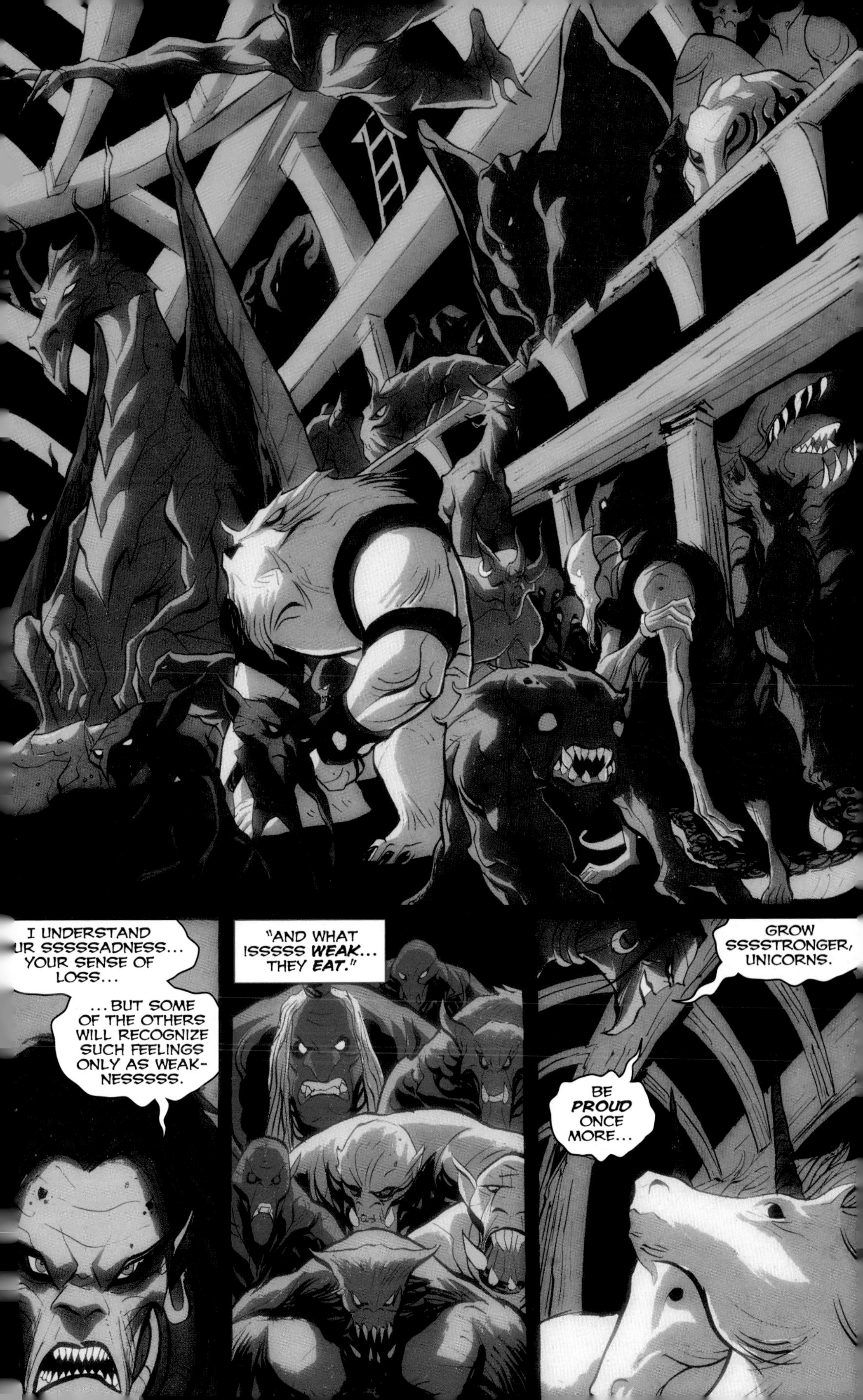
I UNDERSTAND UR SSSSSADNESS... YOUR SENSE OF LOSS...
...BUT SOME OF THE OTHERS WILL RECOGNIZE SUCH FEELINGS ONLY AS WEAK-NESSSSS.
"AND WHAT ISSSSS **WEAK**... THEY **EAT**."
GROW SSSSTRONGER, UNICORNS.
BE **PROUD** ONCE MORE...

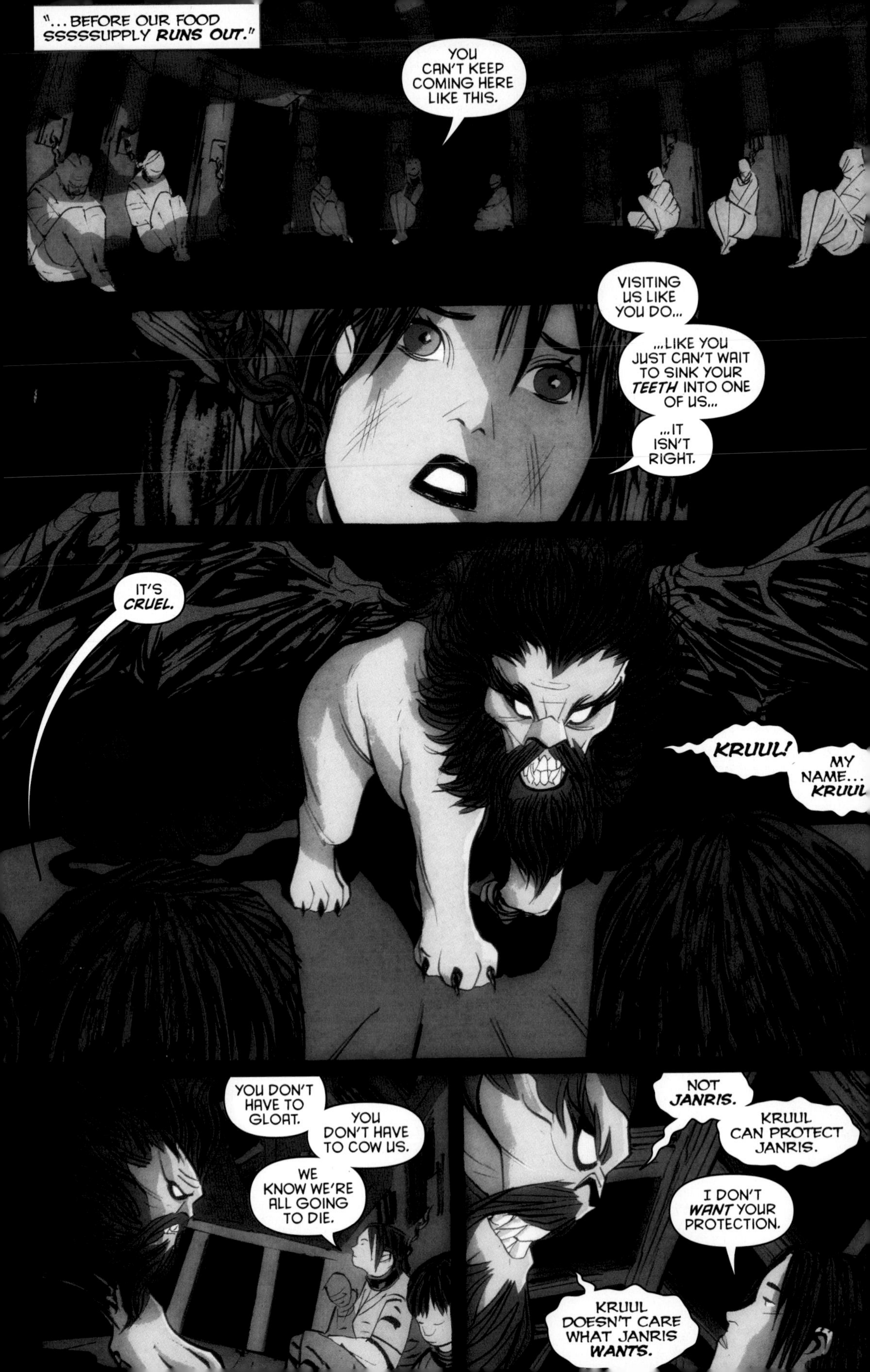
"... BEFORE OUR FOOD SSSSSUPPLY RUNS OUT."
YOU CAN'T KEEP COMING HERE LIKE THIS.
VISITING US LIKE YOU DO...
...LIKE YOU JUST CAN'T WAIT TO SINK YOUR TEETH INTO ONE OF US...
...IT ISN'T RIGHT.
IT'S CRUEL.
KRUUL!
MY NAME... KRUUL
YOU DON'T HAVE TO GLOAT.
YOU DON'T HAVE TO COW US.
WE KNOW WE'RE ALL GOING TO DIE.
NOT JANRIS.
KRUUL CAN PROTECT JANRIS.
I DON'T WANT YOUR PROTECTION.
KRUUL DOESN'T CARE WHAT JANRIS WANTS.

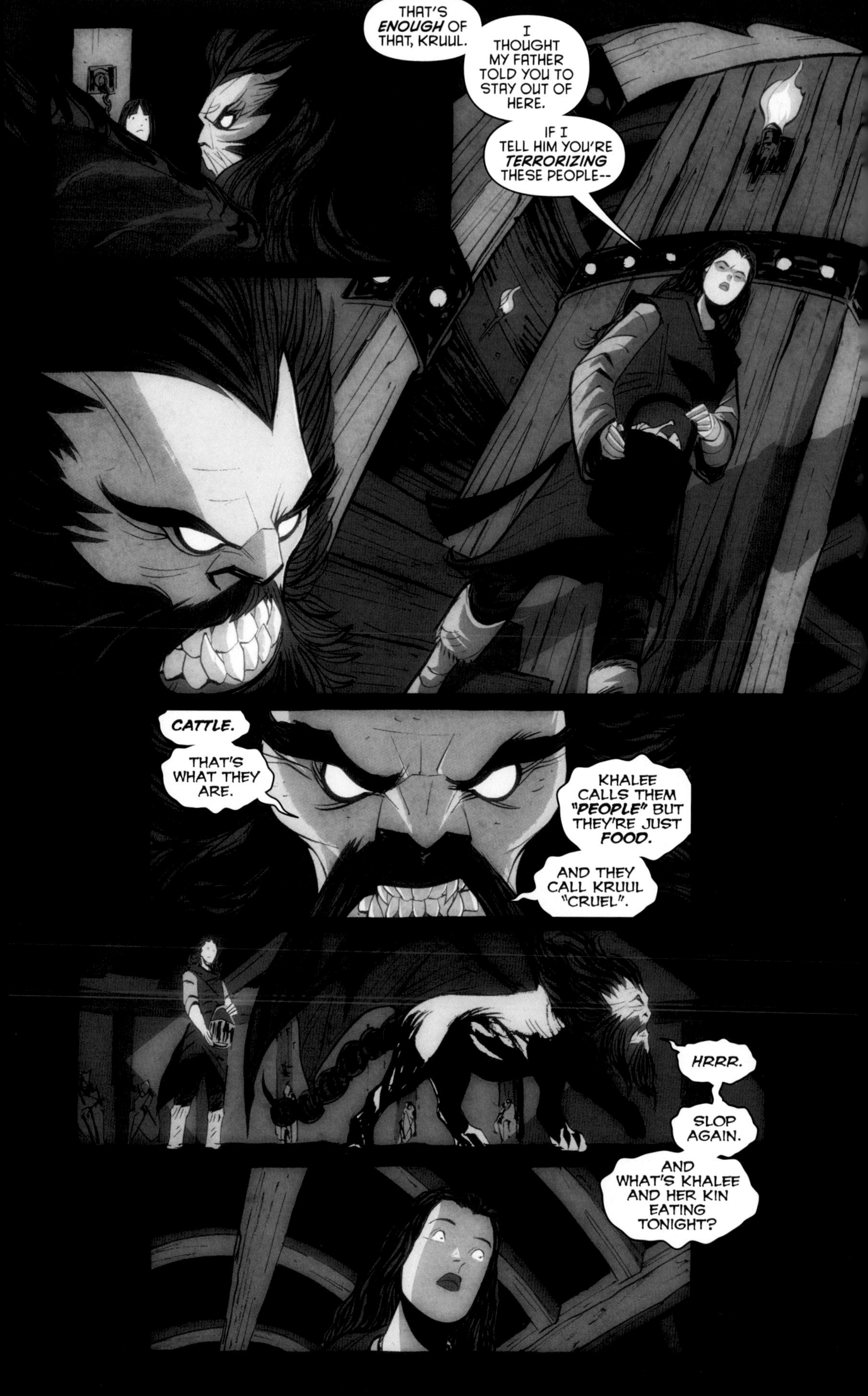
THAT'S ENOUGH OF THAT, KRUUL.
I THOUGHT MY FATHER TOLD YOU TO STAY OUT OF HERE.
IF I TELL HIM YOU'RE TERRORIZING THESE PEOPLE--
CATTLE.
THAT'S WHAT THEY ARE.
KHALEE CALLS THEM "PEOPLE" BUT THEY'RE JUST FOOD.
AND THEY CALL KRUUL "CRUEL".
HRRR.
SLOP AGAIN.
AND WHAT'S KHALEE AND HER KIN EATING TONIGHT?

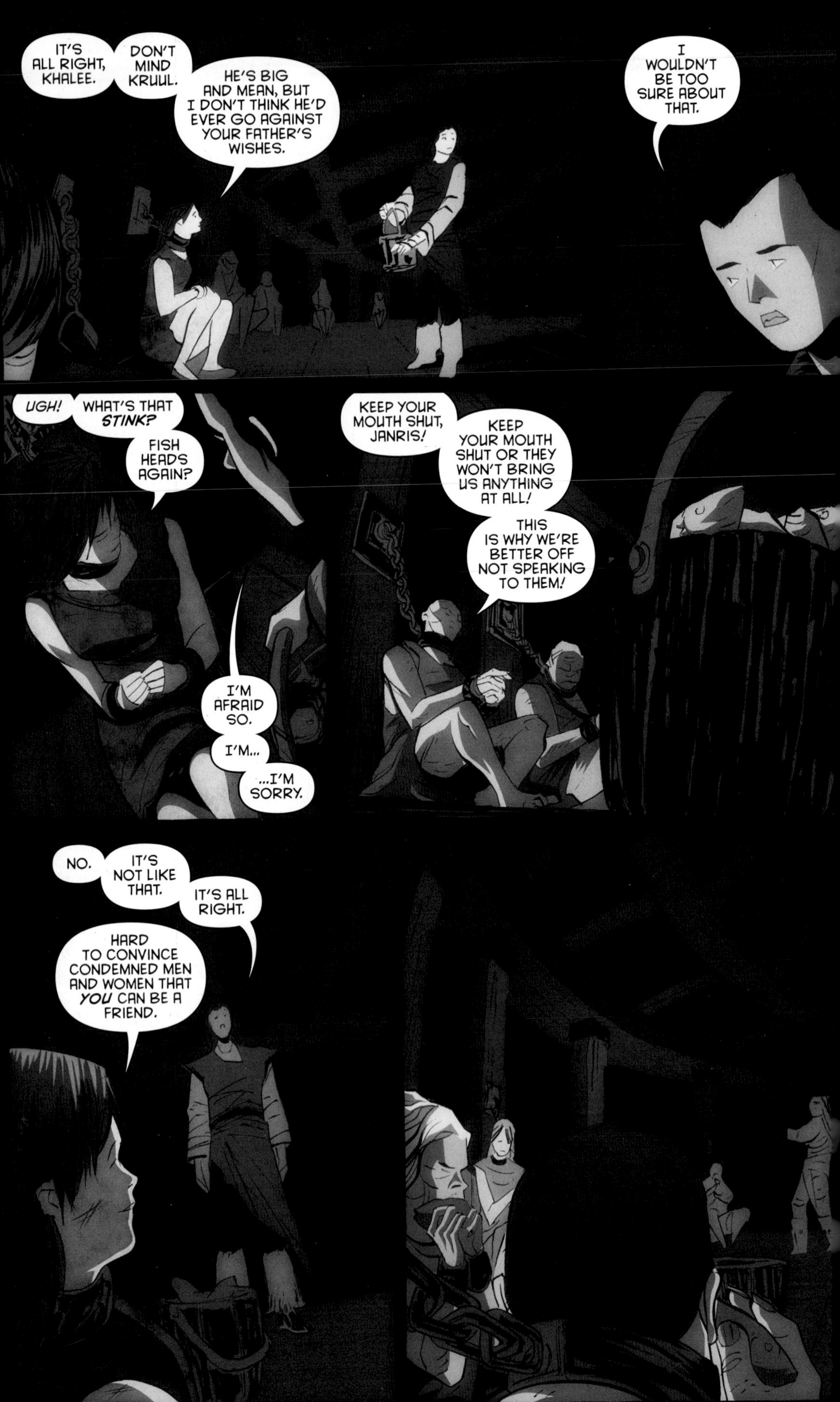
IT'S ALL RIGHT, KHALEE.
DON'T MIND KRUUL.
HE'S BIG AND MEAN, BUT I DON'T THINK HE'D EVER GO AGAINST YOUR FATHER'S WISHES.
I WOULDN'T BE TOO SURE ABOUT THAT.
UGH!
WHAT'S THAT STINK?
FISH HEADS AGAIN?
I'M AFRAID SO.
I'M...
...I'M SORRY.
KEEP YOUR MOUTH SHUT, JANRIS!
KEEP YOUR MOUTH SHUT OR THEY WON'T BRING US ANYTHING AT ALL!
THIS IS WHY WE'RE BETTER OFF NOT SPEAKING TO THEM!
NO.
IT'S NOT LIKE THAT.
IT'S ALL RIGHT.
HARD TO CONVINCE CONDEMNED MEN AND WOMEN THAT YOU CAN BE A FRIEND.

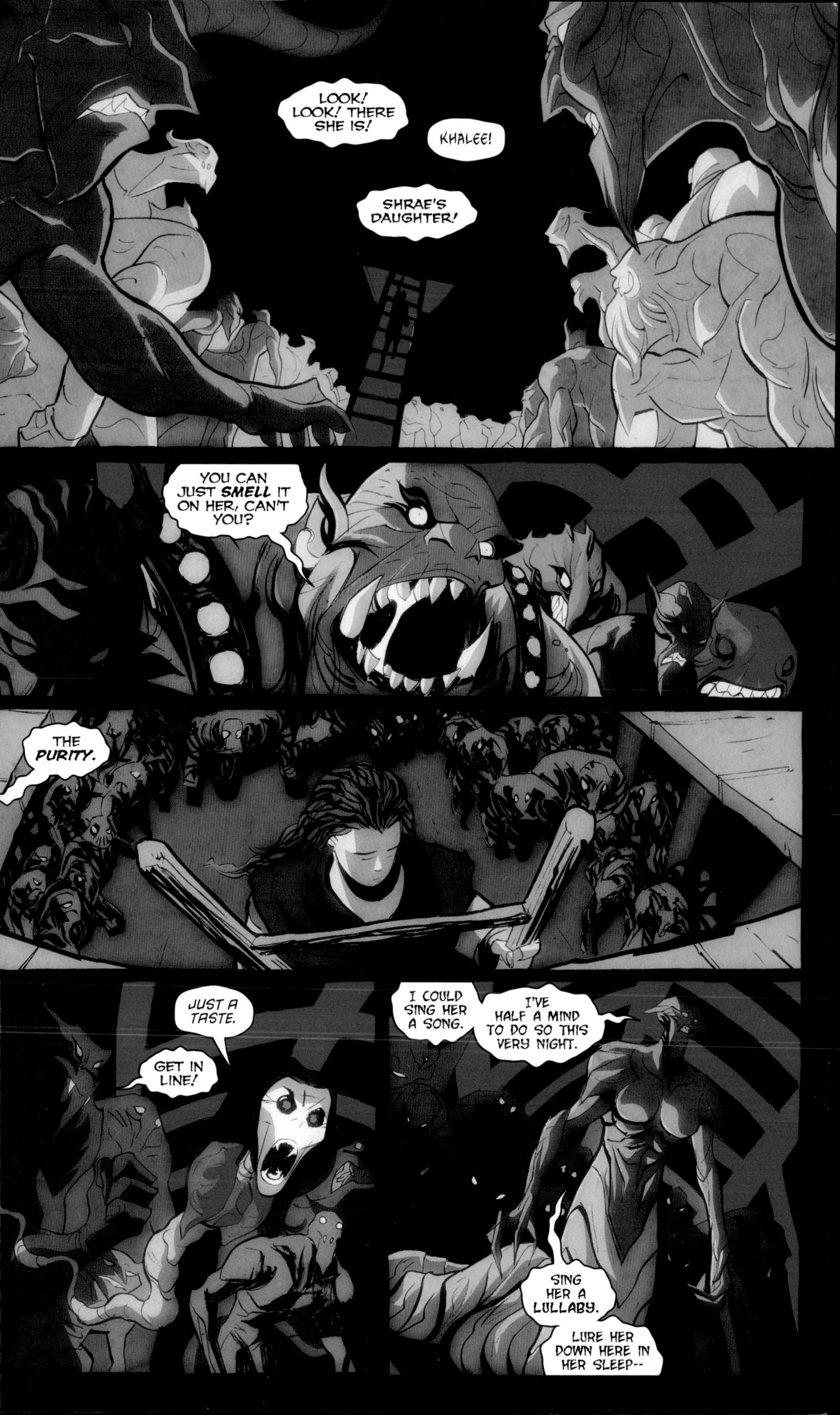
LOOK! LOOK! THERE SHE IS!
KHALEE!
SHRAE'S DAUGHTER!
YOU CAN JUST SMELL IT ON HER, CAN'T YOU?
THE PURITY.
JUST A TASTE.
GET IN LINE!
I COULD SING HER A SONG.
I'VE HALF A MIND TO DO SO THIS VERY NIGHT.
SING HER A LULLABY.
LURE HER DOWN HERE IN HER SLEEP--

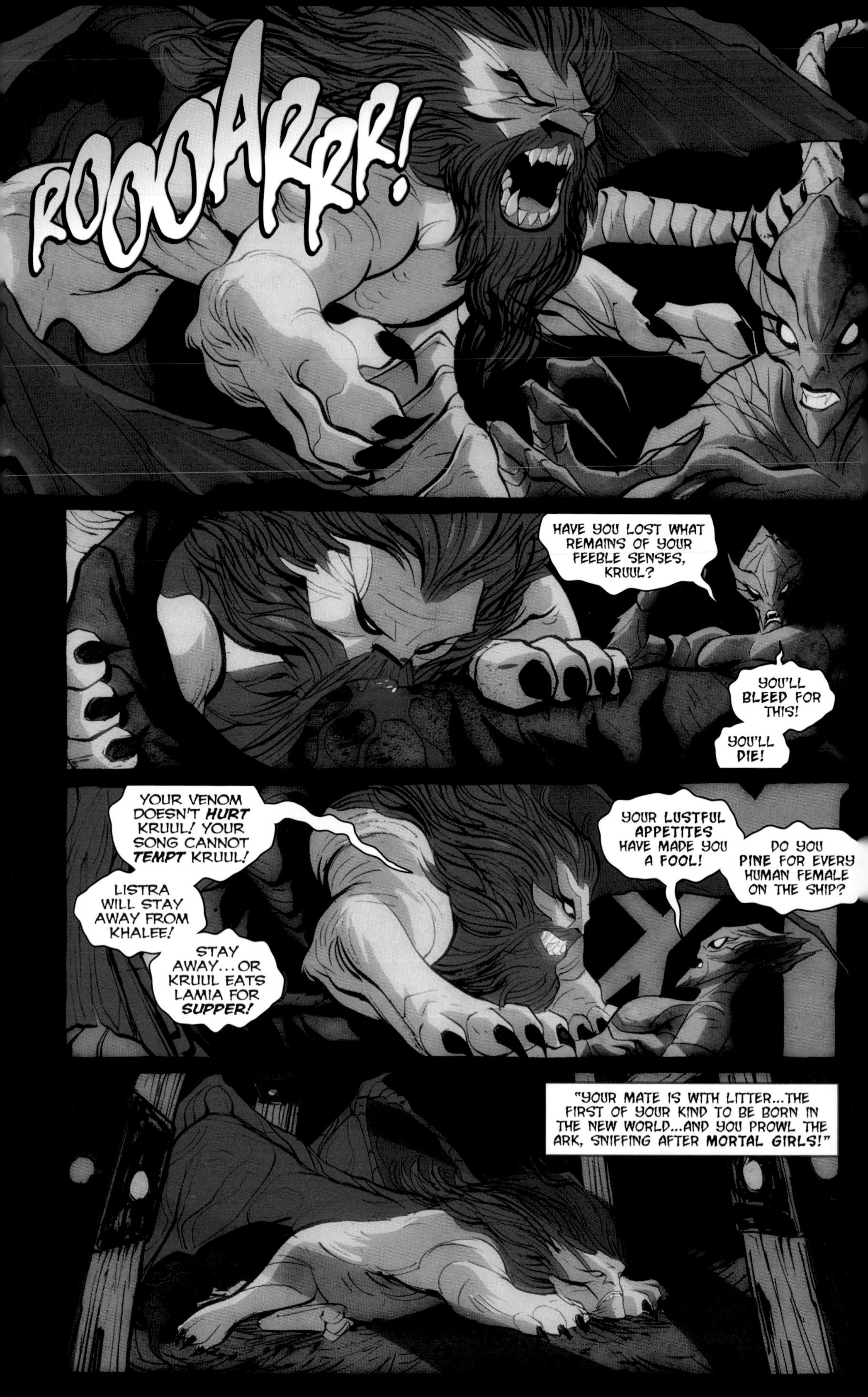
ROOOARRR!
HAVE YOU LOST WHAT REMAINS OF YOUR FEEBLE SENSES, KRUUL?
YOU'LL BLEED FOR THIS!
YOU'LL DIE!
YOUR VENOM DOESN'T HURT KRUUL! YOUR SONG CANNOT TEMPT KRUUL!
LISTRA WILL STAY AWAY FROM KHALEE!
STAY AWAY...OR KRUUL EATS LAMIA FOR SUPPER!
YOUR LUSTFUL APPETITES HAVE MADE YOU A FOOL!
DO YOU PINE FOR EVERY HUMAN FEMALE ON THE SHIP?
"YOUR MATE IS WITH LITTER...THE FIRST OF YOUR KIND TO BE BORN IN THE NEW WORLD...AND YOU PROWL THE ARK, SNIFFING AFTER MORTAL GIRLS!"

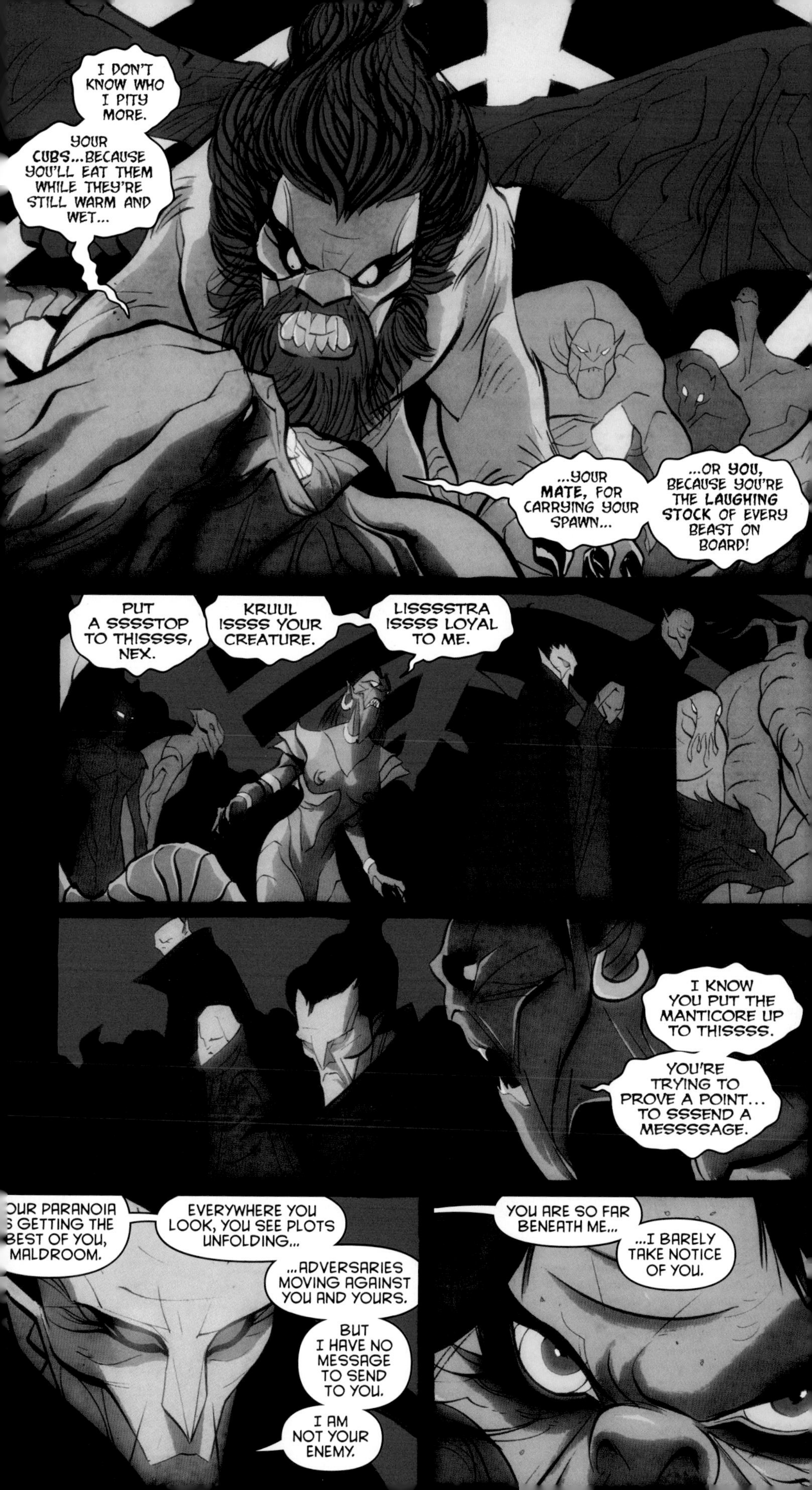
I DON'T KNOW WHO I PITY MORE.
YOUR CUBS...BECAUSE YOU'LL EAT THEM WHILE THEY'RE STILL WARM AND WET...
...YOUR MATE, FOR CARRYING YOUR SPAWN...
...OR YOU, BECAUSE YOU'RE THE LAUGHING STOCK OF EVERY BEAST ON BOARD!
PUT A SSSSTOP TO THISSSS, NEX.
KRUUL ISSSS YOUR CREATURE.
LISSSSTRA ISSSS LOYAL TO ME.
I KNOW YOU PUT THE MANTICORE UP TO THISSSS.
YOU'RE TRYING TO PROVE A POINT... TO SSSEND A MESSSSAGE.
OUR PARANOIA S GETTING THE BEST OF YOU, MALDROOM.
EVERYWHERE YOU LOOK, YOU SEE PLOTS UNFOLDING...
...ADVERSARIES MOVING AGAINST YOU AND YOURS.
BUT I HAVE NO MESSAGE TO SEND TO YOU.
I AM NOT YOUR ENEMY.
YOU ARE SO FAR BENEATH ME...
...I BARELY TAKE NOTICE OF YOU.

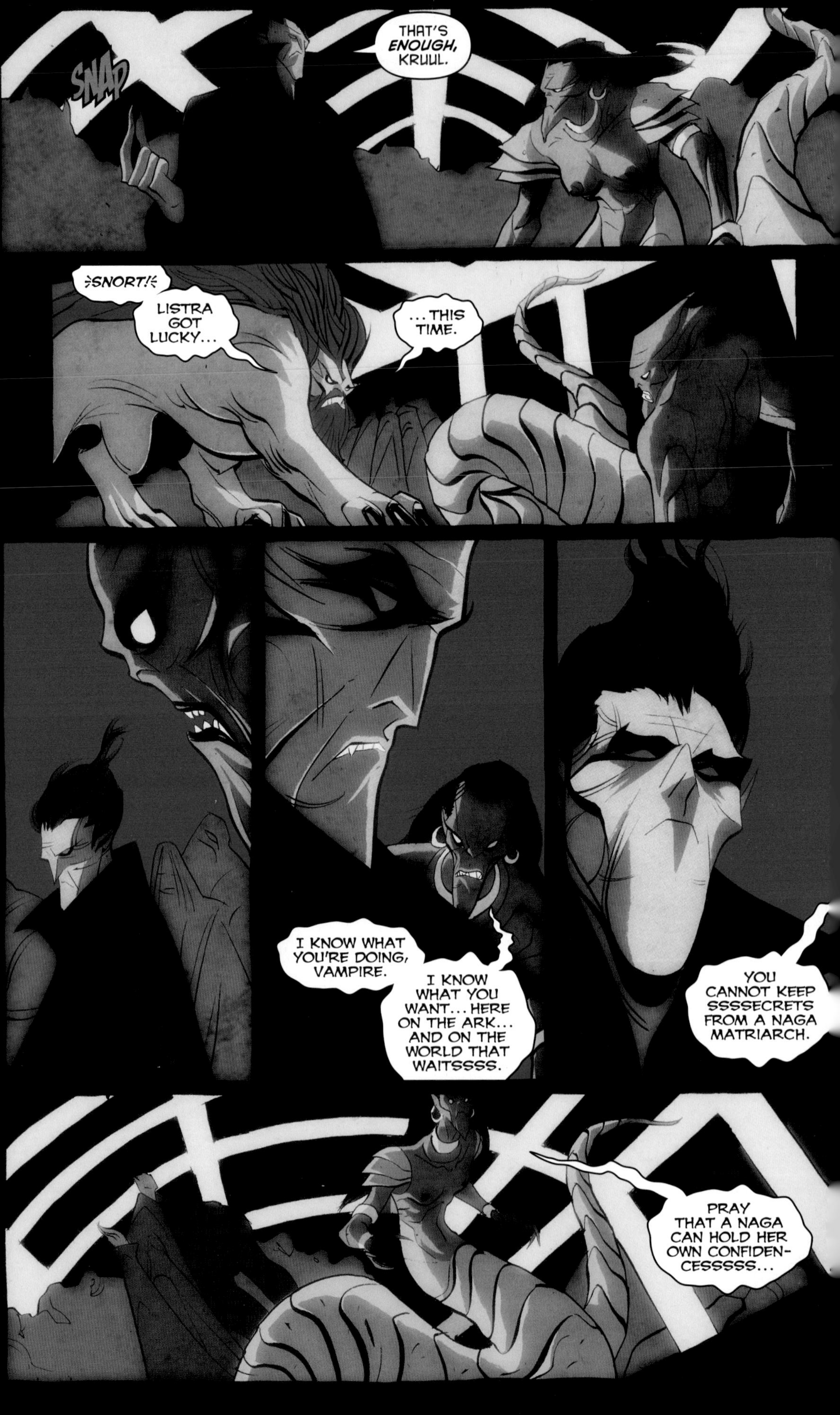
SNAP
THAT'S *ENOUGH,* KRUUL.
SNORT!
LISTRA GOT LUCKY...
...THIS TIME.
I KNOW WHAT YOU'RE DOING, VAMPIRE.
I KNOW WHAT YOU WANT... HERE ON THE ARK... AND ON THE WORLD THAT WAITSSSS.
YOU CANNOT KEEP SSSSECRETS FROM A NAGA MATRIARCH.
PRAY THAT A NAGA CAN HOLD HER OWN CONFIDEN-CESSSSS...

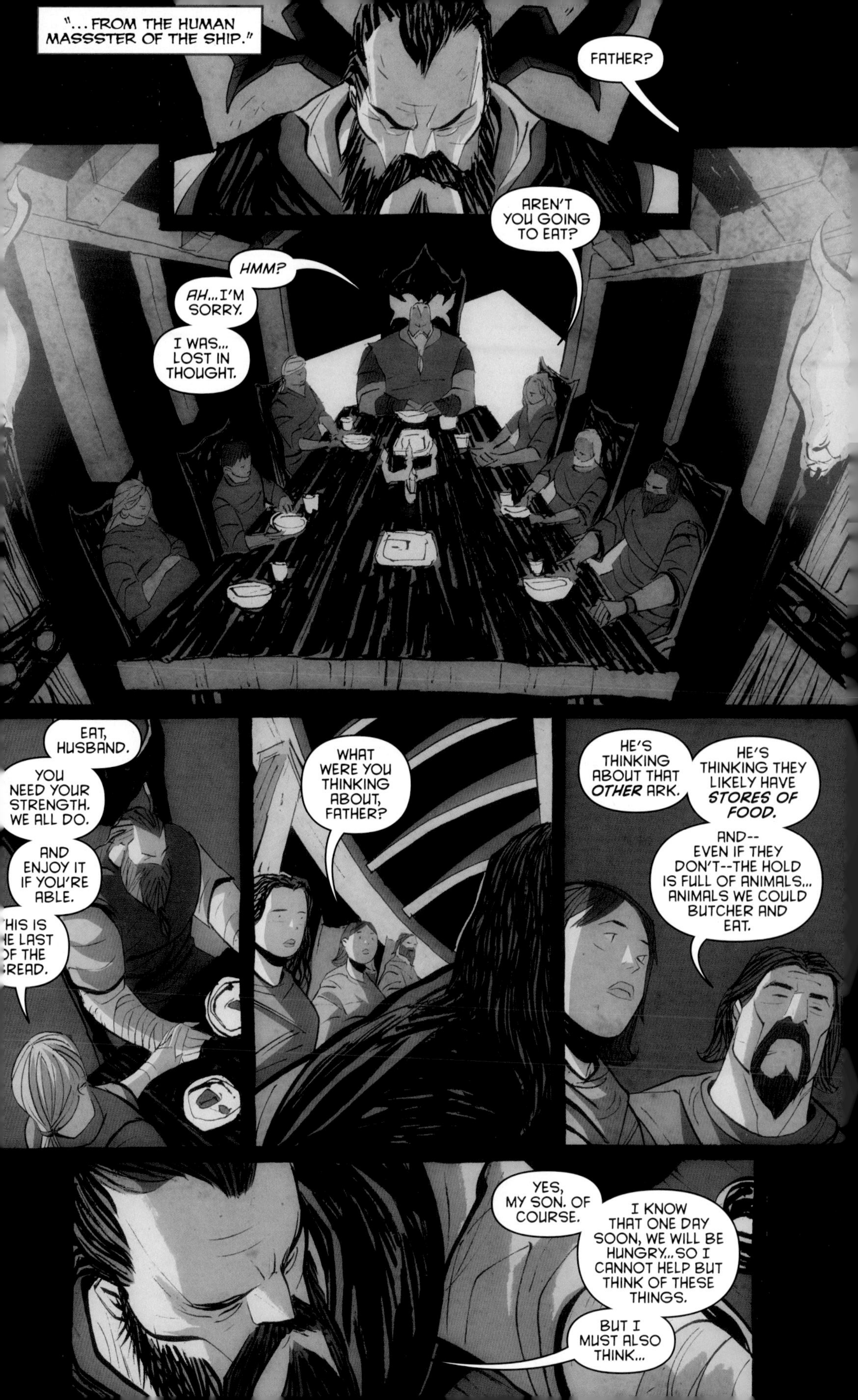

"... FROM THE HUMAN MASSSTER OF THE SHIP."
FATHER?
AREN'T YOU GOING TO EAT?
HMM?
AH... I'M SORRY.
I WAS... LOST IN THOUGHT.
EAT, HUSBAND.
YOU NEED YOUR STRENGTH. WE ALL DO.
AND ENJOY IT IF YOU'RE ABLE.
HIS IS E LAST OF THE READ.
WHAT WERE YOU THINKING ABOUT, FATHER?
HE'S THINKING ABOUT THAT OTHER ARK.
HE'S THINKING THEY LIKELY HAVE STORES OF FOOD.
AND-- EVEN IF THEY DON'T--THE HOLD IS FULL OF ANIMALS... ANIMALS WE COULD BUTCHER AND EAT.
YES, MY SON. OF COURSE.
I KNOW THAT ONE DAY SOON, WE WILL BE HUNGRY... SO I CANNOT HELP BUT THINK OF THESE THINGS.
BUT I MUST ALSO THINK...

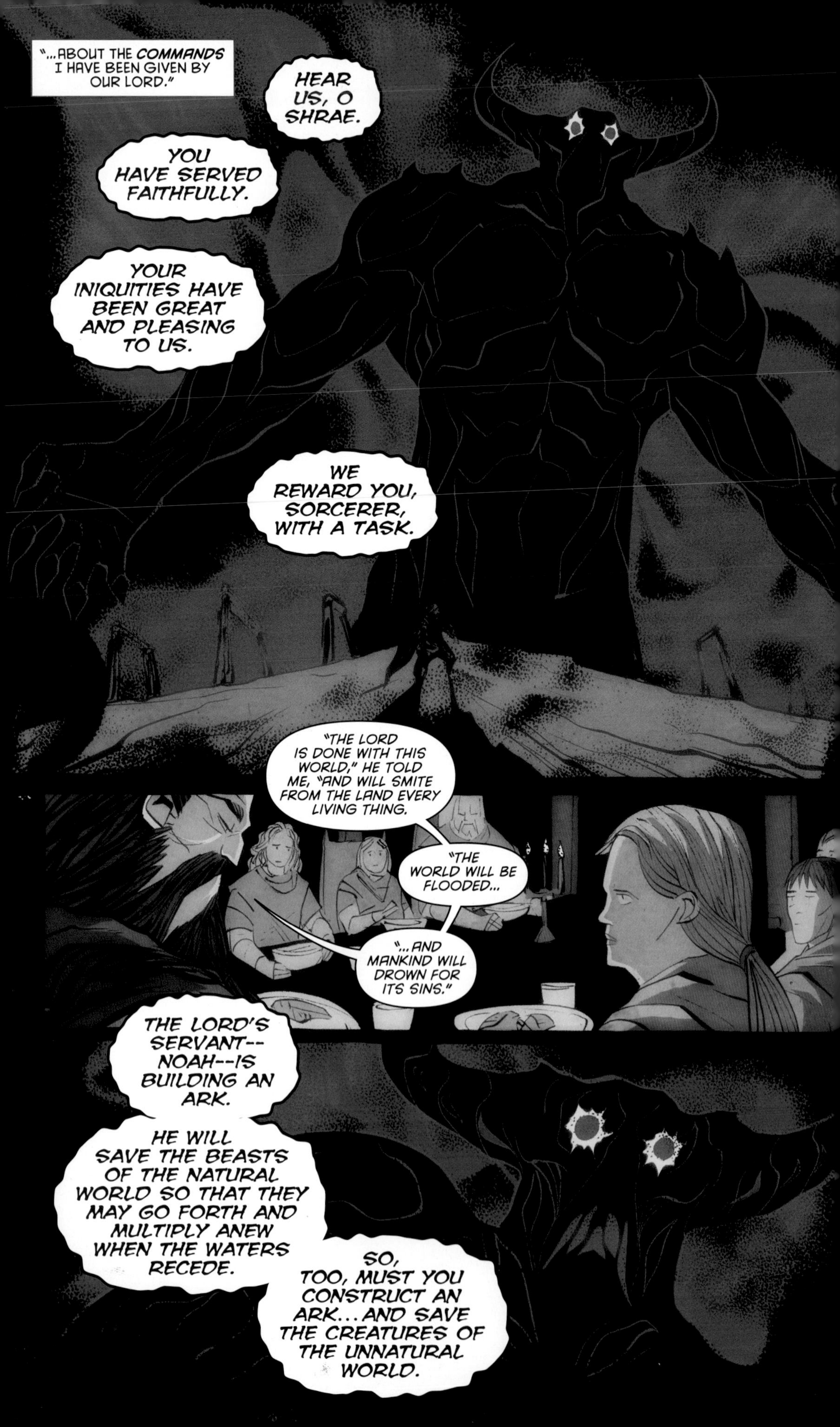
"...ABOUT THE *COMMANDS* I HAVE BEEN GIVEN BY OUR LORD."
HEAR US, O SHRAE.
YOU HAVE SERVED FAITHFULLY.
YOUR INIQUITIES HAVE BEEN GREAT AND PLEASING TO US.
WE REWARD YOU, SORCERER, WITH A TASK.
"THE LORD IS DONE WITH THIS WORLD," HE TOLD ME, "AND WILL SMITE FROM THE LAND EVERY LIVING THING.
"THE WORLD WILL BE FLOODED...
"...AND MANKIND WILL DROWN FOR ITS SINS."
THE LORD'S SERVANT--NOAH--IS BUILDING AN ARK.
HE WILL SAVE THE BEASTS OF THE NATURAL WORLD SO THAT THEY MAY GO FORTH AND MULTIPLY ANEW WHEN THE WATERS RECEDE.
SO, TOO, MUST YOU CONSTRUCT AN ARK...AND SAVE THE CREATURES OF THE UNNATURAL WORLD.

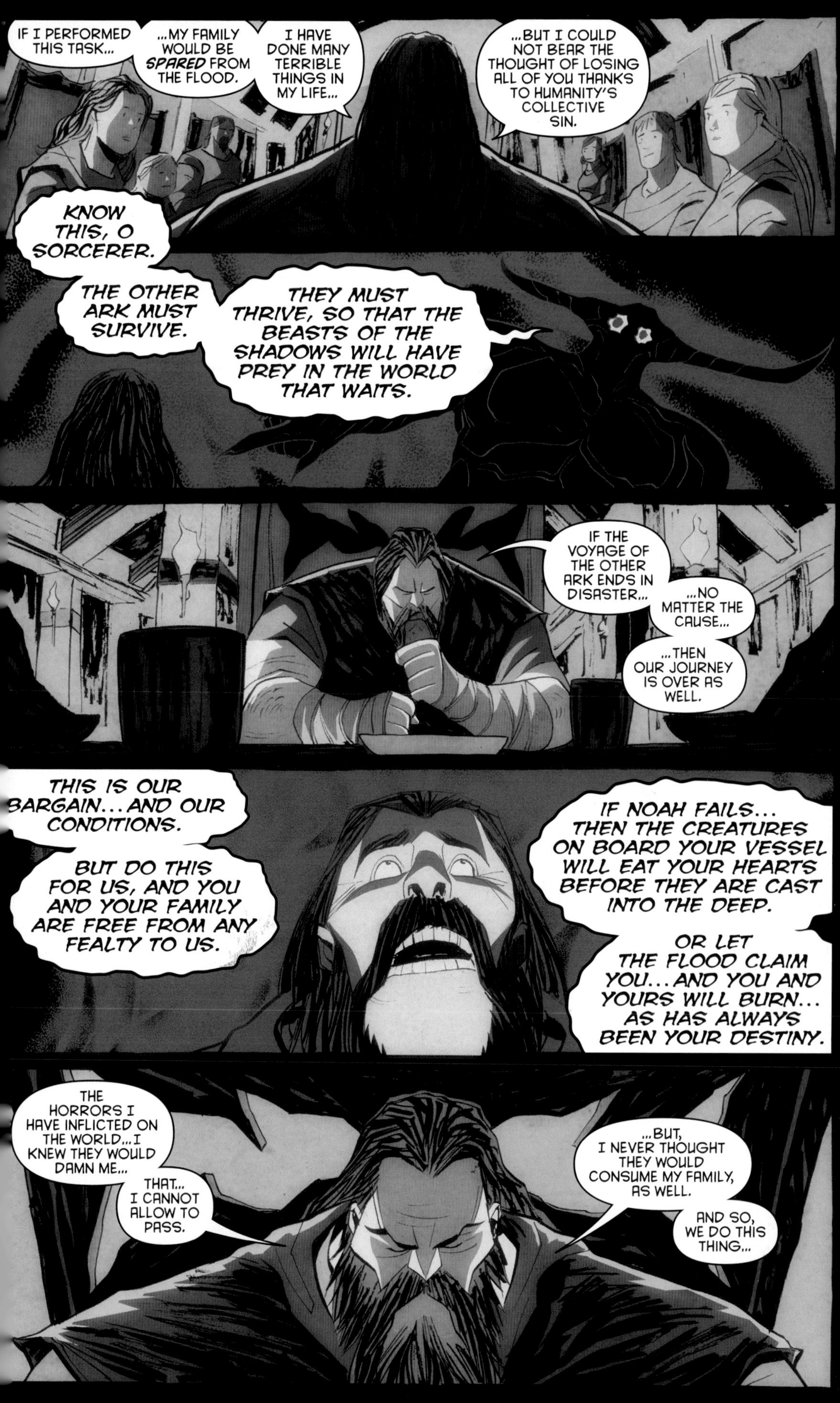
IF I PERFORMED THIS TASK...
...MY FAMILY WOULD BE *SPARED* FROM THE FLOOD.
I HAVE DONE MANY TERRIBLE THINGS IN MY LIFE...
...BUT I COULD NOT BEAR THE THOUGHT OF LOSING ALL OF YOU THANKS TO HUMANITY'S COLLECTIVE SIN.
KNOW THIS, O SORCERER.
THE OTHER ARK MUST SURVIVE.
THEY MUST THRIVE, SO THAT THE BEASTS OF THE SHADOWS WILL HAVE PREY IN THE WORLD THAT WAITS.
IF THE VOYAGE OF THE OTHER ARK ENDS IN DISASTER...
...NO MATTER THE CAUSE...
...THEN OUR JOURNEY IS OVER AS WELL.
THIS IS OUR BARGAIN... AND OUR CONDITIONS.
BUT DO THIS FOR US, AND YOU AND YOUR FAMILY ARE FREE FROM ANY FEALTY TO US.
IF NOAH FAILS... THEN THE CREATURES ON BOARD YOUR VESSEL WILL EAT YOUR HEARTS BEFORE THEY ARE CAST INTO THE DEEP.
OR LET THE FLOOD CLAIM YOU... AND YOU AND YOURS WILL BURN... AS HAS ALWAYS BEEN YOUR DESTINY.
THE HORRORS I HAVE INFLICTED ON THE WORLD...I KNEW THEY WOULD DAMN ME...
THAT... I CANNOT ALLOW TO PASS.
...BUT, I NEVER THOUGHT THEY WOULD CONSUME MY FAMILY, AS WELL.
AND SO, WE DO THIS THING...

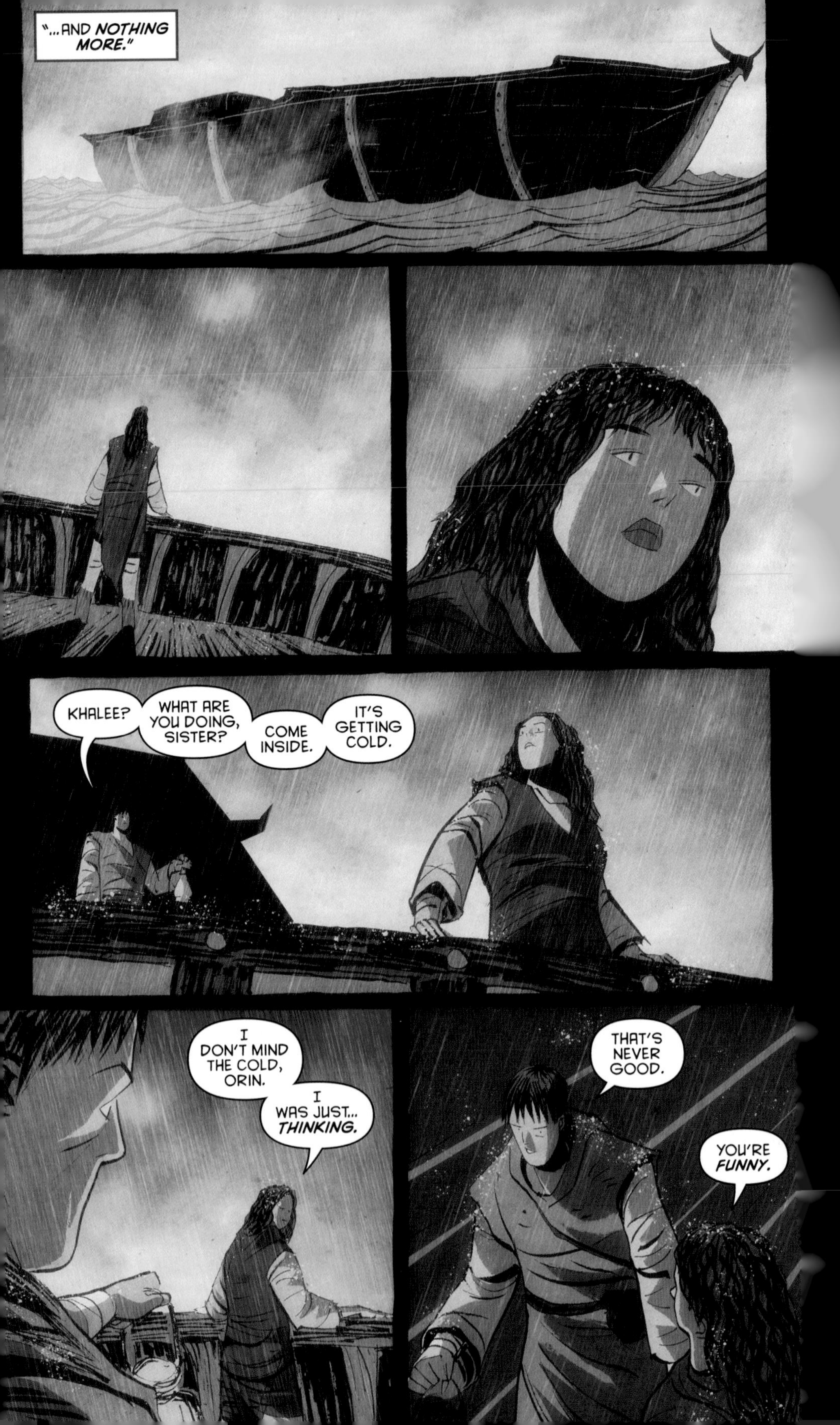
"...AND NOTHING MORE."
KHALEE?
WHAT ARE YOU DOING, SISTER?
COME INSIDE.
IT'S GETTING COLD.
I DON'T MIND THE COLD, ORIN.
I WAS JUST... THINKING.
THAT'S NEVER GOOD.
YOU'RE FUNNY.

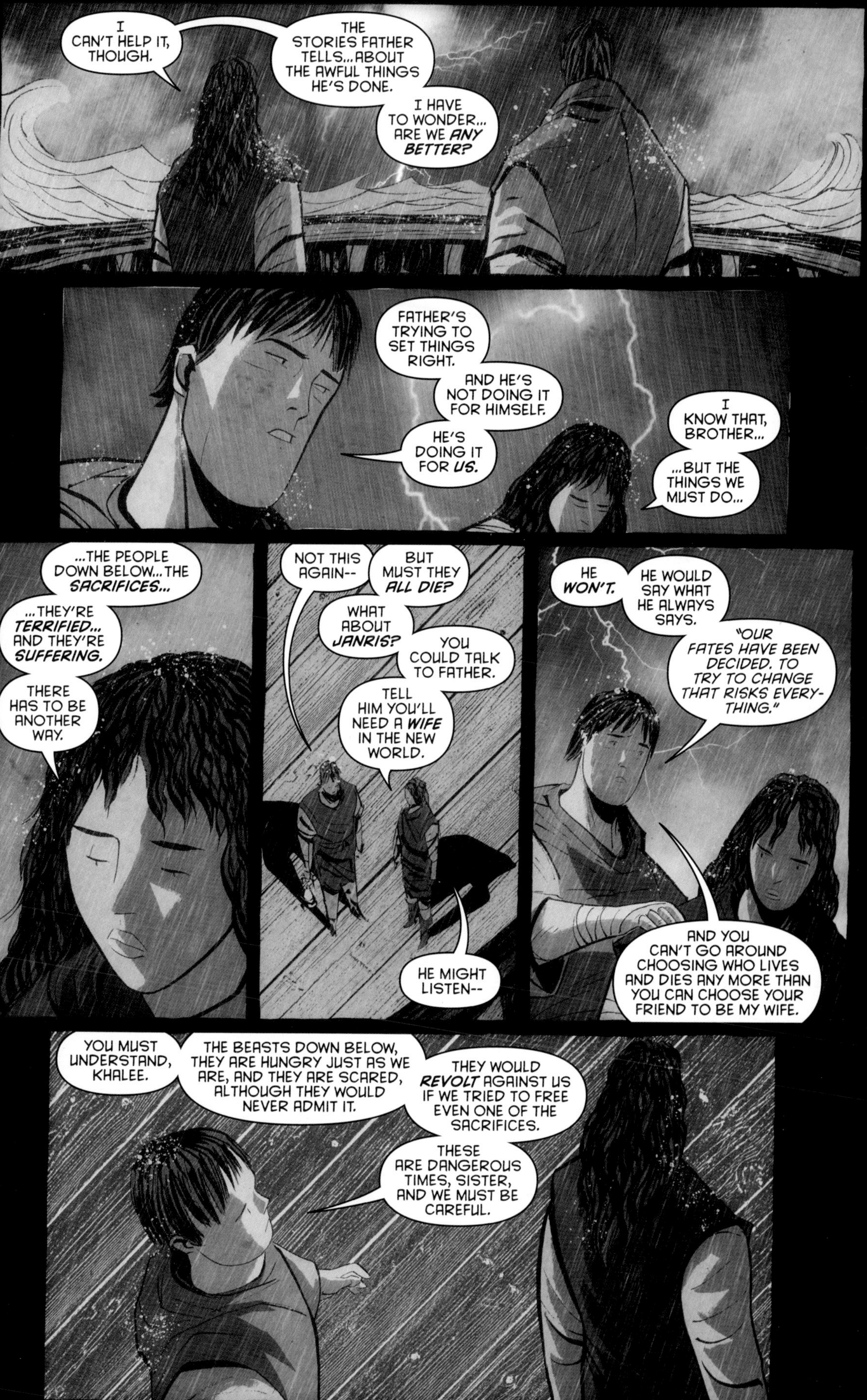
I CAN'T HELP IT, THOUGH.
THE STORIES FATHER TELLS...ABOUT THE AWFUL THINGS HE'S DONE.
I HAVE TO WONDER... ARE WE *ANY BETTER?*
FATHER'S TRYING TO SET THINGS RIGHT.
AND HE'S NOT DOING IT FOR HIMSELF.
HE'S DOING IT FOR *US.*
I KNOW THAT, BROTHER...
...BUT THE THINGS WE MUST DO...
...THE PEOPLE DOWN BELOW...THE *SACRIFICES...*
...THEY'RE *TERRIFIED...* AND THEY'RE *SUFFERING.*
THERE HAS TO BE ANOTHER WAY.
NOT THIS AGAIN--
BUT MUST THEY *ALL DIE?*
WHAT ABOUT *JANRIS?*
YOU COULD TALK TO FATHER.
TELL HIM YOU'LL NEED A *WIFE* IN THE NEW WORLD.
HE MIGHT LISTEN--
HE *WON'T.*
HE WOULD SAY WHAT HE ALWAYS SAYS.
"OUR FATES HAVE BEEN DECIDED. TO TRY TO CHANGE THAT RISKS EVERY-THING."
AND YOU CAN'T GO AROUND CHOOSING WHO LIVES AND DIES ANY MORE THAN YOU CAN CHOOSE YOUR FRIEND TO BE MY WIFE.
YOU MUST UNDERSTAND, KHALEE.
THE BEASTS DOWN BELOW, THEY ARE HUNGRY JUST AS WE ARE, AND THEY ARE SCARED, ALTHOUGH THEY WOULD NEVER ADMIT IT.
THEY WOULD *REVOLT* AGAINST US IF WE TRIED TO FREE EVEN ONE OF THE SACRIFICES.
THESE ARE DANGEROUS TIMES, SISTER, AND WE MUST BE CAREFUL.

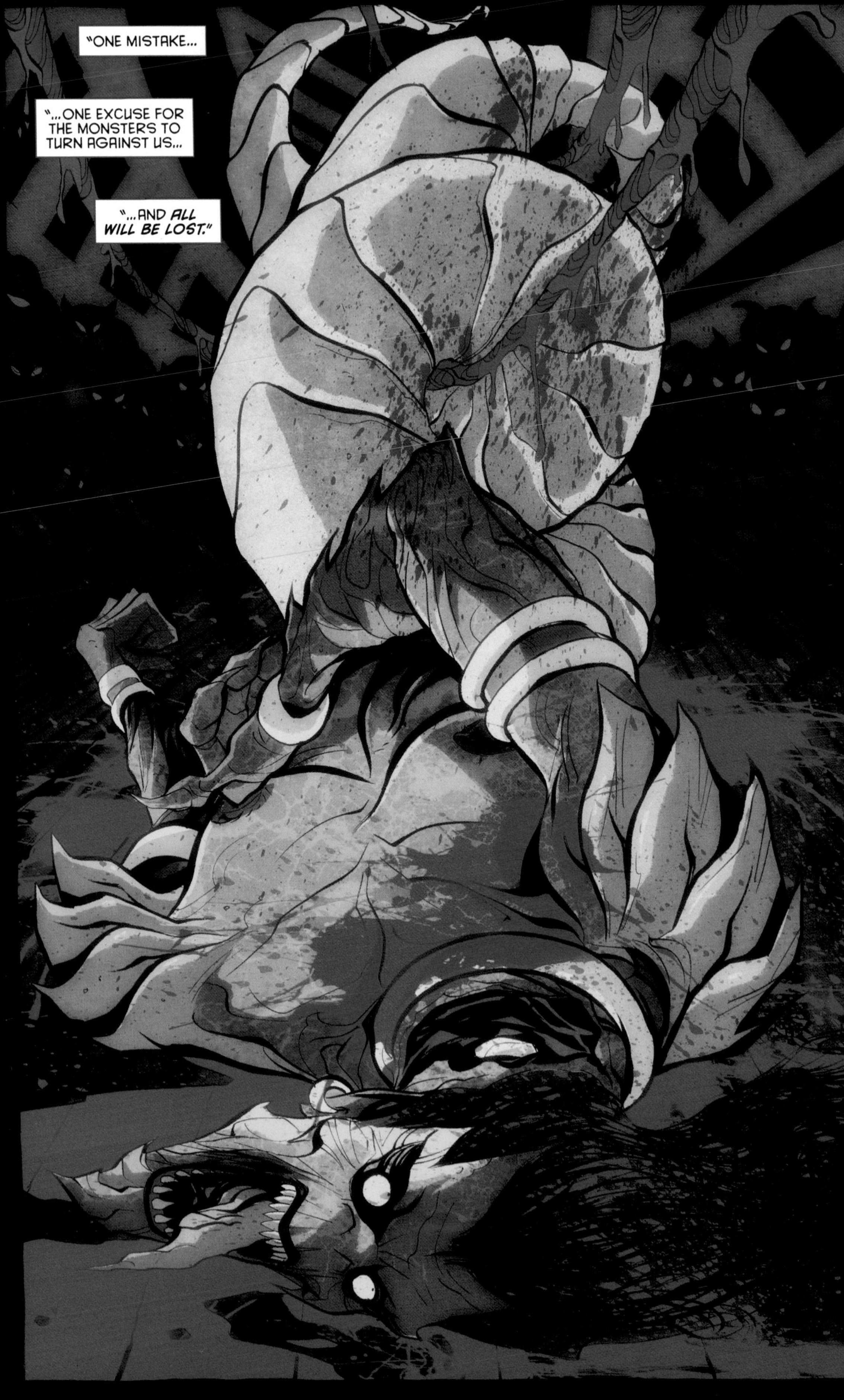
"ONE MISTAKE...
"...ONE EXCUSE FOR THE MONSTERS TO TURN AGAINST US...
"...AND ALL WILL BE LOST."

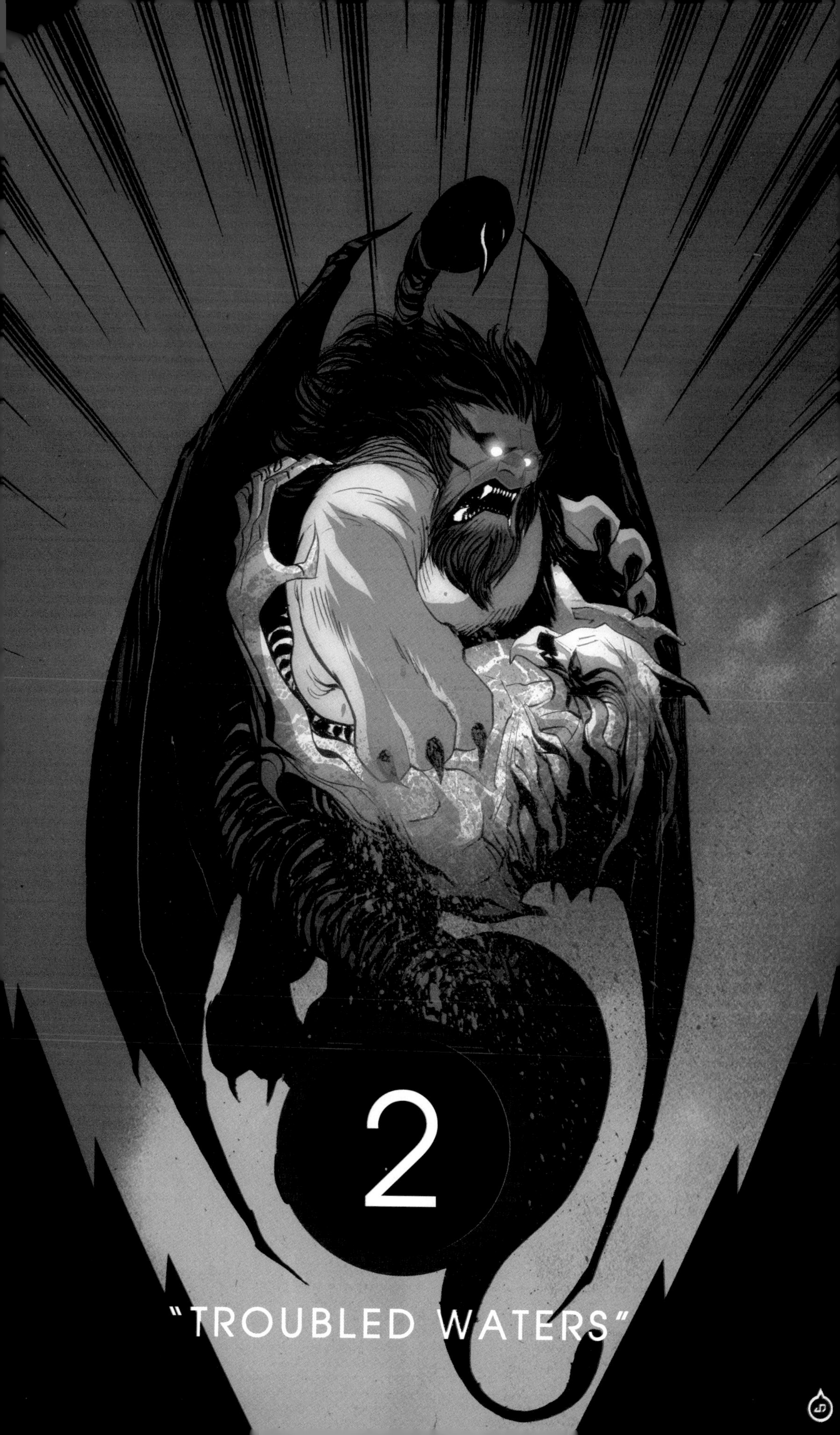
2
"TROUBLED WATERS"

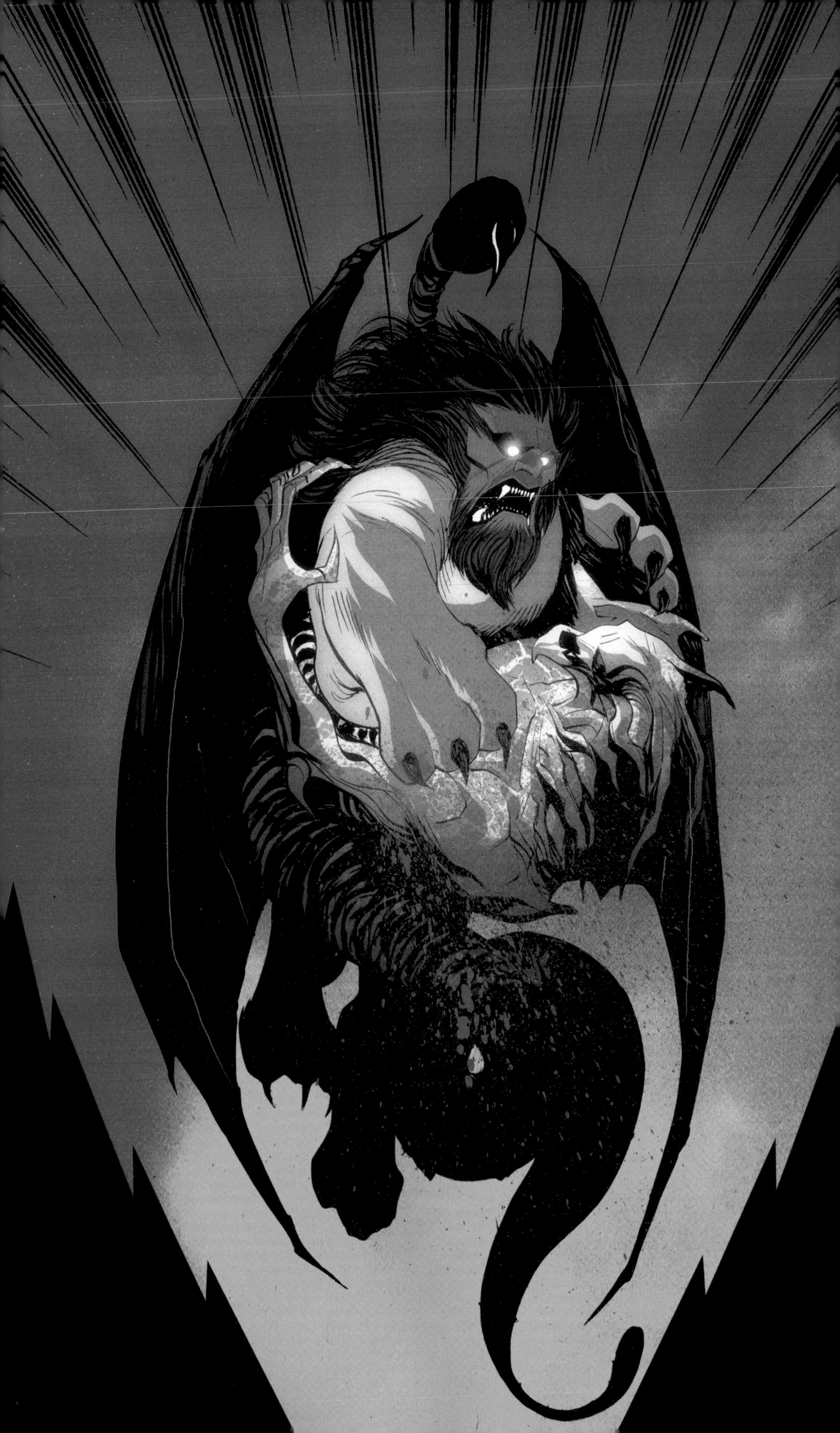

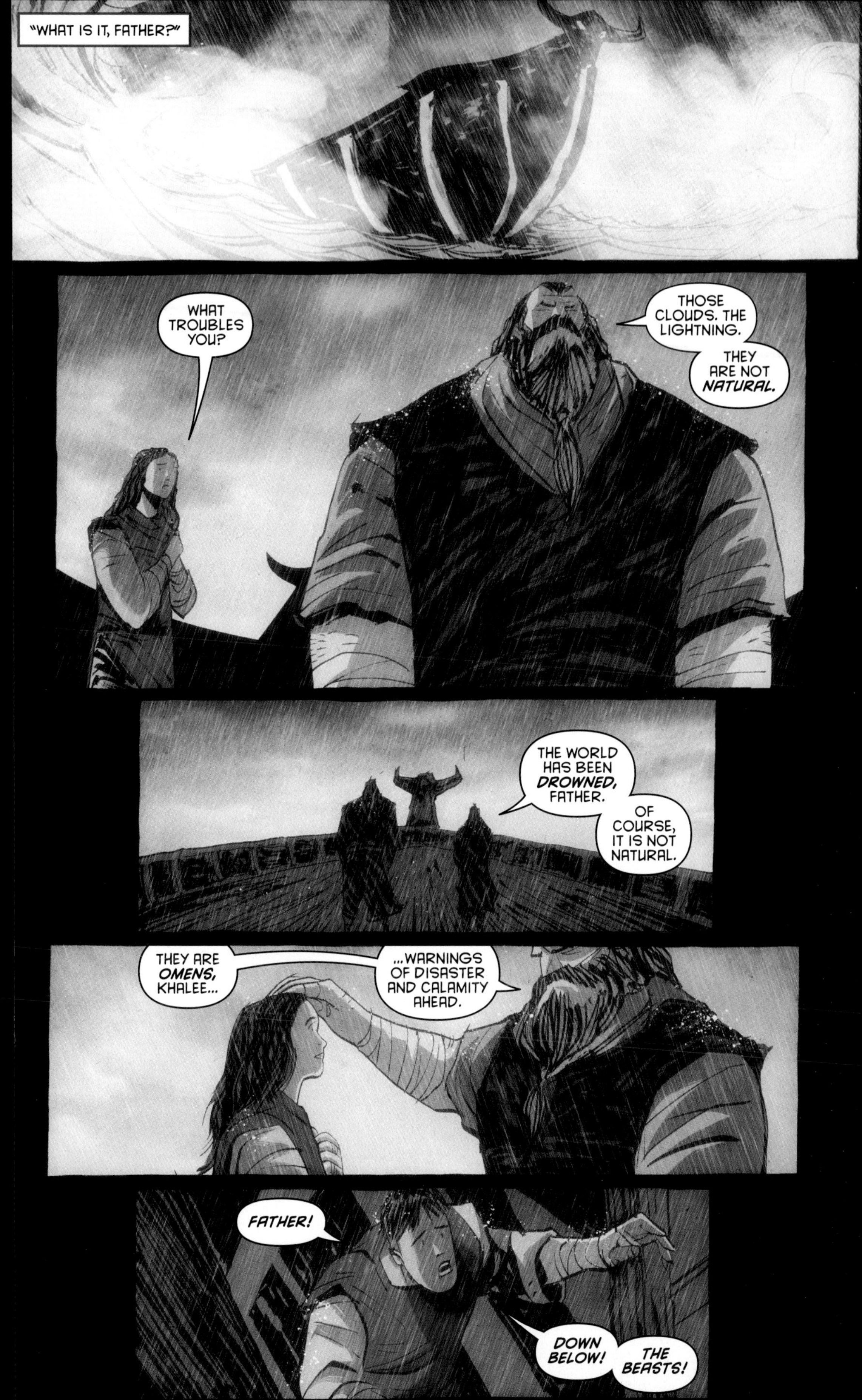
"WHAT IS IT, FATHER?"
WHAT TROUBLES YOU?
THOSE CLOUDS. THE LIGHTNING.
THEY ARE NOT NATURAL.
THE WORLD HAS BEEN DROWNED, FATHER.
OF COURSE, IT IS NOT NATURAL.
THEY ARE OMENS, KHALEE...
...WARNINGS OF DISASTER AND CALAMITY AHEAD.
FATHER!
DOWN BELOW!
THE BEASTS!

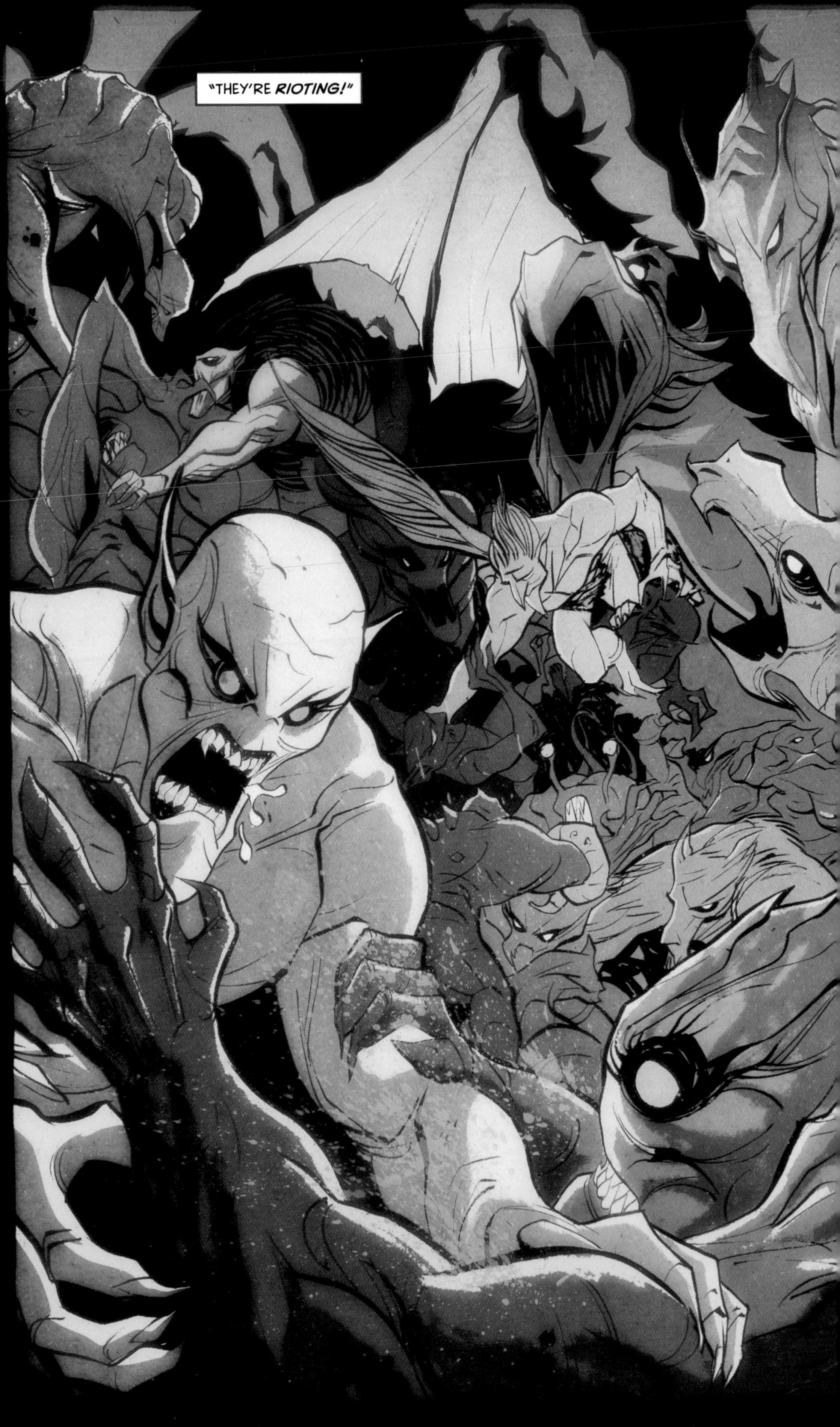
"THEY'RE RIOTING!"

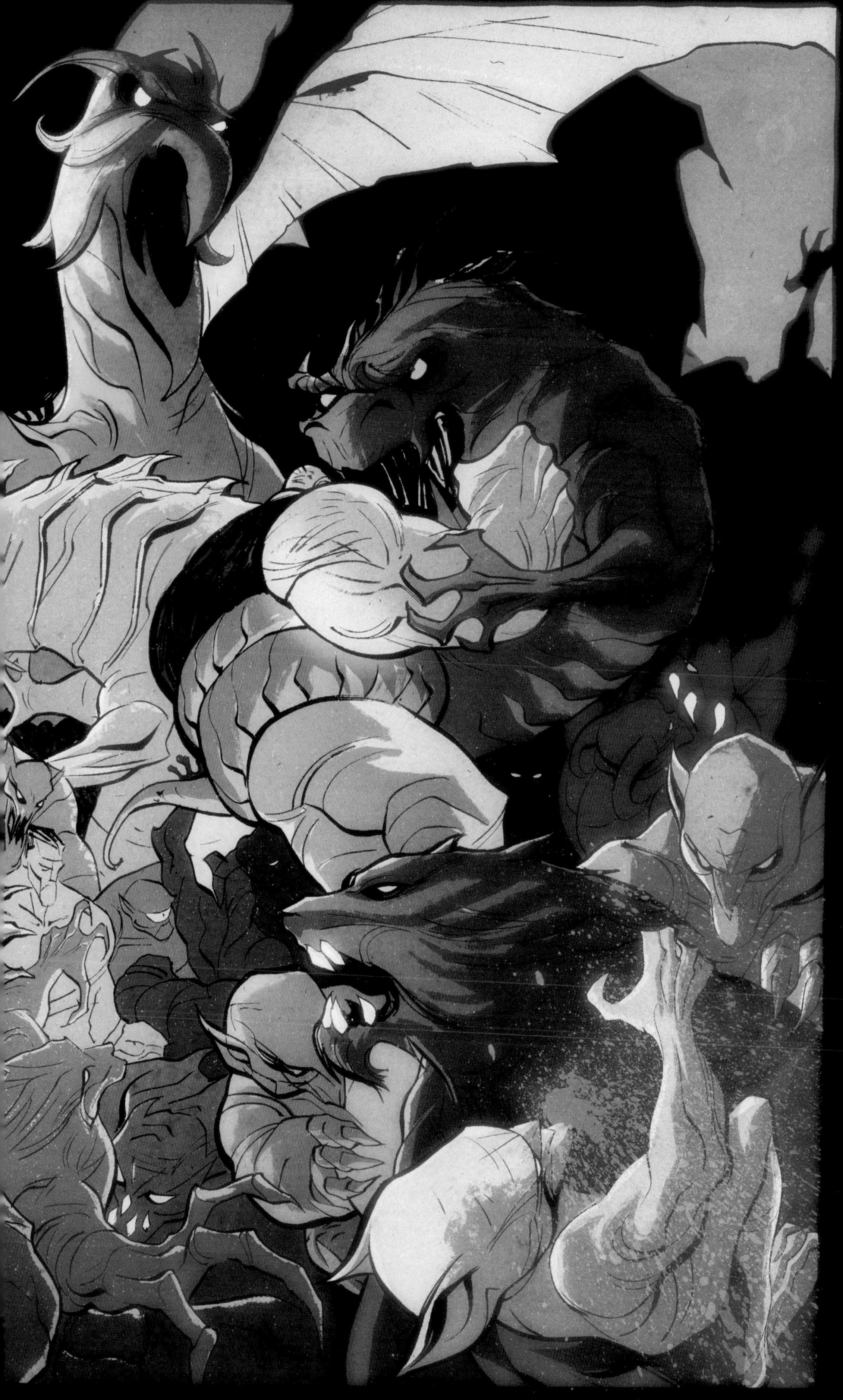

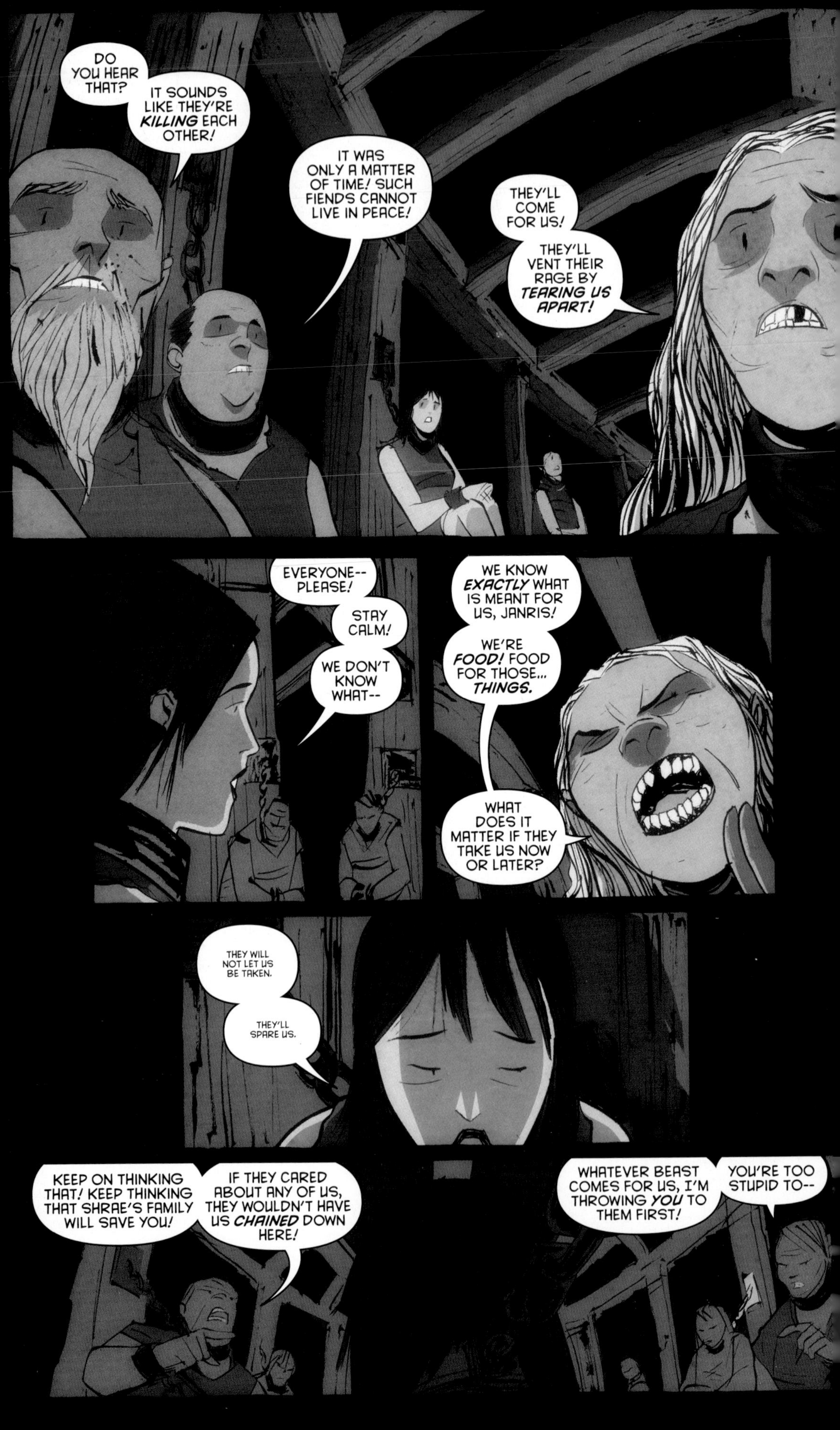

DO YOU HEAR THAT?
IT SOUNDS LIKE THEY'RE *KILLING* EACH OTHER!
IT WAS ONLY A MATTER OF TIME! SUCH FIENDS CANNOT LIVE IN PEACE!
THEY'LL COME FOR US!
THEY'LL VENT THEIR RAGE BY *TEARING US APART!*
EVERYONE-- PLEASE!
STAY CALM!
WE DON'T KNOW WHAT--
WE KNOW *EXACTLY* WHAT IS MEANT FOR US, JANRIS!
WE'RE *FOOD!* FOOD FOR THOSE... *THINGS.*
WHAT DOES IT MATTER IF THEY TAKE US NOW OR LATER?
THEY WILL NOT LET US BE TAKEN.
THEY'LL SPARE US.
KEEP ON THINKING THAT! KEEP THINKING THAT SHRAE'S FAMILY WILL SAVE YOU!
IF THEY CARED ABOUT ANY OF US, THEY WOULDN'T HAVE US *CHAINED* DOWN HERE!
WHATEVER BEAST COMES FOR US, I'M THROWING *YOU* TO THEM FIRST!
YOU'RE TOO STUPID TO--

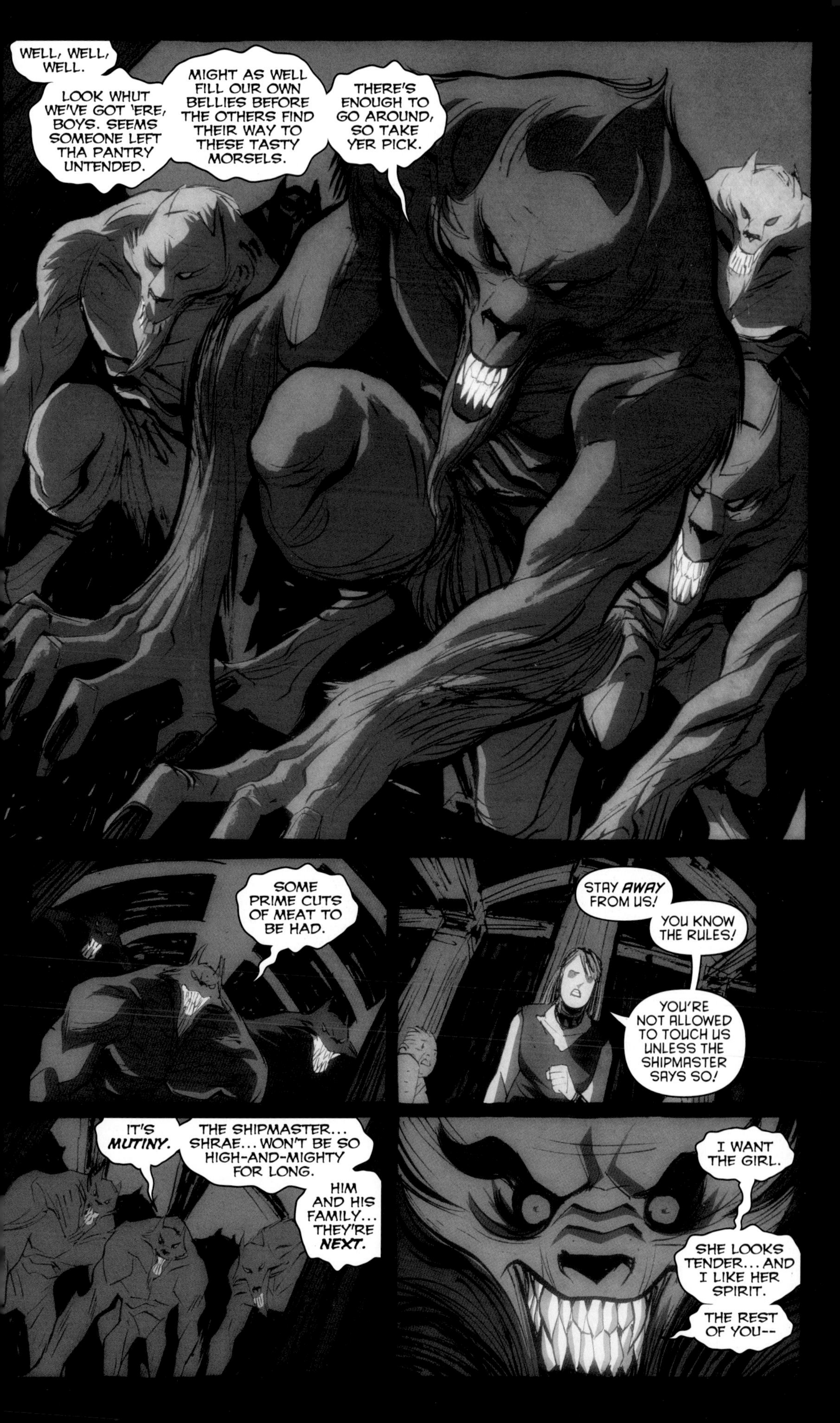
WELL, WELL, WELL.
LOOK WHUT WE'VE GOT 'ERE, BOYS. SEEMS SOMEONE LEFT THA PANTRY UNTENDED.
MIGHT AS WELL FILL OUR OWN BELLIES BEFORE THE OTHERS FIND THEIR WAY TO THESE TASTY MORSELS.
THERE'S ENOUGH TO GO AROUND, SO TAKE YER PICK.
SOME PRIME CUTS OF MEAT TO BE HAD.
STAY *AWAY* FROM US!
YOU KNOW THE RULES!
YOU'RE NOT ALLOWED TO TOUCH US UNLESS THE SHIPMASTER SAYS SO!
IT'S ***MUTINY.***
THE SHIPMASTER... SHRAE... WON'T BE SO HIGH-AND-MIGHTY FOR LONG.
HIM AND HIS FAMILY... THEY'RE ***NEXT.***
I WANT THE GIRL.
SHE LOOKS TENDER... AND I LIKE HER SPIRIT.
THE REST OF YOU--

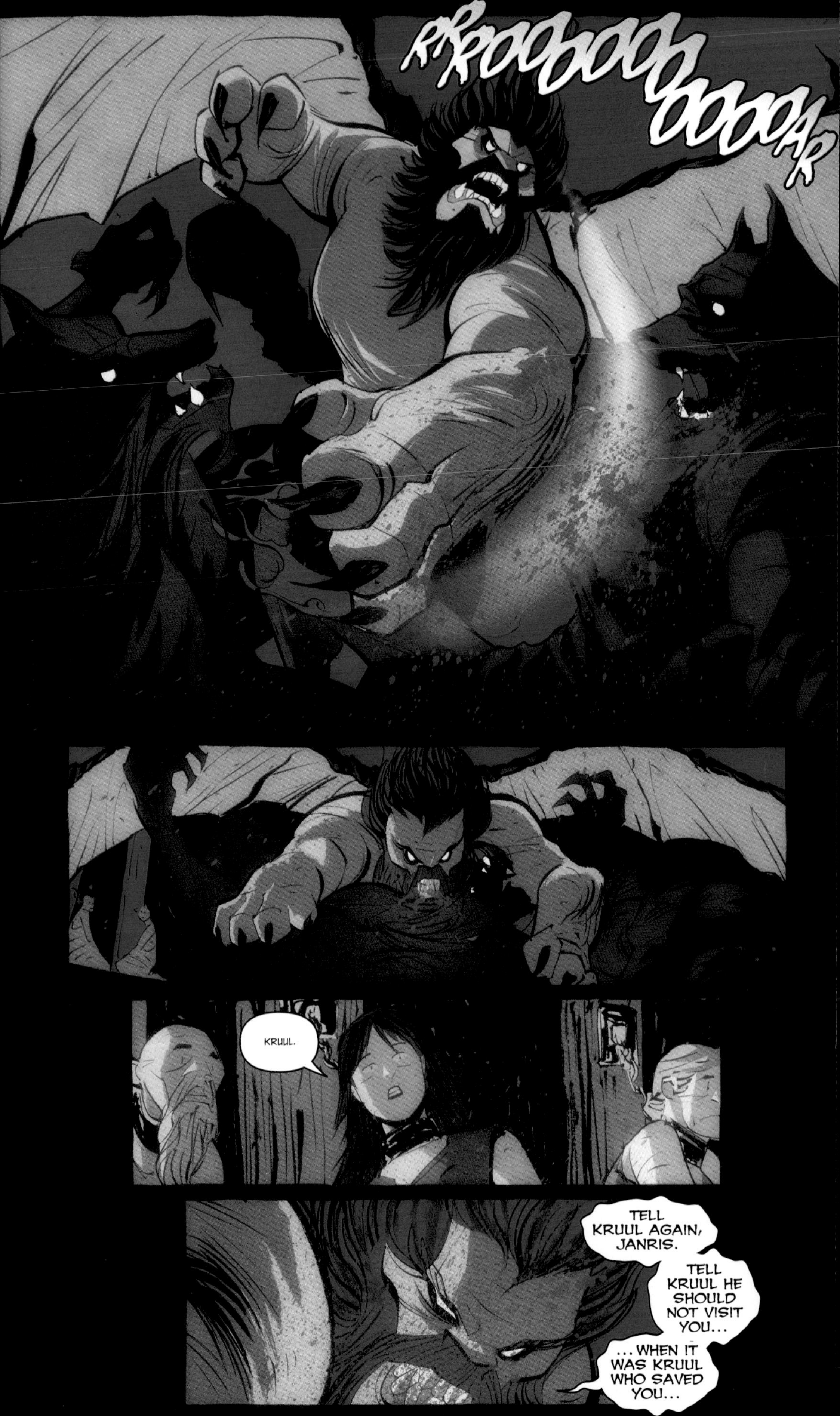
RRROOOOOOOOOOOOAR
KRUUL.
TELL KRUUL AGAIN, JANRIS.
TELL KRUUL HE SHOULD NOT VISIT YOU...
...WHEN IT WAS KRUUL WHO SAVED YOU...

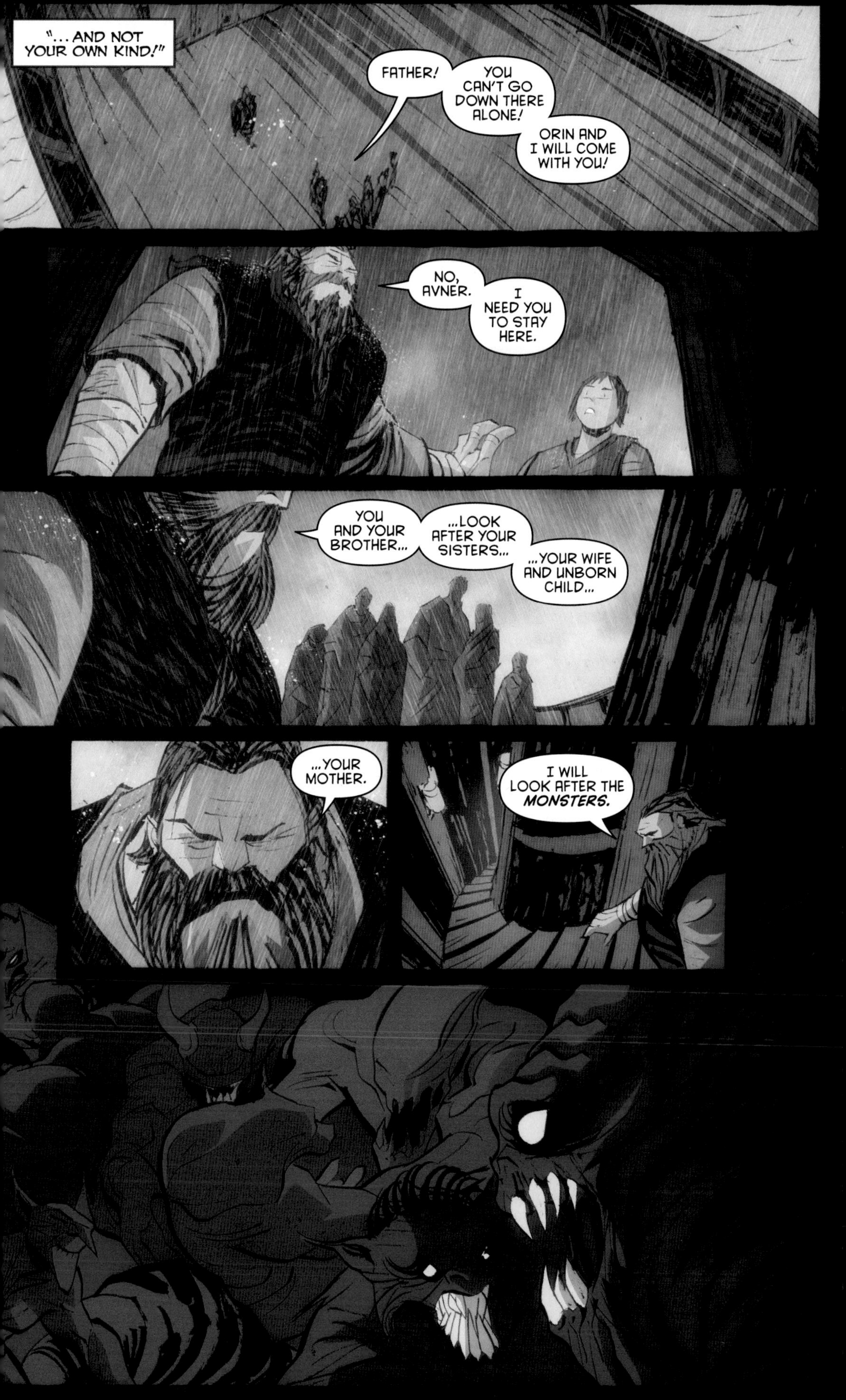
"... AND NOT YOUR OWN KIND!"
FATHER!
YOU CAN'T GO DOWN THERE ALONE!
ORIN AND I WILL COME WITH YOU!
NO, AVNER.
I NEED YOU TO STAY HERE.
YOU AND YOUR BROTHER...
...LOOK AFTER YOUR SISTERS...
...YOUR WIFE AND UNBORN CHILD...
...YOUR MOTHER.
I WILL LOOK AFTER THE *MONSTERS.*

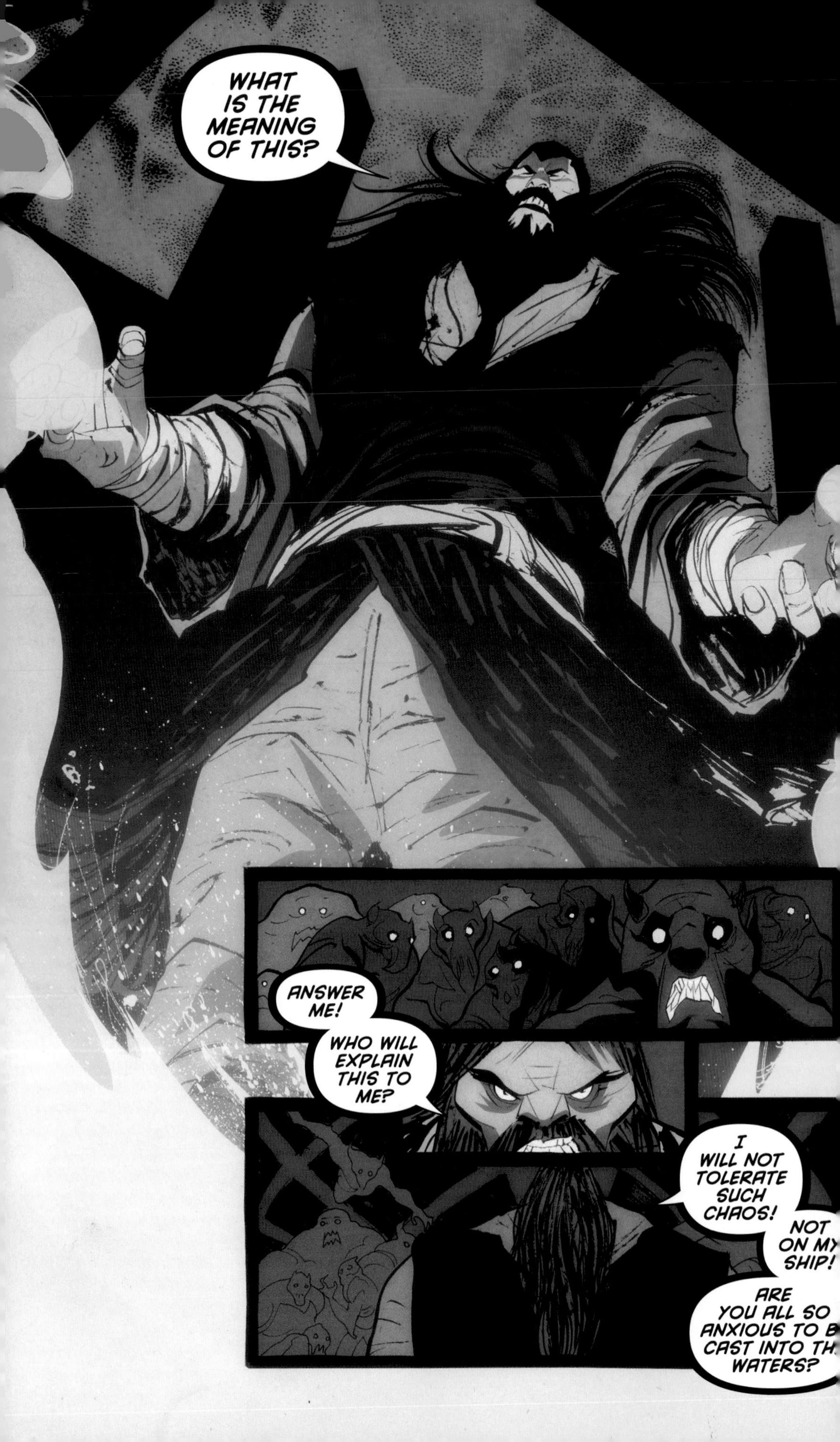
WHAT IS THE MEANING OF THIS?
ANSWER ME!
WHO WILL EXPLAIN THIS TO ME?
I WILL NOT TOLERATE SUCH CHAOS!
NOT ON MY SHIP!
ARE YOU ALL SO ANXIOUS TO BE CAST INTO THE WATERS?

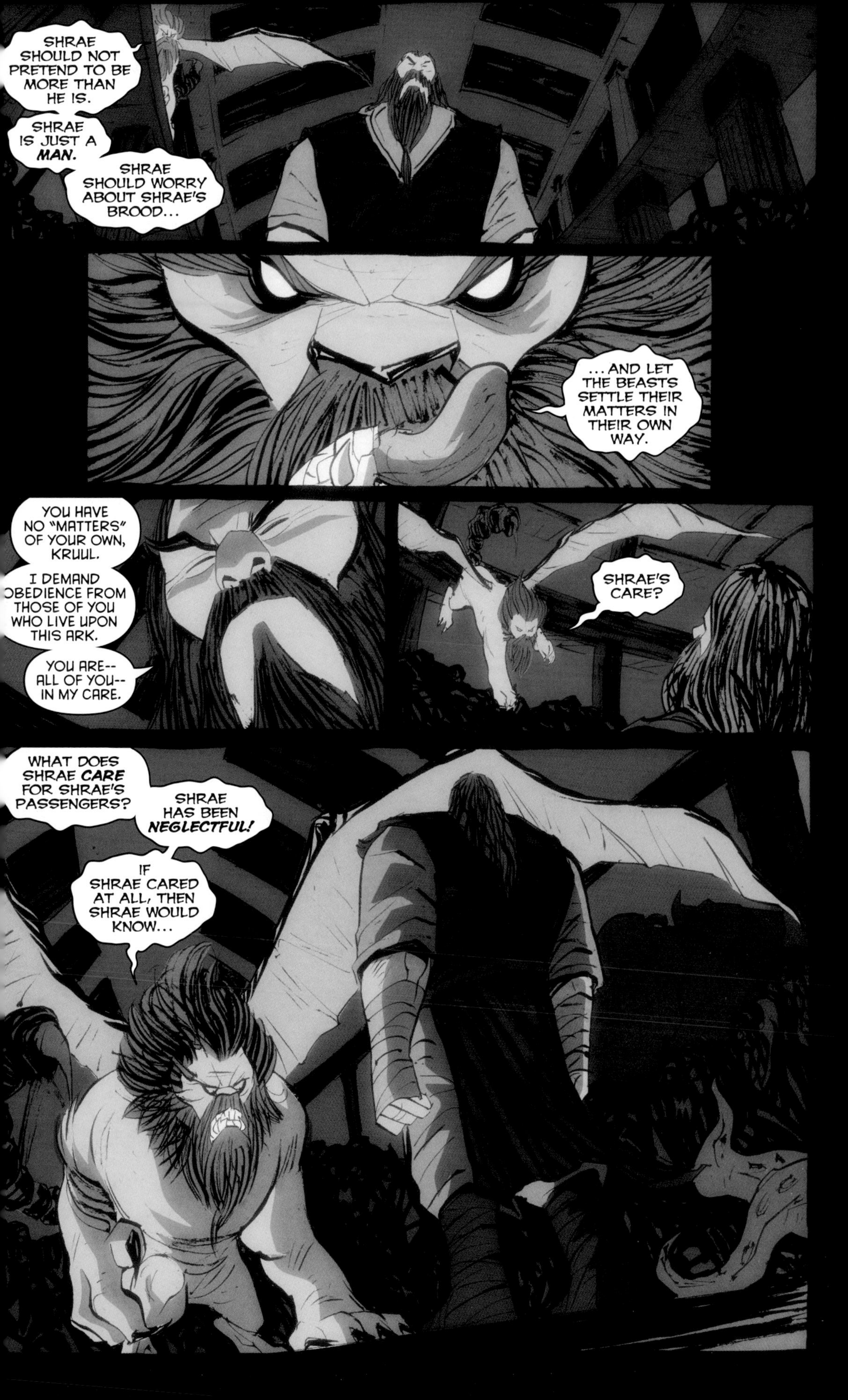
SHRAE SHOULD NOT PRETEND TO BE MORE THAN HE IS.
SHRAE IS JUST A ***MAN.***
SHRAE SHOULD WORRY ABOUT SHRAE'S BROOD...
...AND LET THE BEASTS SETTLE THEIR MATTERS IN THEIR OWN WAY.
YOU HAVE NO "MATTERS" OF YOUR OWN, KRUUL.
I DEMAND OBEDIENCE FROM THOSE OF YOU WHO LIVE UPON THIS ARK.
YOU ARE-- ALL OF YOU-- IN MY CARE.
SHRAE'S CARE?
WHAT DOES SHRAE ***CARE*** FOR SHRAE'S PASSENGERS?
SHRAE HAS BEEN ***NEGLECTFUL!***
IF SHRAE CARED AT ALL, THEN SHRAE WOULD KNOW...

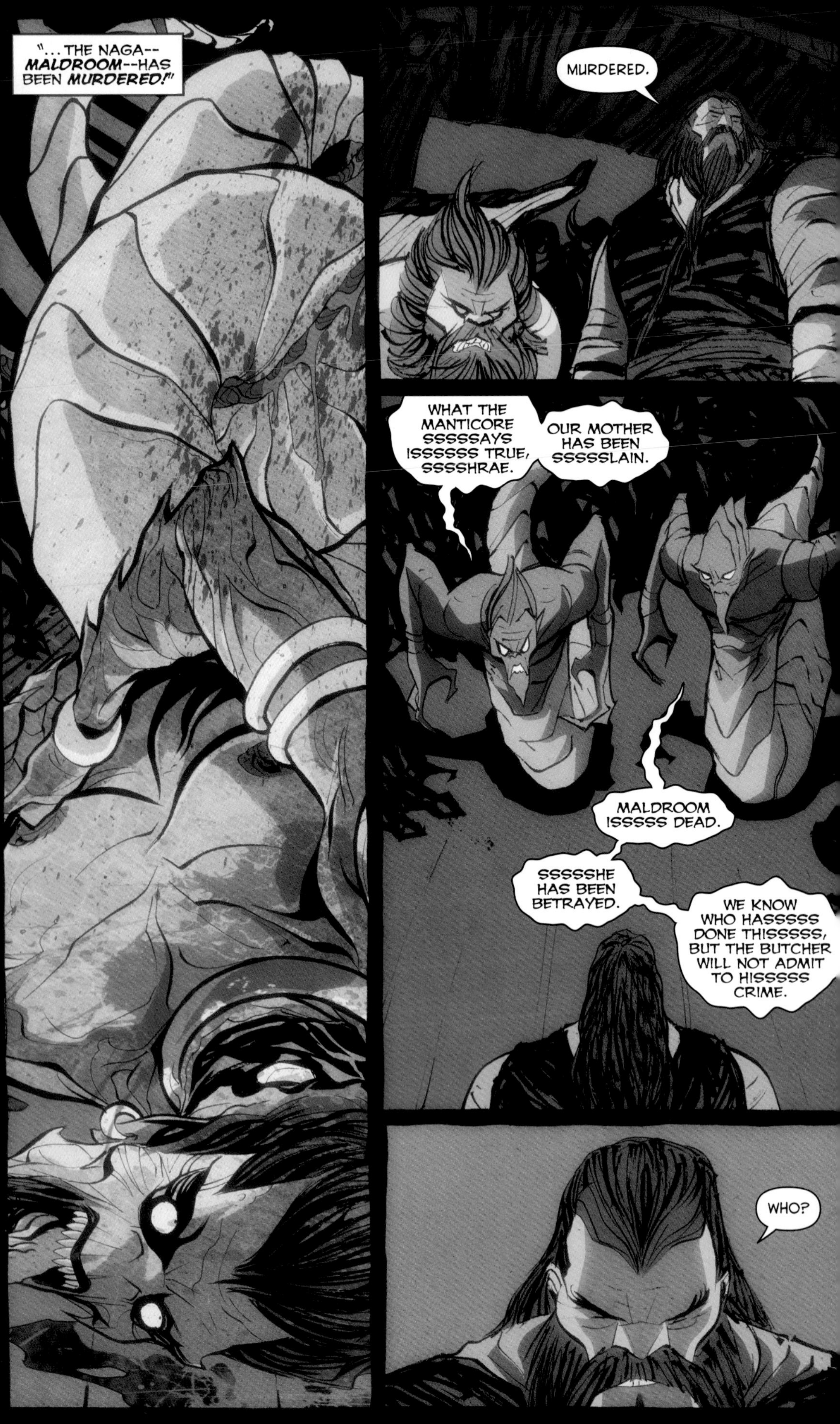
"...THE NAGA-- MALDROOM--HAS BEEN MURDERED!"
MURDERED.
WHAT THE MANTICORE SSSSSAYS ISSSSSS TRUE, SSSSHRAE.
OUR MOTHER HAS BEEN SSSSSLAIN.
MALDROOM ISSSSS DEAD.
SSSSSHE HAS BEEN BETRAYED.
WE KNOW WHO HASSSSS DONE THISSSSS, BUT THE BUTCHER WILL NOT ADMIT TO HISSSSS CRIME.
WHO?

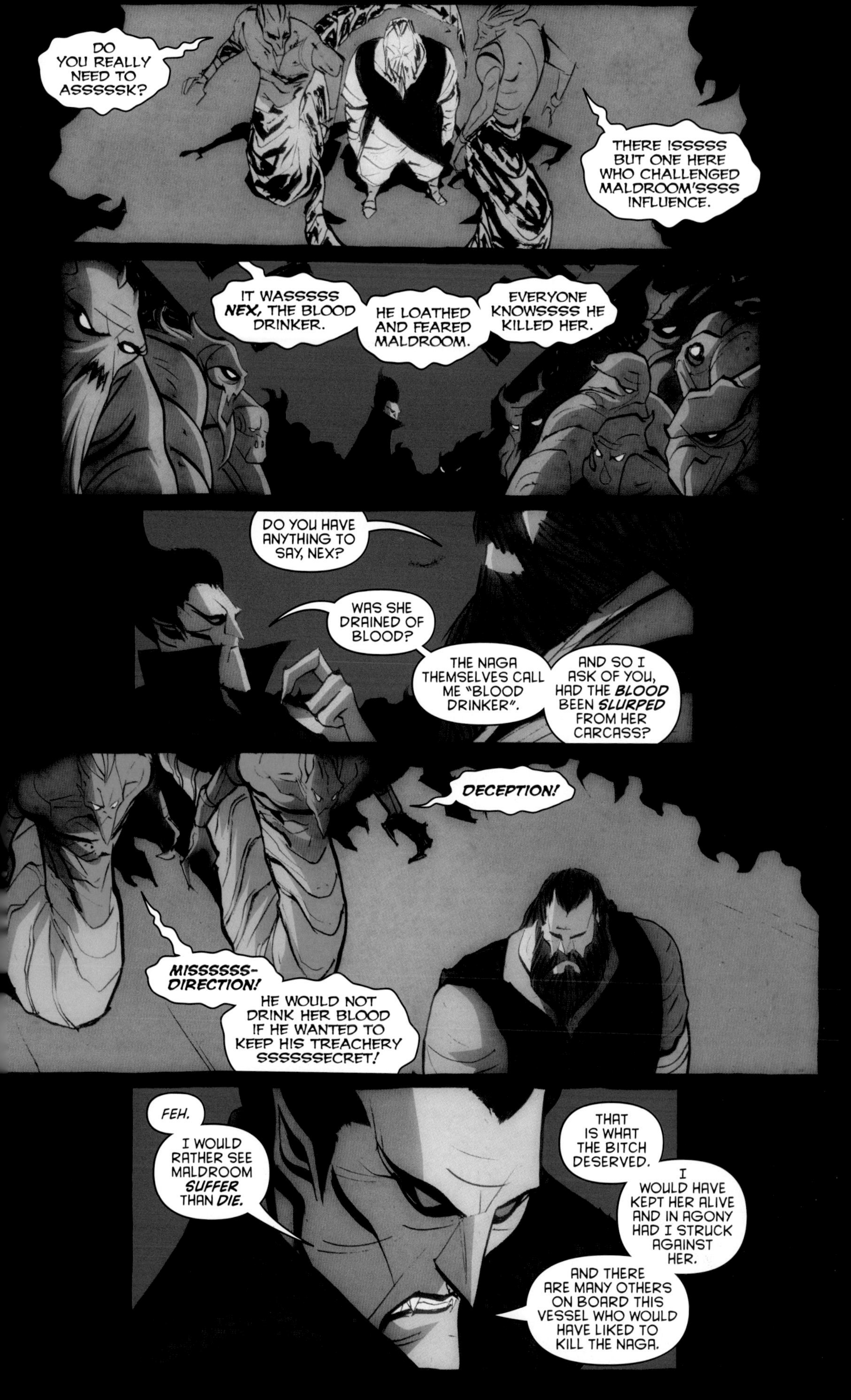
DO YOU REALLY NEED TO ASSSSSK?
THERE ISSSSS BUT ONE HERE WHO CHALLENGED MALDROOM'SSSS INFLUENCE.
IT WASSSSS NEX, THE BLOOD DRINKER.
HE LOATHED AND FEARED MALDROOM.
EVERYONE KNOWSSSS HE KILLED HER.
DO YOU HAVE ANYTHING TO SAY, NEX?
WAS SHE DRAINED OF BLOOD?
THE NAGA THEMSELVES CALL ME "BLOOD DRINKER".
AND SO I ASK OF YOU, HAD THE BLOOD BEEN SLURPED FROM HER CARCASS?
DECEPTION!
MISSSSSS-DIRECTION!
HE WOULD NOT DRINK HER BLOOD IF HE WANTED TO KEEP HIS TREACHERY SSSSSSECRET!
FEH.
I WOULD RATHER SEE MALDROOM SUFFER THAN DIE.
THAT IS WHAT THE BITCH DESERVED.
I WOULD HAVE KEPT HER ALIVE AND IN AGONY HAD I STRUCK AGAINST HER.
AND THERE ARE MANY OTHERS ON BOARD THIS VESSEL WHO WOULD HAVE LIKED TO KILL THE NAGA.

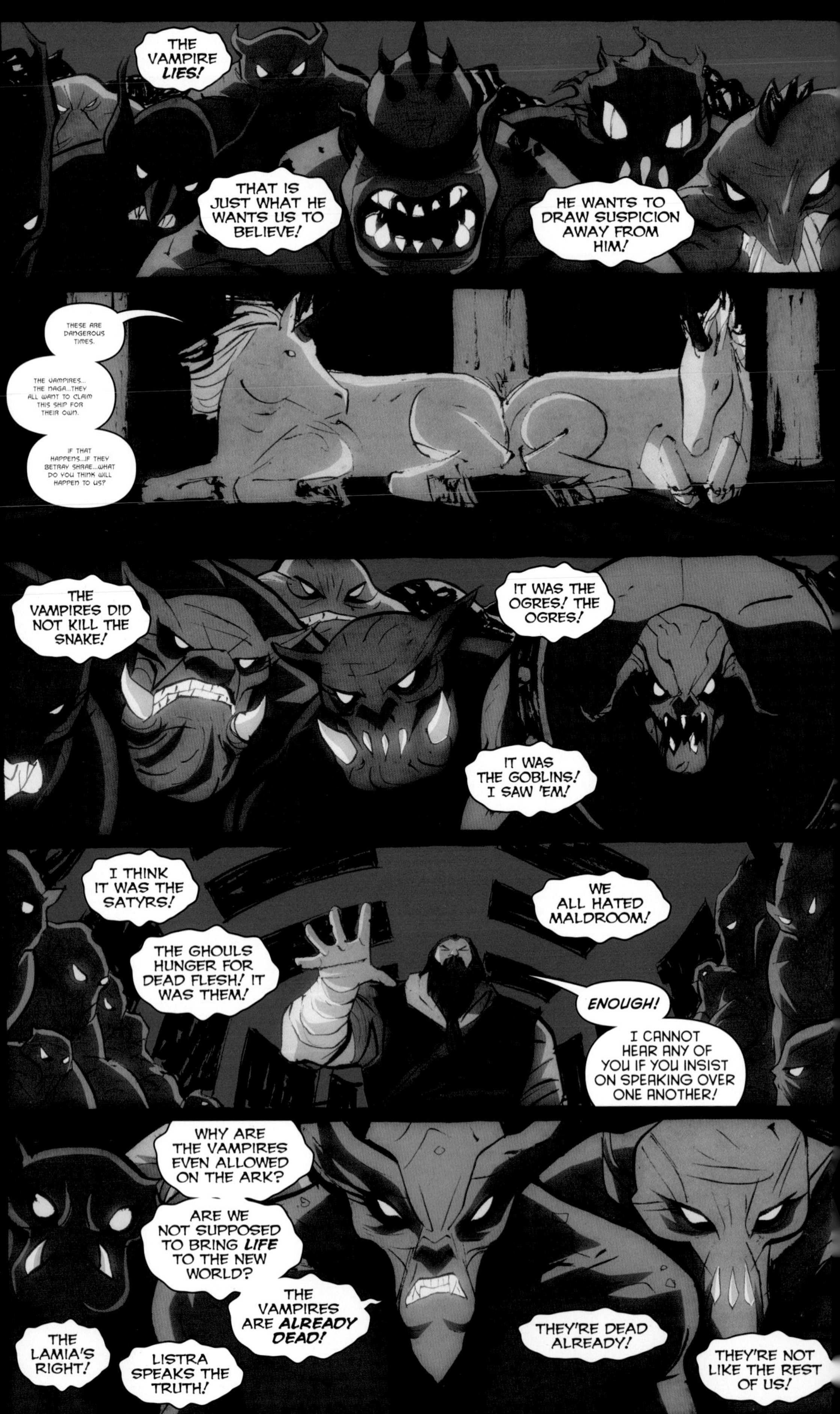
THE VAMPIRE LIES!
THAT IS JUST WHAT HE WANTS US TO BELIEVE!
HE WANTS TO DRAW SUSPICION AWAY FROM HIM!
THESE ARE DANGEROUS TIMES.
THE VAMPIRES... THE NAGA...THEY ALL WANT TO CLAIM THIS SHIP FOR THEIR OWN.
IF THAT HAPPENS...IF THEY BETRAY SHRAE...WHAT DO YOU THINK WILL HAPPEN TO US?
THE VAMPIRES DID NOT KILL THE SNAKE!
IT WAS THE OGRES! THE OGRES!
IT WAS THE GOBLINS! I SAW 'EM!
I THINK IT WAS THE SATYRS!
WE ALL HATED MALDROOM!
THE GHOULS HUNGER FOR DEAD FLESH! IT WAS THEM!
ENOUGH!
I CANNOT HEAR ANY OF YOU IF YOU INSIST ON SPEAKING OVER ONE ANOTHER!
WHY ARE THE VAMPIRES EVEN ALLOWED ON THE ARK?
ARE WE NOT SUPPOSED TO BRING LIFE TO THE NEW WORLD?
THE VAMPIRES ARE ALREADY DEAD!
THEY'RE DEAD ALREADY!
THE LAMIA'S RIGHT!
LISTRA SPEAKS THE TRUTH!
THEY'RE NOT LIKE THE REST OF US!

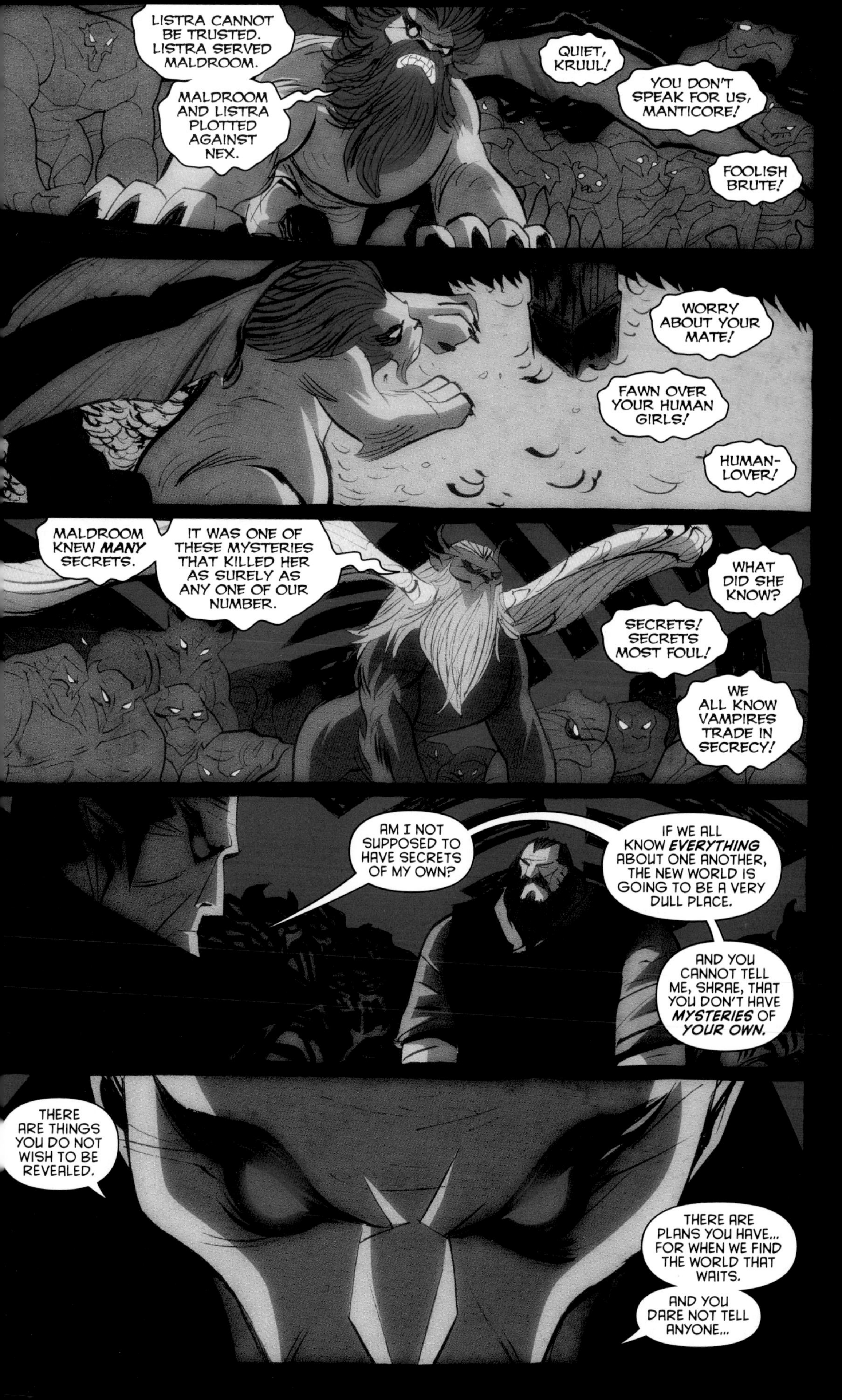
LISTRA CANNOT BE TRUSTED. LISTRA SERVED MALDROOM.
MALDROOM AND LISTRA PLOTTED AGAINST NEX.
QUIET, KRUUL!
YOU DON'T SPEAK FOR US, MANTICORE!
FOOLISH BRUTE!
WORRY ABOUT YOUR MATE!
FAWN OVER YOUR HUMAN GIRLS!
HUMAN-LOVER!
MALDROOM KNEW *MANY* SECRETS.
IT WAS ONE OF THESE MYSTERIES THAT KILLED HER AS SURELY AS ANY ONE OF OUR NUMBER.
WHAT DID SHE KNOW?
SECRETS! SECRETS MOST FOUL!
WE ALL KNOW VAMPIRES TRADE IN SECRECY!
AM I NOT SUPPOSED TO HAVE SECRETS OF MY OWN?
IF WE ALL KNOW *EVERYTHING* ABOUT ONE ANOTHER, THE NEW WORLD IS GOING TO BE A VERY DULL PLACE.
AND YOU CANNOT TELL ME, SHRAE, THAT YOU DON'T HAVE *MYSTERIES* OF *YOUR OWN.*
THERE ARE THINGS YOU DO NOT WISH TO BE REVEALED.
THERE ARE PLANS YOU HAVE... FOR WHEN WE FIND THE WORLD THAT WAITS.
AND YOU DARE NOT TELL ANYONE...

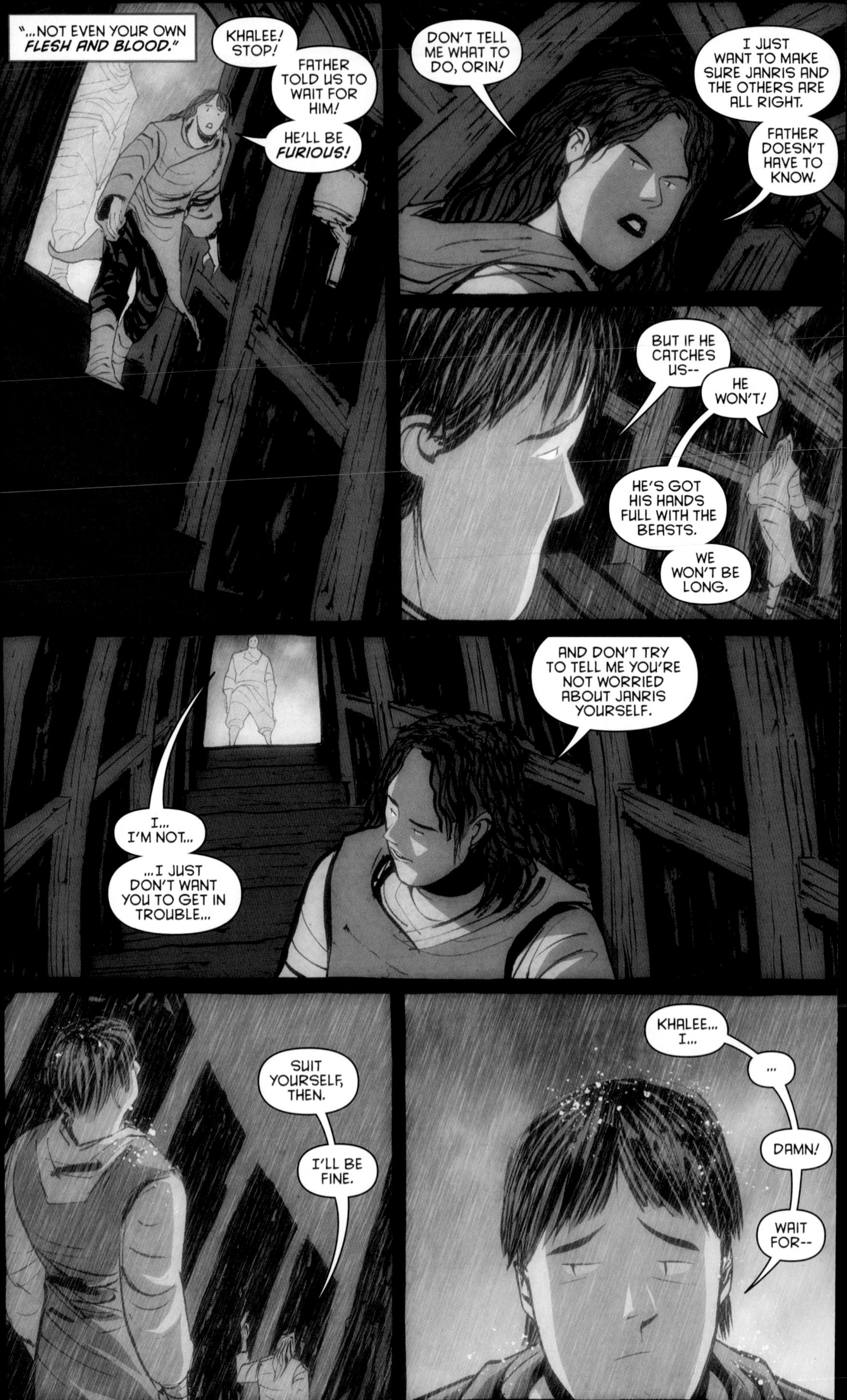
"...NOT EVEN YOUR OWN FLESH AND BLOOD."
KHALEE! STOP!
FATHER TOLD US TO WAIT FOR HIM!
HE'LL BE FURIOUS!
DON'T TELL ME WHAT TO DO, ORIN!
I JUST WANT TO MAKE SURE JANRIS AND THE OTHERS ARE ALL RIGHT.
FATHER DOESN'T HAVE TO KNOW.
BUT IF HE CATCHES US--
HE WON'T!
HE'S GOT HIS HANDS FULL WITH THE BEASTS.
WE WON'T BE LONG.
AND DON'T TRY TO TELL ME YOU'RE NOT WORRIED ABOUT JANRIS YOURSELF.
I... I'M NOT...
...I JUST DON'T WANT YOU TO GET IN TROUBLE...
SUIT YOURSELF, THEN.
I'LL BE FINE.
KHALEE... I...
...
DAMN!
WAIT FOR--

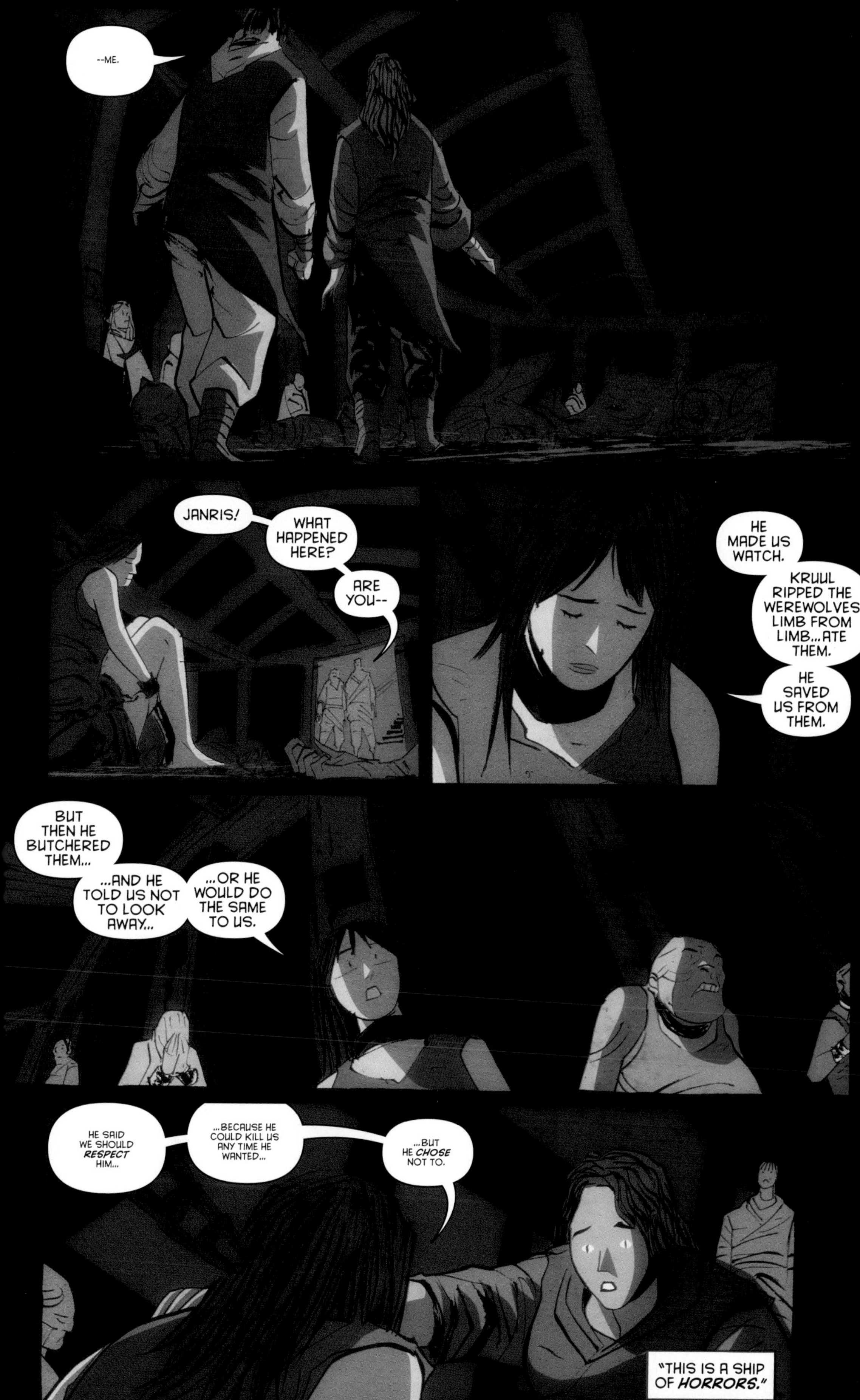
--ME.
JANRIS!
WHAT HAPPENED HERE?
ARE YOU--
HE MADE US WATCH.
KRUUL RIPPED THE WEREWOLVES LIMB FROM LIMB...ATE THEM.
HE SAVED US FROM THEM.
BUT THEN HE BUTCHERED THEM...
...AND HE TOLD US NOT TO LOOK AWAY...
...OR HE WOULD DO THE SAME TO US.
HE SAID WE SHOULD *RESPECT* HIM...
...BECAUSE HE COULD KILL US ANY TIME HE WANTED...
...BUT HE *CHOSE* NOT TO.
"THIS IS A SHIP OF *HORRORS.*"

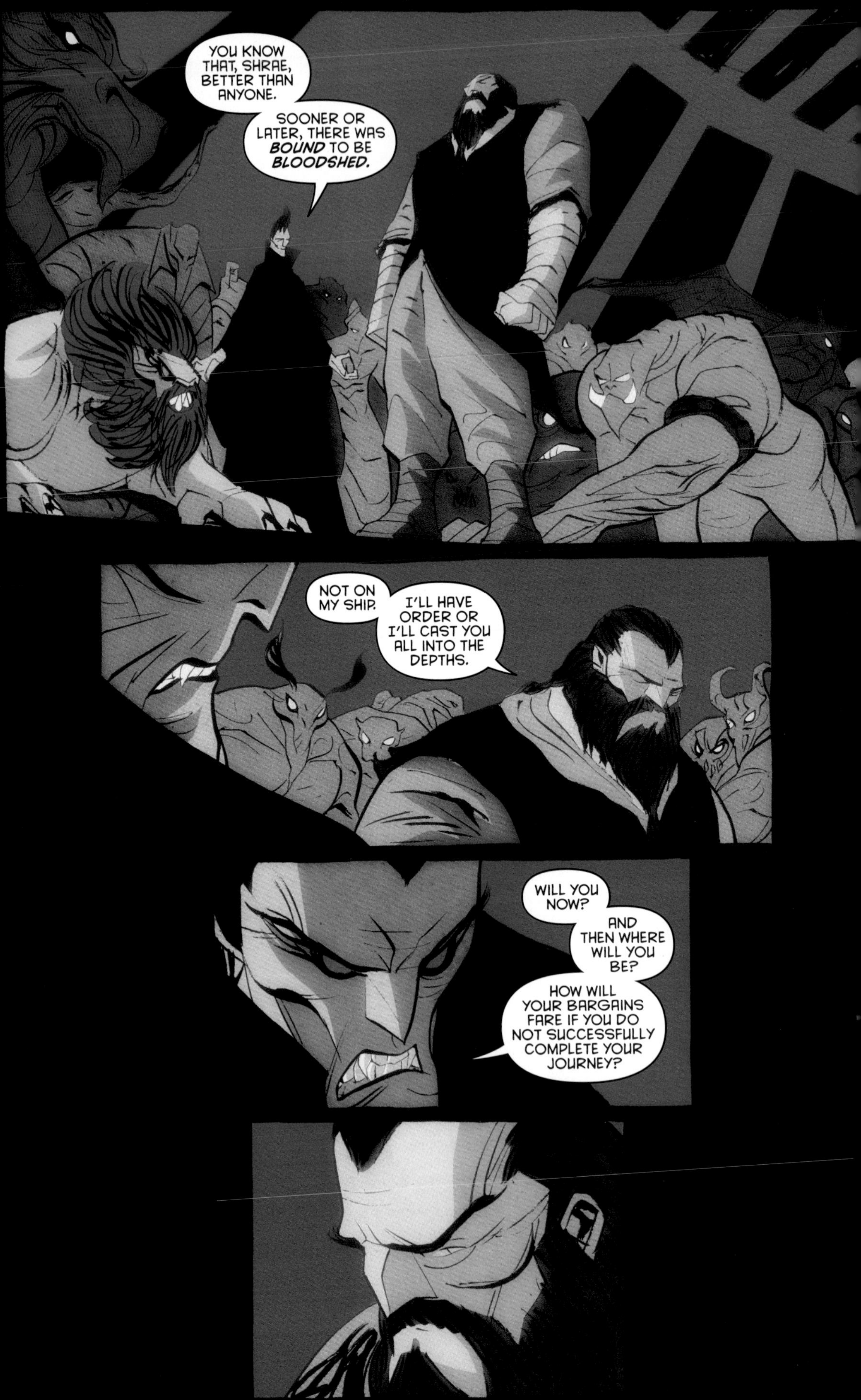
YOU KNOW THAT, SHRAE, BETTER THAN ANYONE.
SOONER OR LATER, THERE WAS ***BOUND*** TO BE ***BLOODSHED.***
NOT ON MY SHIP.
I'LL HAVE ORDER OR I'LL CAST YOU ALL INTO THE DEPTHS.
WILL YOU NOW?
AND THEN WHERE WILL YOU BE?
HOW WILL YOUR BARGAINS FARE IF YOU DO NOT SUCCESSFULLY COMPLETE YOUR JOURNEY?

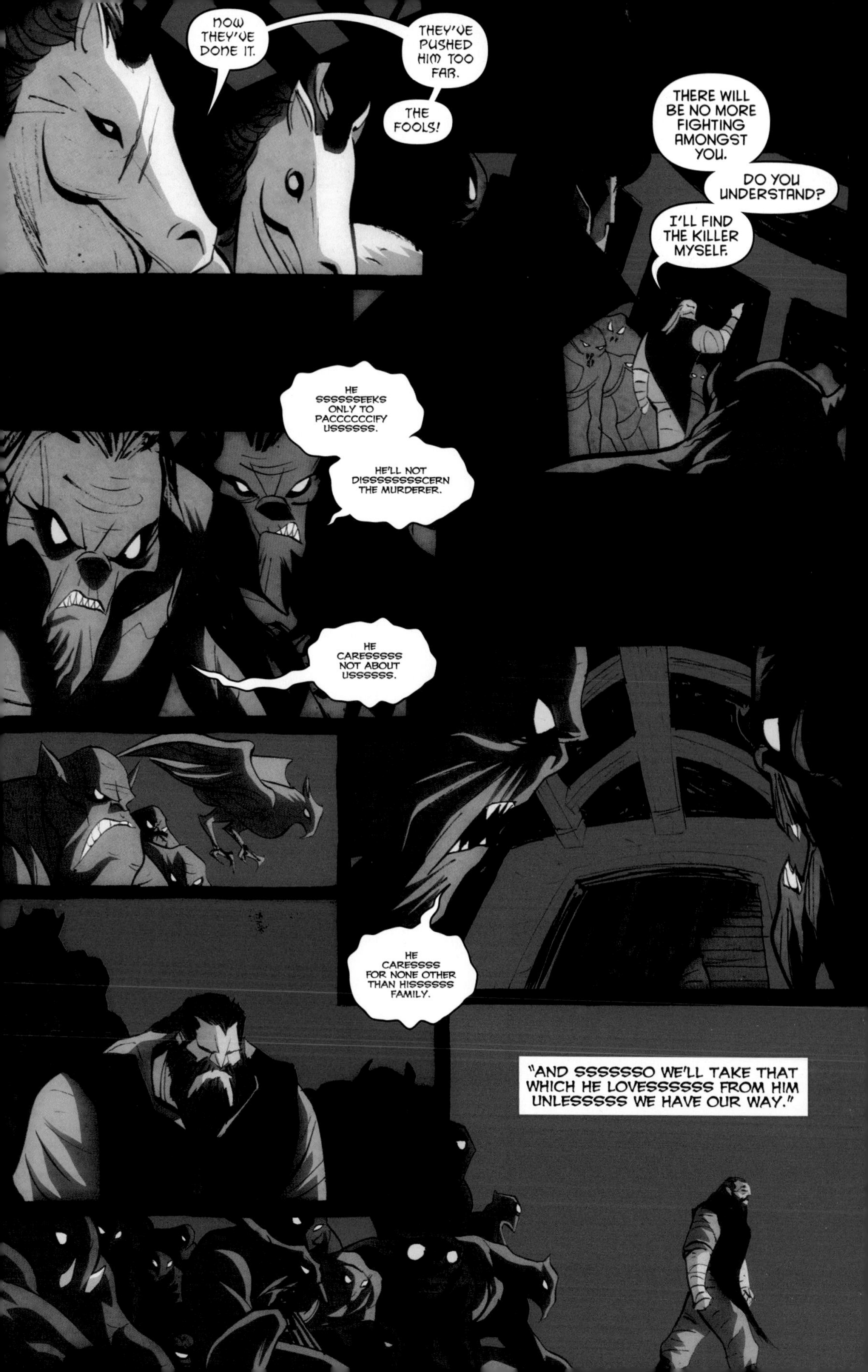
NOW THEY'VE DONE IT.
THEY'VE PUSHED HIM TOO FAR.
THE FOOLS!
THERE WILL BE NO MORE FIGHTING AMONGST YOU.
DO YOU UNDERSTAND?
I'LL FIND THE KILLER MYSELF.
HE SSSSSSEEKS ONLY TO PACCCCCCIFY USSSSSS.
HE'LL NOT DISSSSSSSSSCERN THE MURDERER.
HE CARESSSSS NOT ABOUT USSSSSS.
HE CARESSSS FOR NONE OTHER THAN HISSSSSS FAMILY.
"AND SSSSSSO WE'LL TAKE THAT WHICH HE LOVESSSSSS FROM HIM UNLESSSSS WE HAVE OUR WAY."

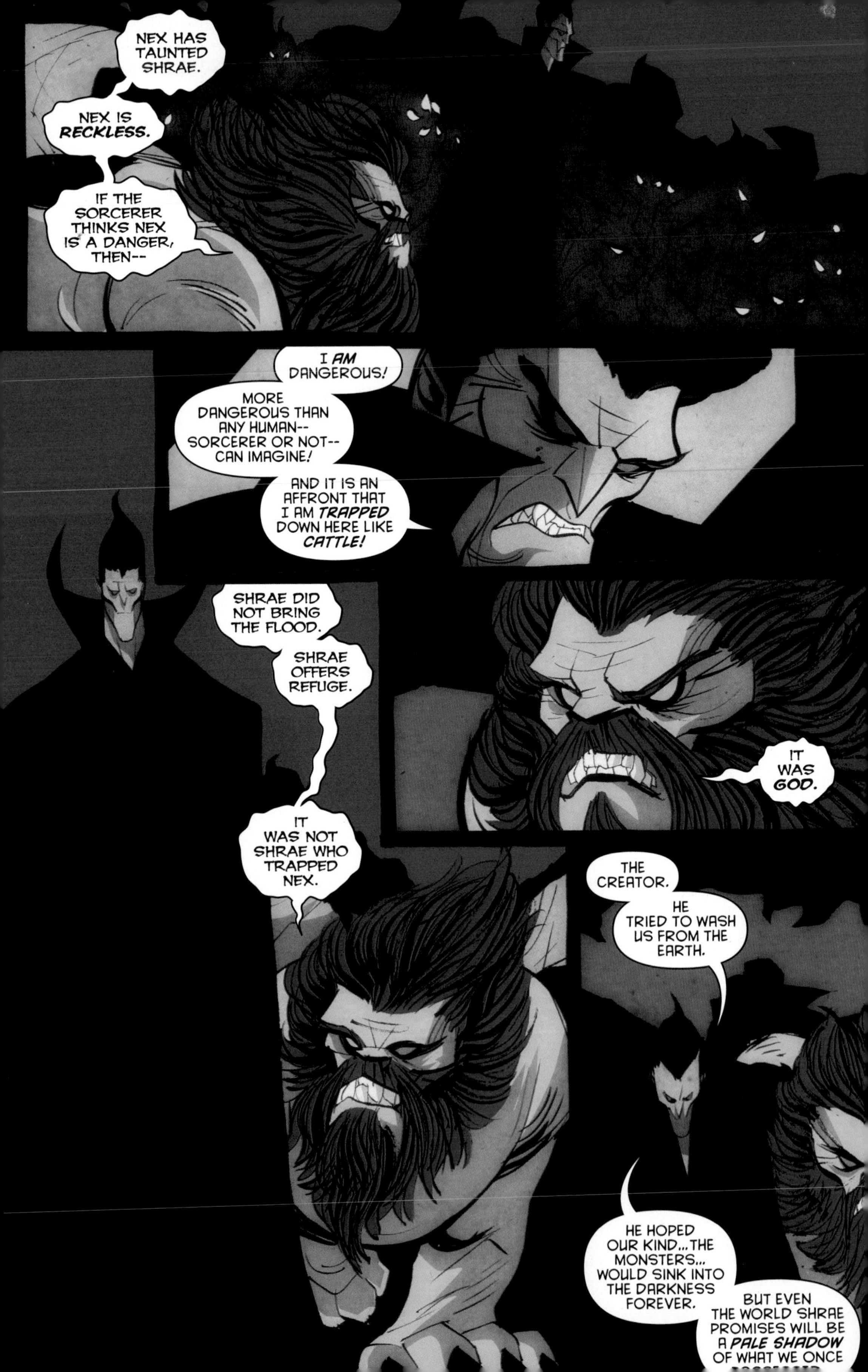
NEX HAS TAUNTED SHRAE.
NEX IS RECKLESS.
IF THE SORCERER THINKS NEX IS A DANGER, THEN--
I AM DANGEROUS!
MORE DANGEROUS THAN ANY HUMAN-- SORCERER OR NOT-- CAN IMAGINE!
AND IT IS AN AFFRONT THAT I AM TRAPPED DOWN HERE LIKE CATTLE!
SHRAE DID NOT BRING THE FLOOD.
SHRAE OFFERS REFUGE.
IT WAS NOT SHRAE WHO TRAPPED NEX.
IT WAS GOD.
THE CREATOR.
HE TRIED TO WASH US FROM THE EARTH.
HE HOPED OUR KIND... THE MONSTERS... WOULD SINK INTO THE DARKNESS FOREVER.
BUT EVEN THE WORLD SHRAE PROMISES WILL BE A PALE SHADOW OF WHAT WE ONCE

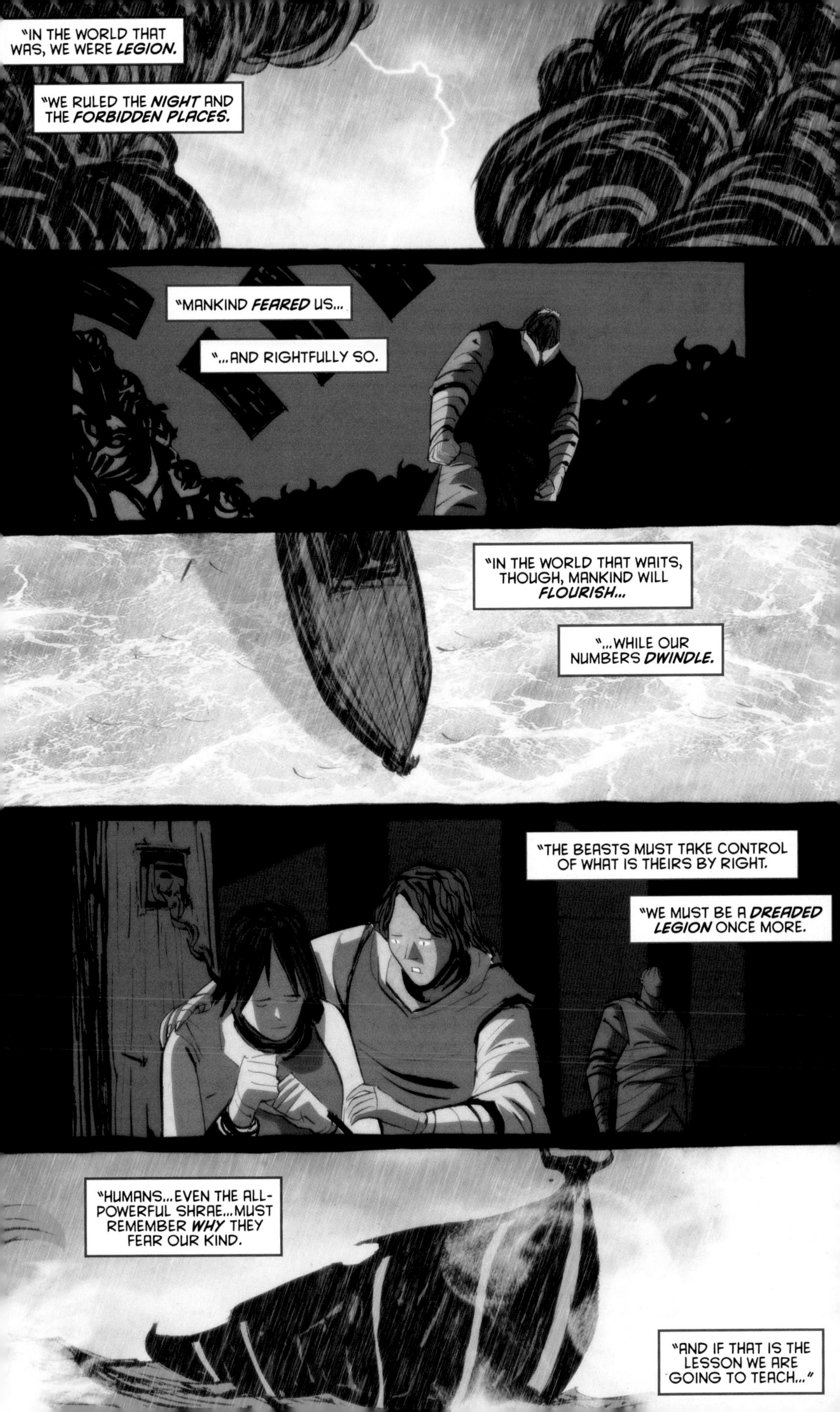
"IN THE WORLD THAT WAS, WE WERE LEGION.
"WE RULED THE NIGHT AND THE FORBIDDEN PLACES.
"MANKIND FEARED US...
"...AND RIGHTFULLY SO.
"IN THE WORLD THAT WAITS, THOUGH, MANKIND WILL FLOURISH...
"...WHILE OUR NUMBERS DWINDLE.
"THE BEASTS MUST TAKE CONTROL OF WHAT IS THEIRS BY RIGHT.
"WE MUST BE A DREADED LEGION ONCE MORE.
"HUMANS...EVEN THE ALL-POWERFUL SHRAE...MUST REMEMBER WHY THEY FEAR OUR KIND.
"AND IF THAT IS THE LESSON WE ARE GOING TO TEACH..."

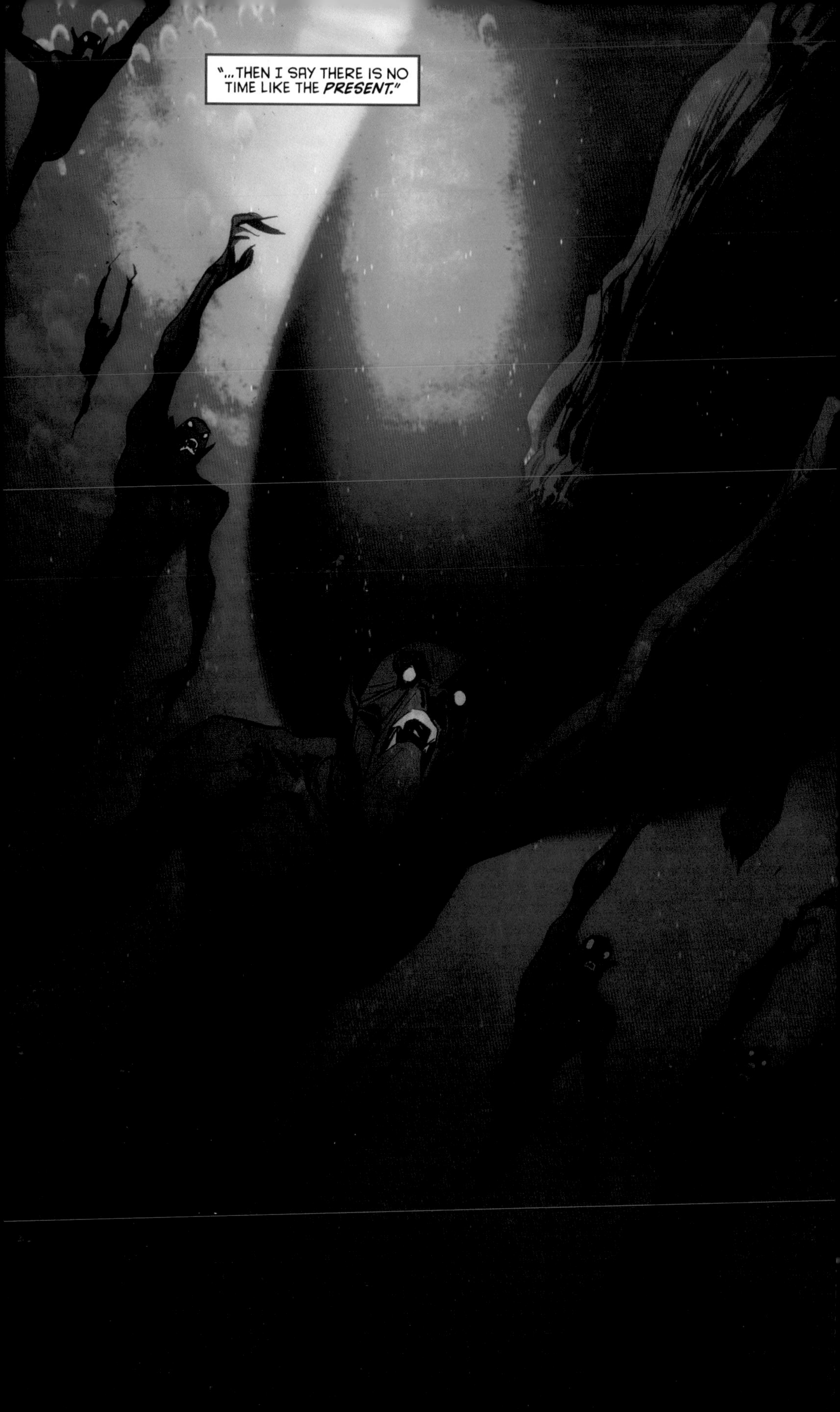
"...THEN I SAY THERE IS NO TIME LIKE THE *PRESENT.*"

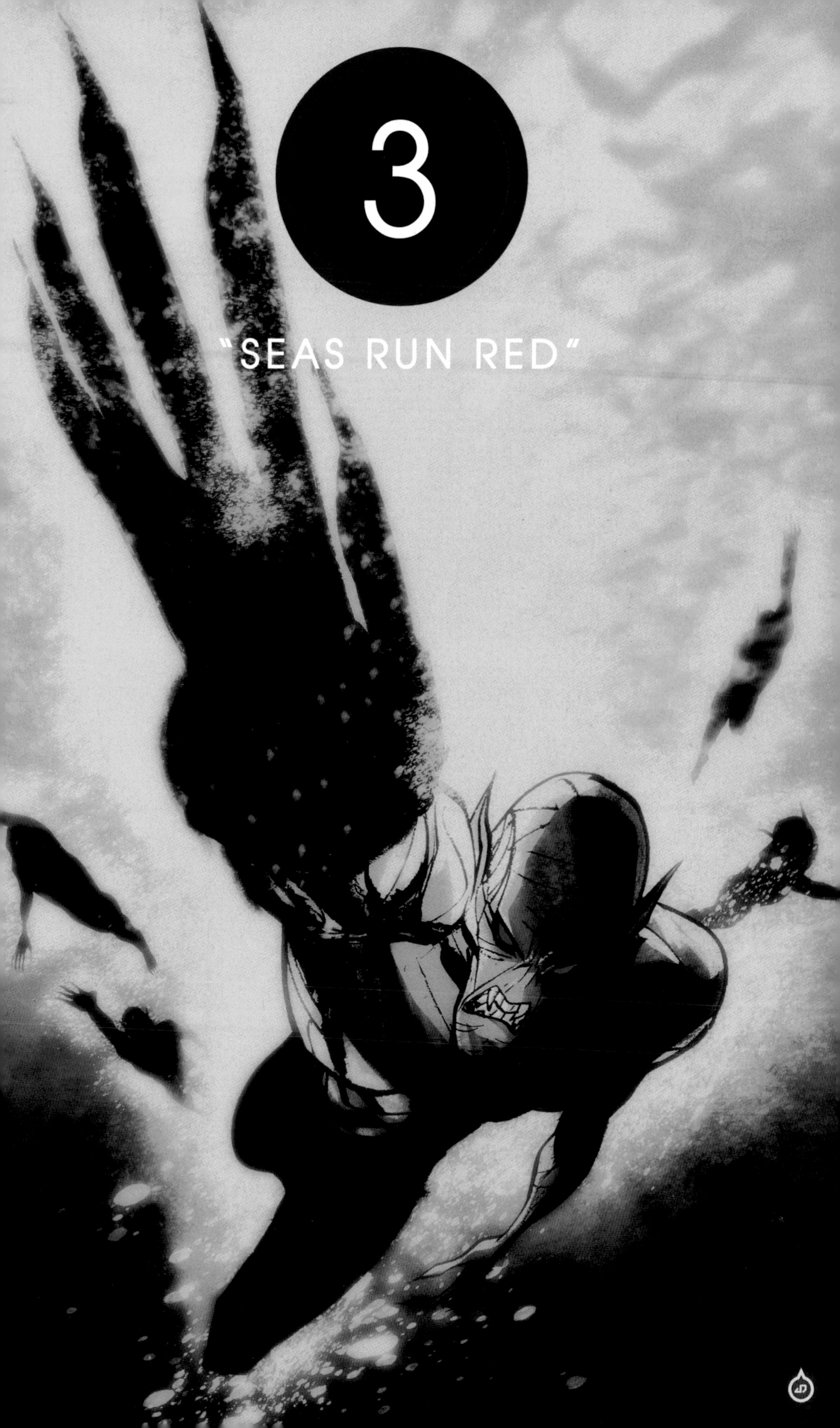
3
"SEAS RUN RED"

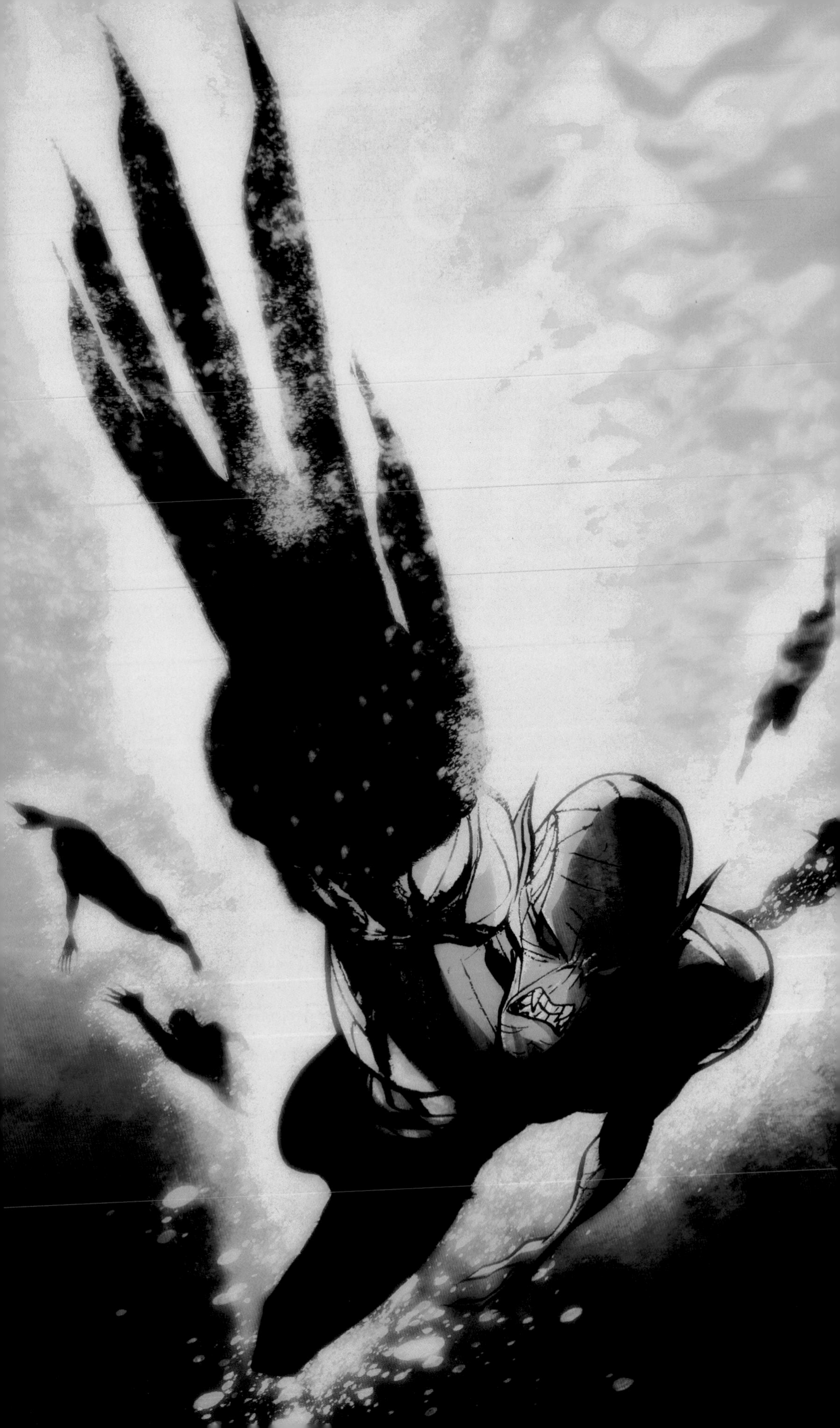

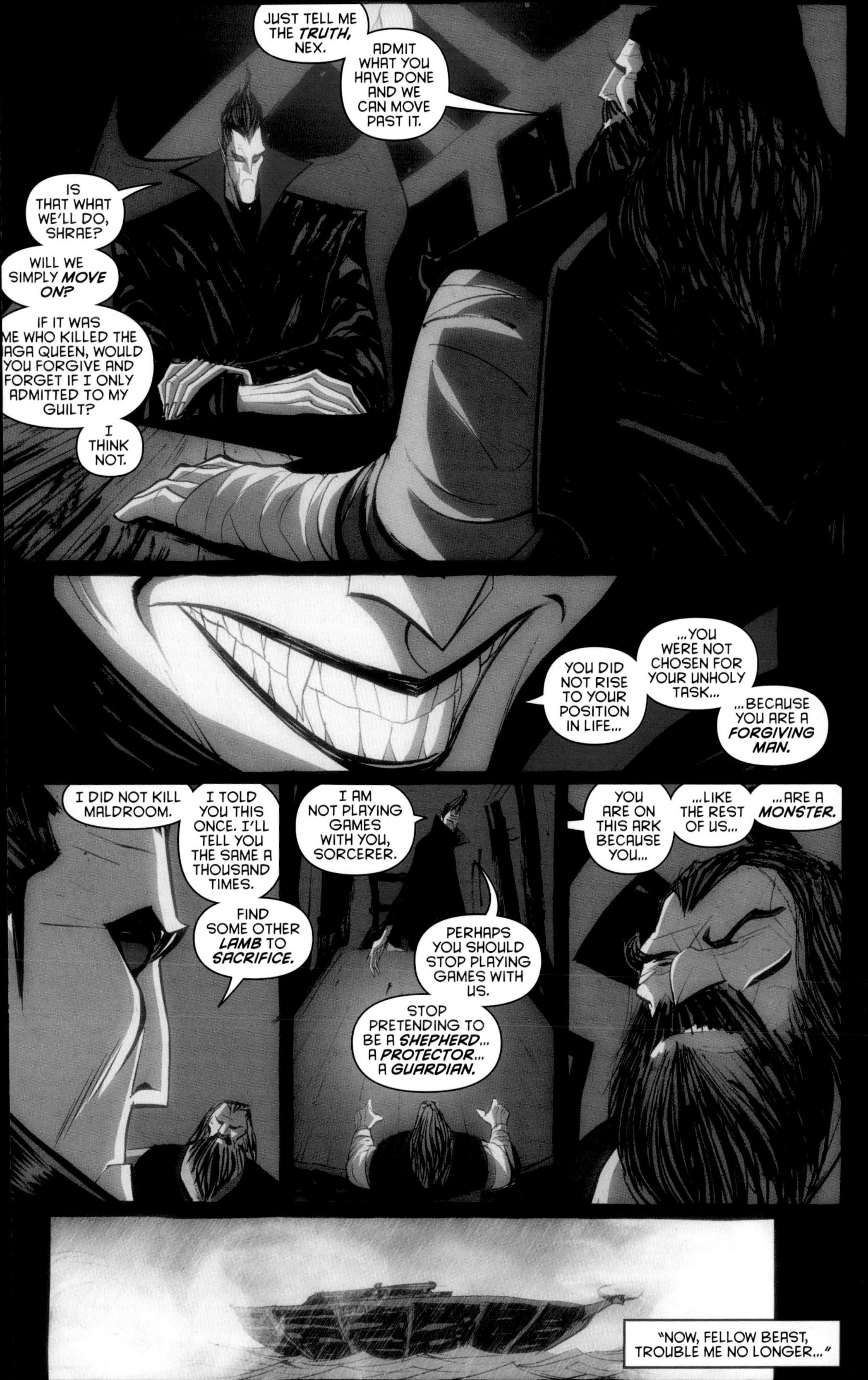
JUST TELL ME THE TRUTH, NEX.
ADMIT WHAT YOU HAVE DONE AND WE CAN MOVE PAST IT.
IS THAT WHAT WE'LL DO, SHRAE?
WILL WE SIMPLY MOVE ON?
IF IT WAS ME WHO KILLED THE AGA QUEEN, WOULD YOU FORGIVE AND FORGET IF I ONLY ADMITTED TO MY GUILT?
I THINK NOT.
YOU DID NOT RISE TO YOUR POSITION IN LIFE...
...YOU WERE NOT CHOSEN FOR YOUR UNHOLY TASK...
...BECAUSE YOU ARE A FORGIVING MAN.
I DID NOT KILL MALDROOM.
I TOLD YOU THIS ONCE. I'LL TELL YOU THE SAME A THOUSAND TIMES.
FIND SOME OTHER LAMB TO SACRIFICE.
I AM NOT PLAYING GAMES WITH YOU, SORCERER.
PERHAPS YOU SHOULD STOP PLAYING GAMES WITH US.
STOP PRETENDING TO BE A SHEPHERD... A PROTECTOR... A GUARDIAN.
YOU ARE ON THIS ARK BECAUSE YOU...
...LIKE THE REST OF US...
...ARE A MONSTER.
"NOW, FELLOW BEAST, TROUBLE ME NO LONGER..."

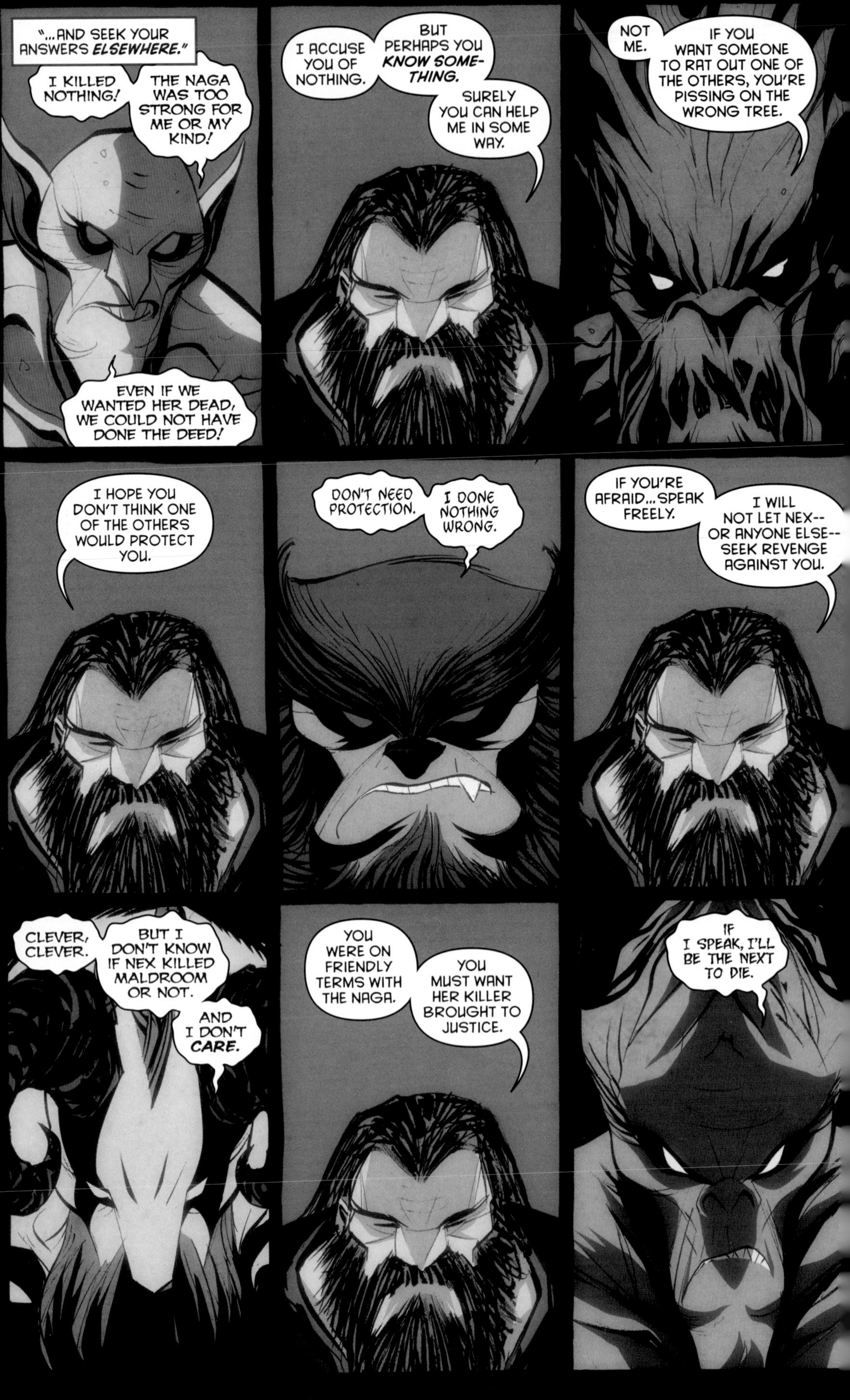
"...AND SEEK YOUR ANSWERS *ELSEWHERE.*"
I KILLED NOTHING!
THE NAGA WAS TOO STRONG FOR ME OR MY KIND!
EVEN IF WE WANTED HER DEAD, WE COULD NOT HAVE DONE THE DEED!
I ACCUSE YOU OF NOTHING.
BUT PERHAPS YOU *KNOW SOMETHING.*
SURELY YOU CAN HELP ME IN SOME WAY.
NOT ME.
IF YOU WANT SOMEONE TO RAT OUT ONE OF THE OTHERS, YOU'RE PISSING ON THE WRONG TREE.
I HOPE YOU DON'T THINK ONE OF THE OTHERS WOULD PROTECT YOU.
DON'T NEED PROTECTION.
I DONE NOTHING WRONG.
IF YOU'RE AFRAID...SPEAK FREELY.
I WILL NOT LET NEX-- OR ANYONE ELSE-- SEEK REVENGE AGAINST YOU.
CLEVER, CLEVER.
BUT I DON'T KNOW IF NEX KILLED MALDROOM OR NOT.
AND I DON'T *CARE.*
YOU WERE ON FRIENDLY TERMS WITH THE NAGA.
YOU MUST WANT HER KILLER BROUGHT TO JUSTICE.
IF I SPEAK, I'LL BE THE NEXT TO DIE.

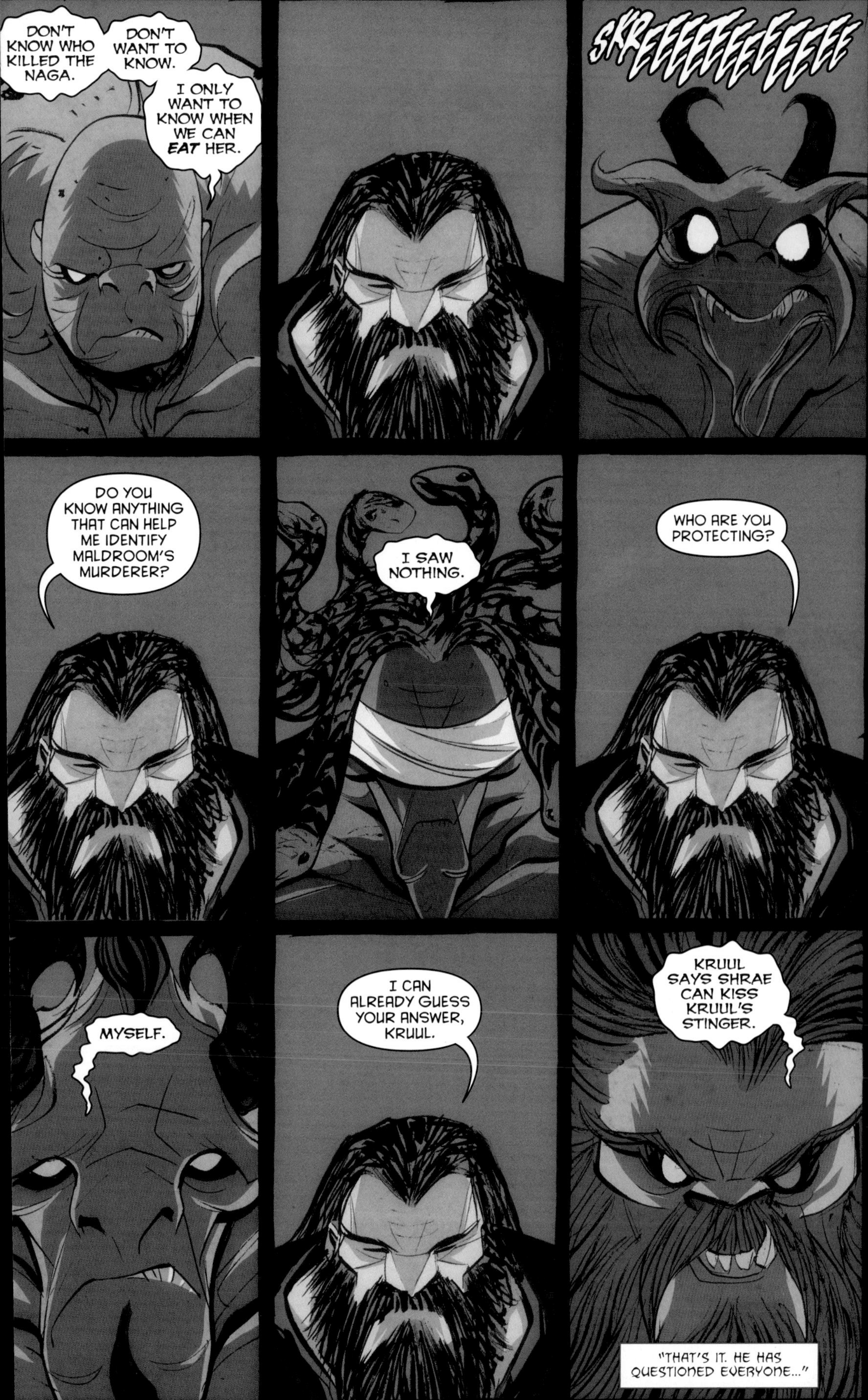
DON'T KNOW WHO KILLED THE NAGA.
DON'T WANT TO KNOW.
I ONLY WANT TO KNOW WHEN WE CAN *EAT* HER.
SKREEEEEEEEEEEE
DO YOU KNOW ANYTHING THAT CAN HELP ME IDENTIFY MALDROOM'S MURDERER?
I SAW NOTHING.
WHO ARE YOU PROTECTING?
MYSELF.
I CAN ALREADY GUESS YOUR ANSWER, KRUUL.
KRUUL SAYS SHRAE CAN KISS KRUUL'S STINGER.
"THAT'S IT. HE HAS QUESTIONED EVERYONE..."

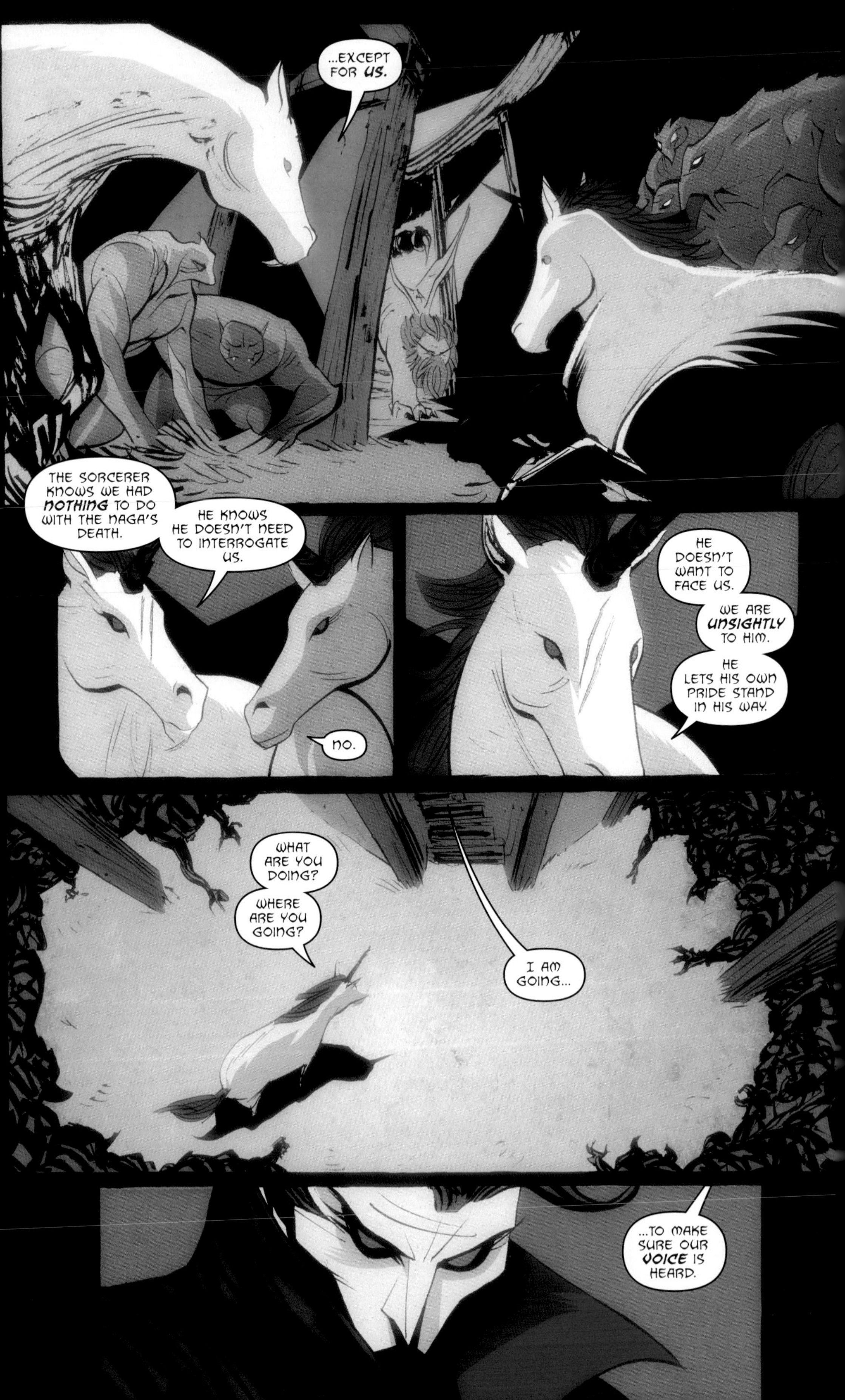
...EXCEPT FOR US.
THE SORCERER KNOWS WE HAD NOTHING TO DO WITH THE NAGA'S DEATH.
HE KNOWS HE DOESN'T NEED TO INTERROGATE US.
NO.
HE DOESN'T WANT TO FACE US.
WE ARE UNSIGHTLY TO HIM.
HE LETS HIS OWN PRIDE STAND IN HIS WAY.
WHAT ARE YOU DOING?
WHERE ARE YOU GOING?
I AM GOING...
...TO MAKE SURE OUR VOICE IS HEARD.

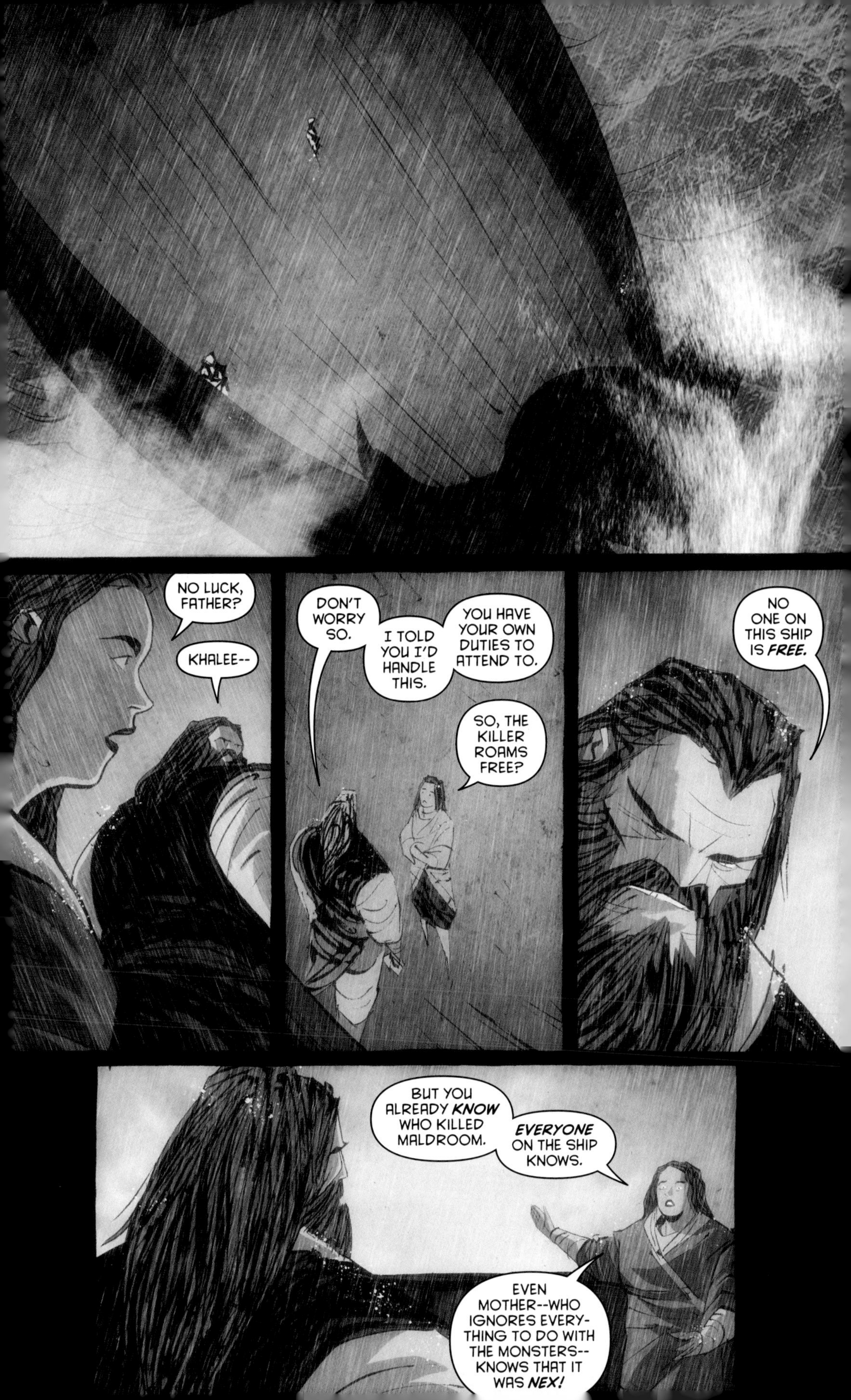
NO LUCK, FATHER?
KHALEE--
DON'T WORRY SO.
I TOLD YOU I'D HANDLE THIS.
YOU HAVE YOUR OWN DUTIES TO ATTEND TO.
SO, THE KILLER ROAMS FREE?
NO ONE ON THIS SHIP IS FREE.
BUT YOU ALREADY KNOW WHO KILLED MALDROOM.
EVERYONE ON THE SHIP KNOWS.
EVEN MOTHER--WHO IGNORES EVERY-THING TO DO WITH THE MONSTERS--KNOWS THAT IT WAS NEX!

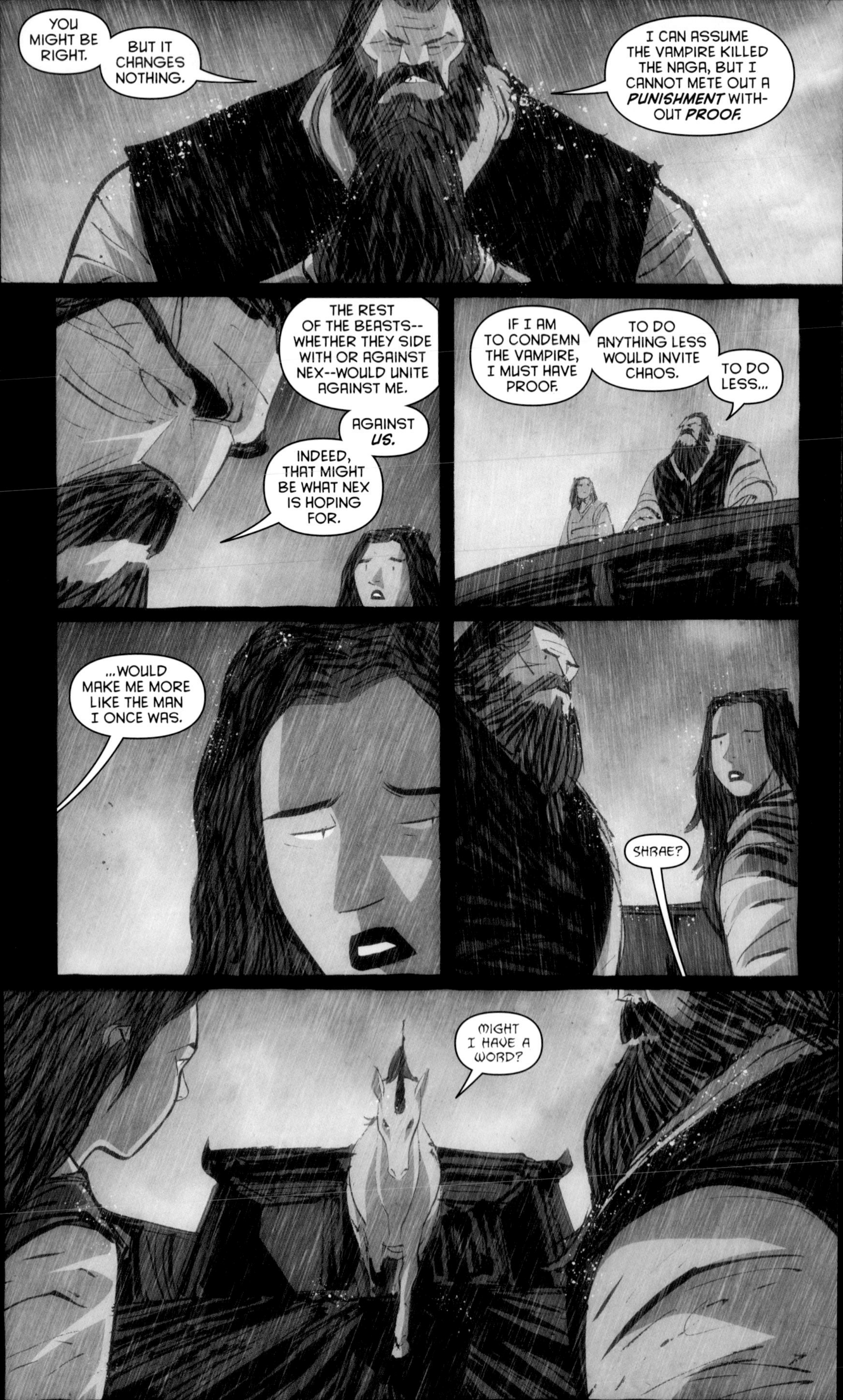
YOU MIGHT BE RIGHT.
BUT IT CHANGES NOTHING.
I CAN ASSUME THE VAMPIRE KILLED THE NAGA, BUT I CANNOT METE OUT A PUNISHMENT WITH-OUT PROOF.
THE REST OF THE BEASTS--WHETHER THEY SIDE WITH OR AGAINST NEX--WOULD UNITE AGAINST ME.
AGAINST US.
INDEED, THAT MIGHT BE WHAT NEX IS HOPING FOR.
IF I AM TO CONDEMN THE VAMPIRE, I MUST HAVE PROOF.
TO DO ANYTHING LESS WOULD INVITE CHAOS.
TO DO LESS...
...WOULD MAKE ME MORE LIKE THE MAN I ONCE WAS.
SHRAE?
MIGHT I HAVE A WORD?

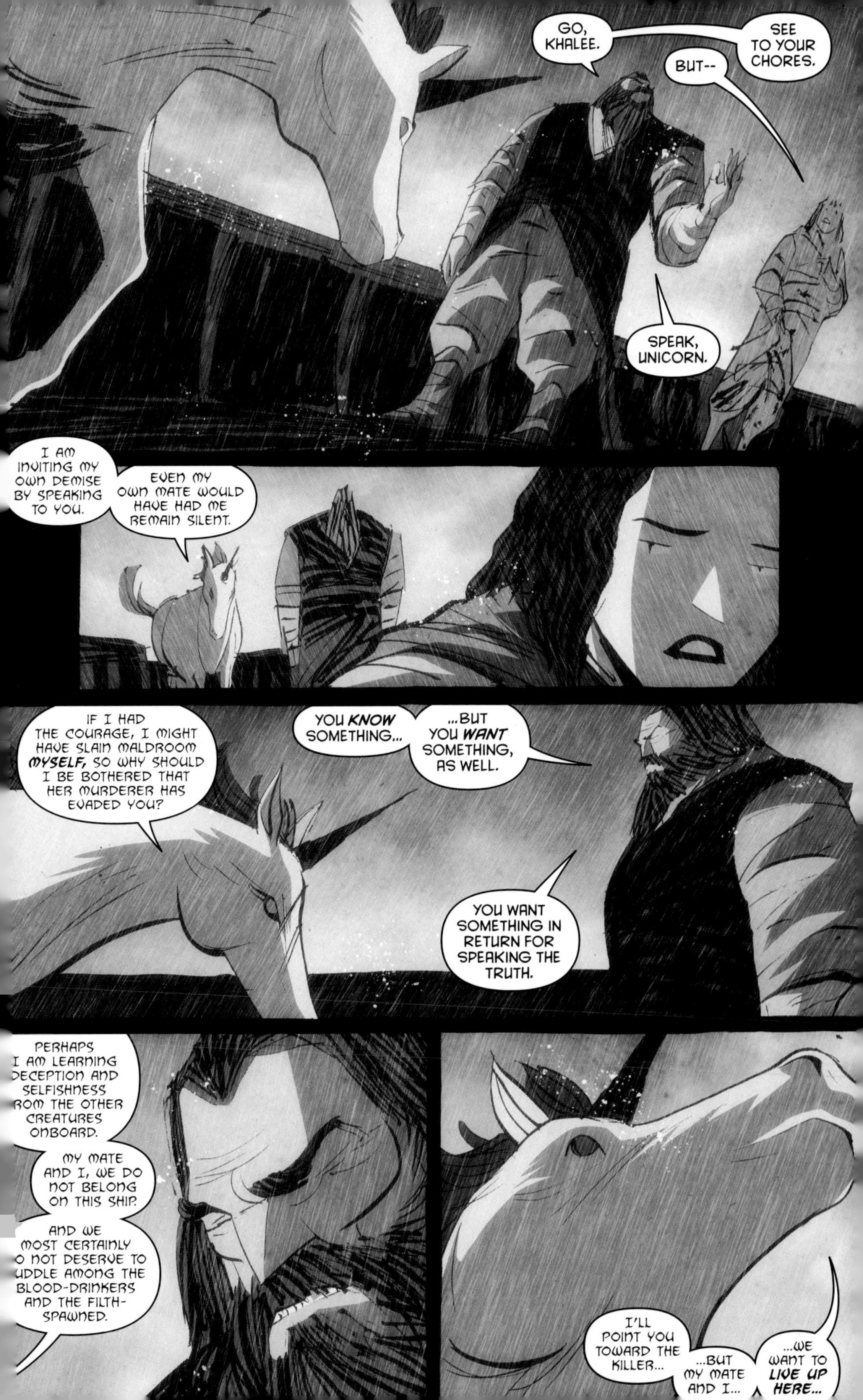
GO, KHALEE.
BUT--
SEE TO YOUR CHORES.
SPEAK, UNICORN.
I AM INVITING MY OWN DEMISE BY SPEAKING TO YOU.
EVEN MY OWN MATE WOULD HAVE HAD ME REMAIN SILENT.
IF I HAD THE COURAGE, I MIGHT HAVE SLAIN MALDROOM *MYSELF,* SO WHY SHOULD I BE BOTHERED THAT HER MURDERER HAS EVADED YOU?
YOU *KNOW* SOMETHING...
...BUT YOU *WANT* SOMETHING, AS WELL.
YOU WANT SOMETHING IN RETURN FOR SPEAKING THE TRUTH.
PERHAPS I AM LEARNING DECEPTION AND SELFISHNESS ROM THE OTHER CREATURES ONBOARD.
MY MATE AND I, WE DO NOT BELONG ON THIS SHIP.
AND WE MOST CERTAINLY O NOT DESERVE TO UDDLE AMONG THE BLOOD-DRINKERS AND THE FILTH-SPAWNED.
I'LL POINT YOU TOWARD THE KILLER...
...BUT MY MATE AND I...
...WE WANT TO *LIVE UP HERE...*

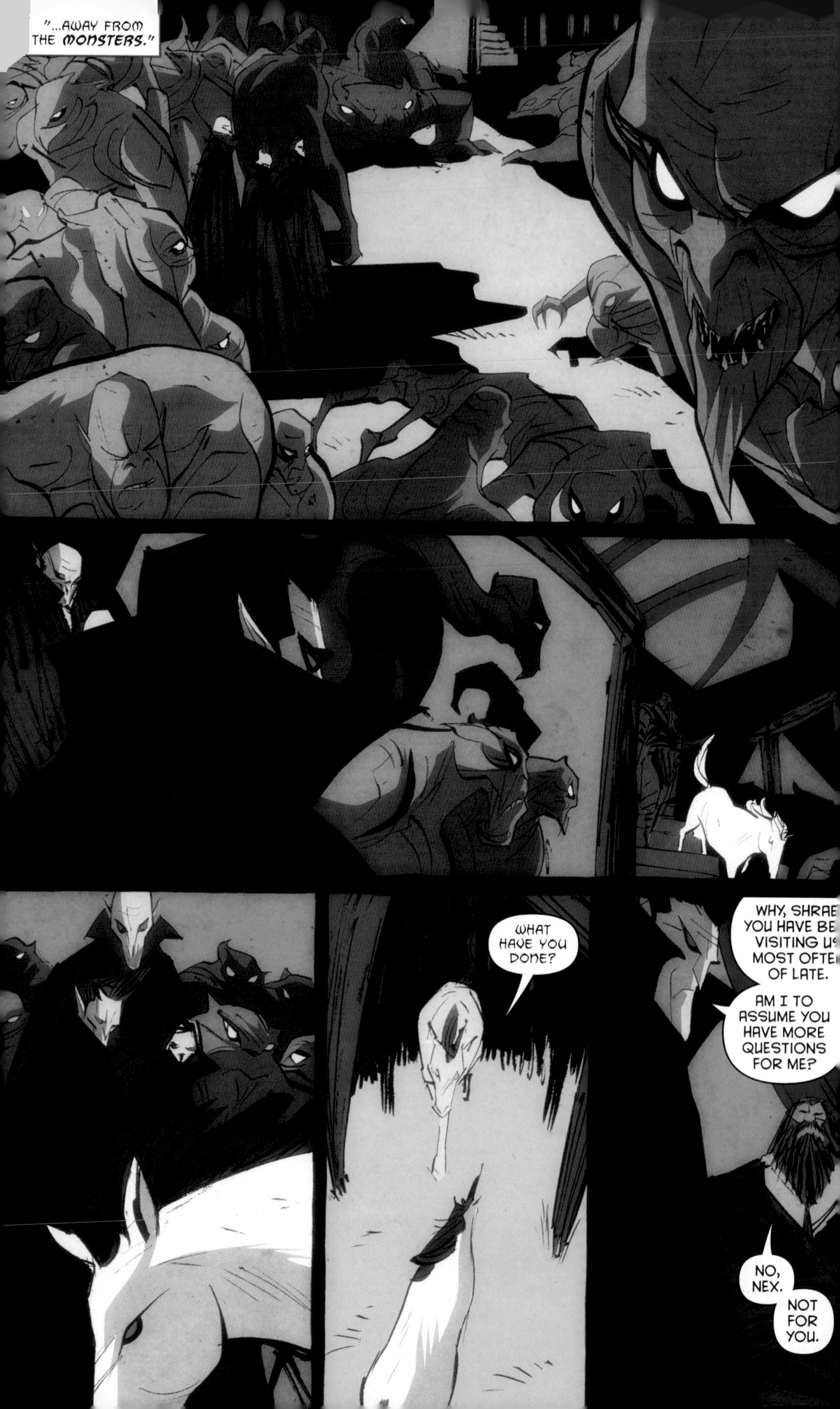
"...AWAY FROM THE MONSTERS."
WHAT HAVE YOU DONE?
WHY, SHRAE YOU HAVE BE VISITING U MOST OFTE OF LATE.
AM I TO ASSUME YOU HAVE MORE QUESTIONS FOR ME?
NO, NEX.
NOT FOR YOU.

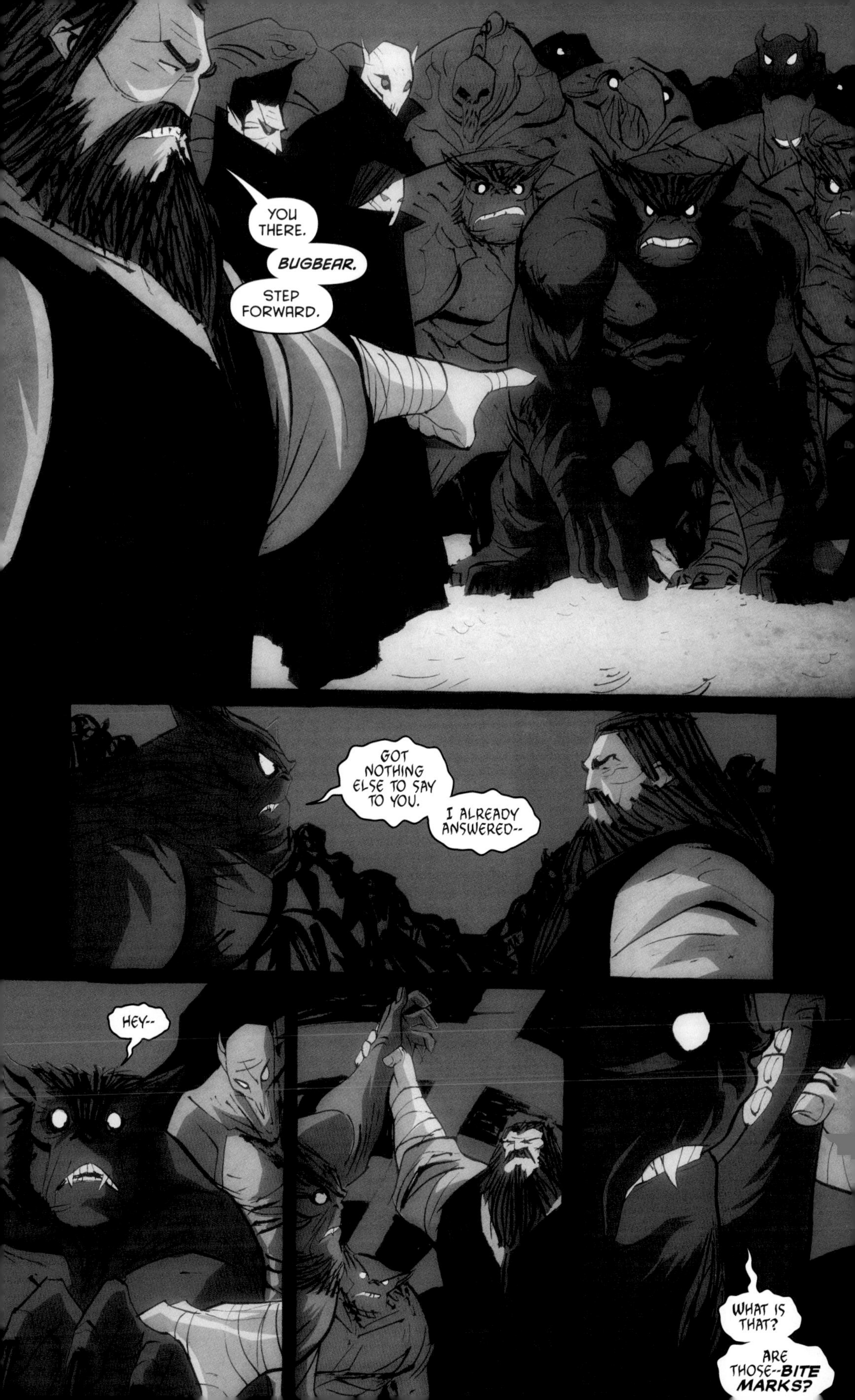
YOU THERE.
BUGBEAR.
STEP FORWARD.
GOT NOTHING ELSE TO SAY TO YOU.
I ALREADY ANSWERED--
HEY--
WHAT IS THAT?
ARE THOSE--BITE MARKS?

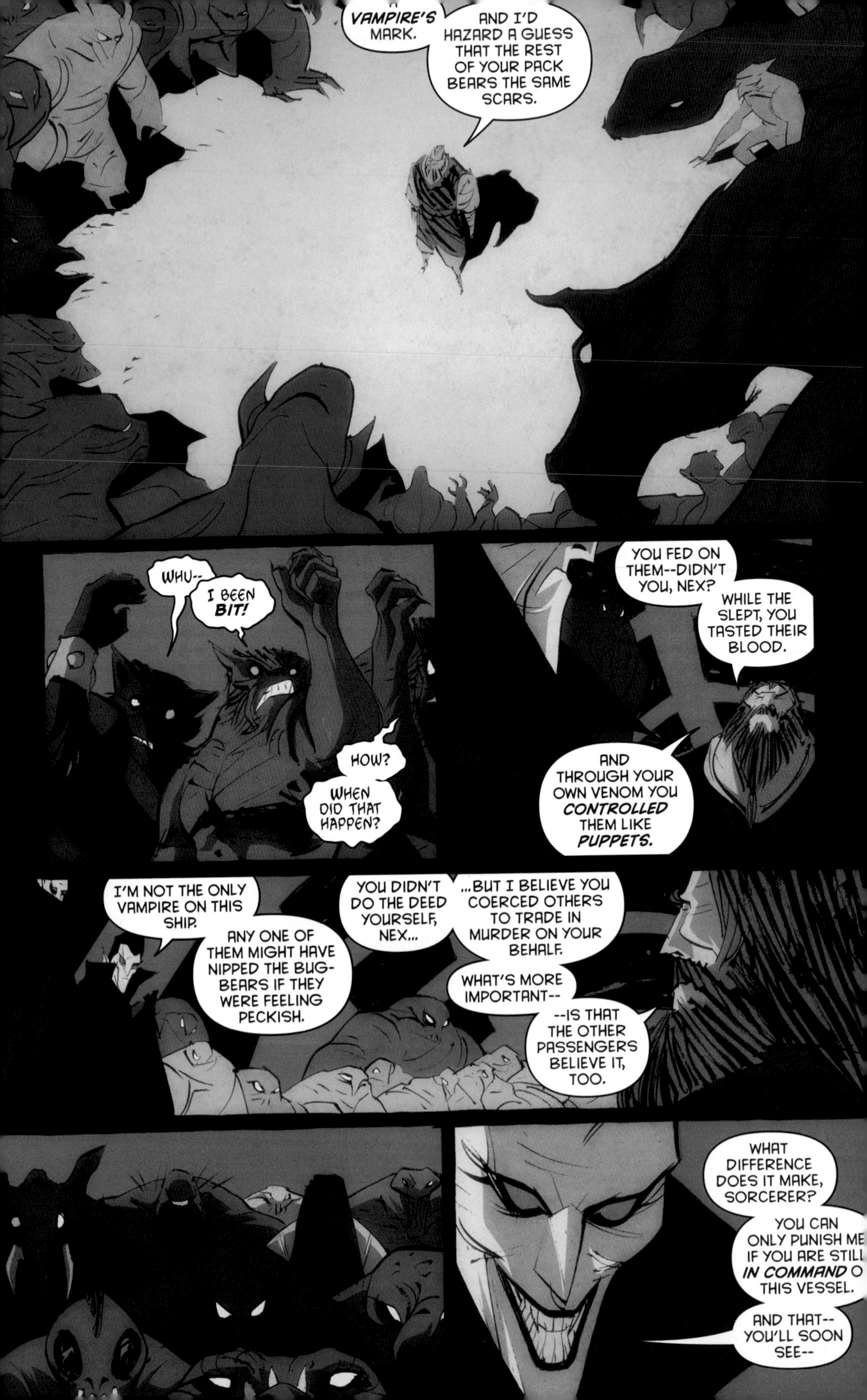
VAMPIRE'S MARK.
AND I'D HAZARD A GUESS THAT THE REST OF YOUR PACK BEARS THE SAME SCARS.
WHU--
I BEEN BIT!
HOW?
WHEN DID THAT HAPPEN?
YOU FED ON THEM--DIDN'T YOU, NEX?
WHILE THE SLEPT, YOU TASTED THEIR BLOOD.
AND THROUGH YOUR OWN VENOM YOU CONTROLLED THEM LIKE PUPPETS.
I'M NOT THE ONLY VAMPIRE ON THIS SHIP.
ANY ONE OF THEM MIGHT HAVE NIPPED THE BUG-BEARS IF THEY WERE FEELING PECKISH.
YOU DIDN'T DO THE DEED YOURSELF, NEX...
...BUT I BELIEVE YOU COERCED OTHERS TO TRADE IN MURDER ON YOUR BEHALF.
WHAT'S MORE IMPORTANT--
--IS THAT THE OTHER PASSENGERS BELIEVE IT, TOO.
WHAT DIFFERENCE DOES IT MAKE, SORCERER?
YOU CAN ONLY PUNISH ME IF YOU ARE STILL IN COMMAND OF THIS VESSEL.
AND THAT-- YOU'LL SOON SEE--

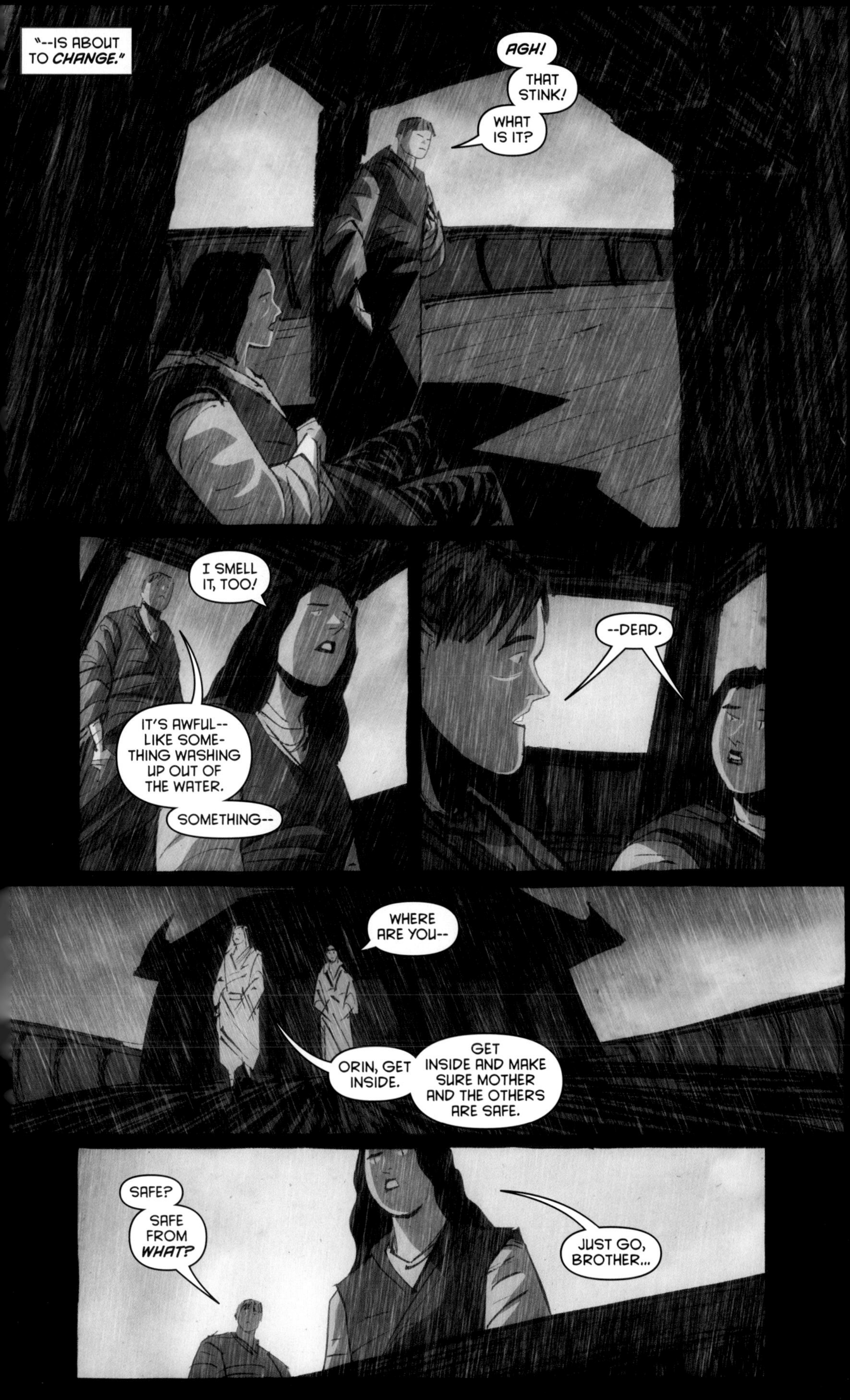
"--IS ABOUT TO *CHANGE.*"
AGH!
THAT STINK!
WHAT IS IT?
I SMELL IT, TOO!
IT'S AWFUL-- LIKE SOME-THING WASHING UP OUT OF THE WATER.
SOMETHING--
--DEAD.
WHERE ARE YOU--
ORIN, GET INSIDE.
GET INSIDE AND MAKE SURE MOTHER AND THE OTHERS ARE SAFE.
SAFE?
SAFE FROM *WHAT?*
JUST GO, BROTHER...

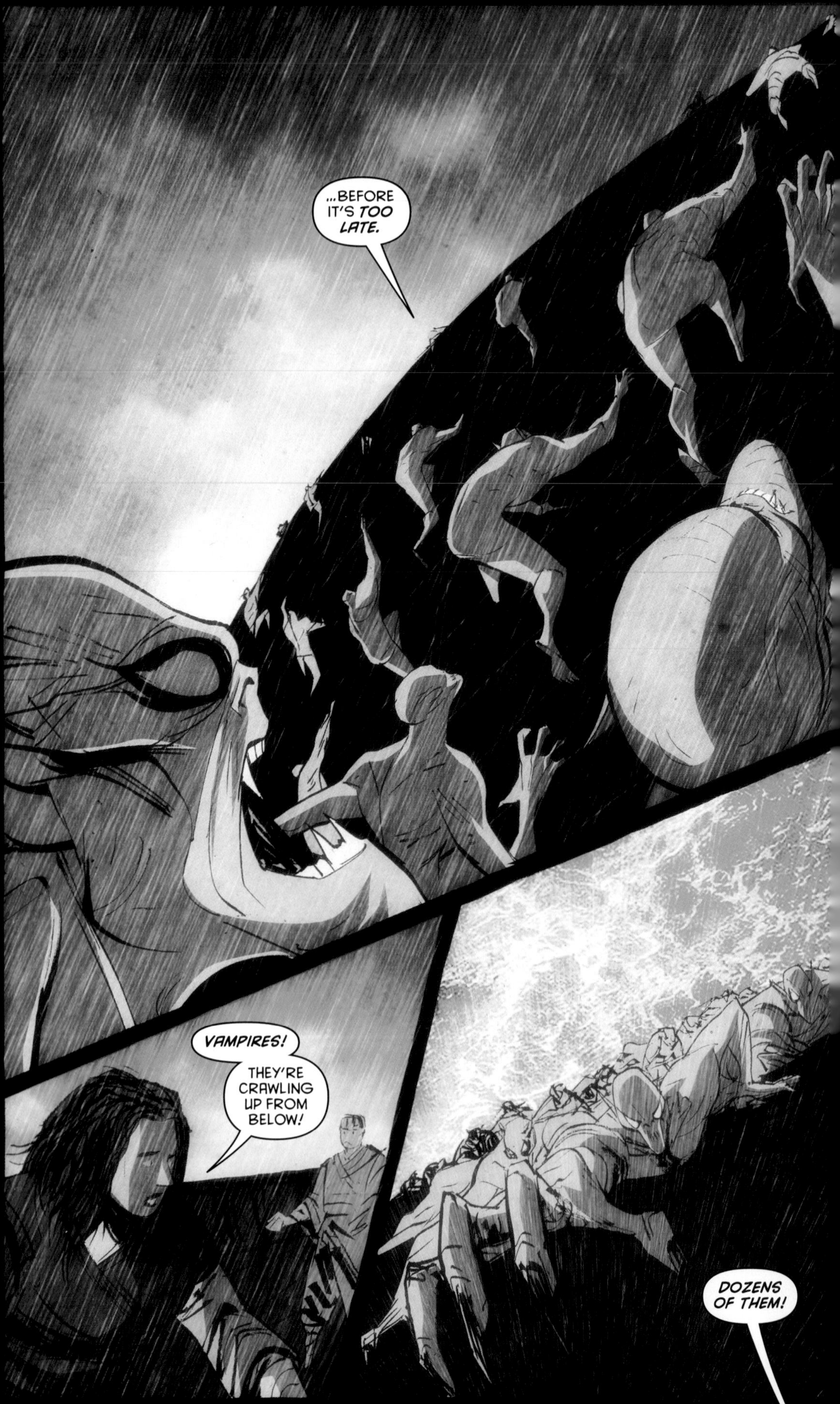
...BEFORE IT'S *TOO LATE.*
VAMPIRES!
THEY'RE CRAWLING UP FROM BELOW!
DOZENS OF THEM!

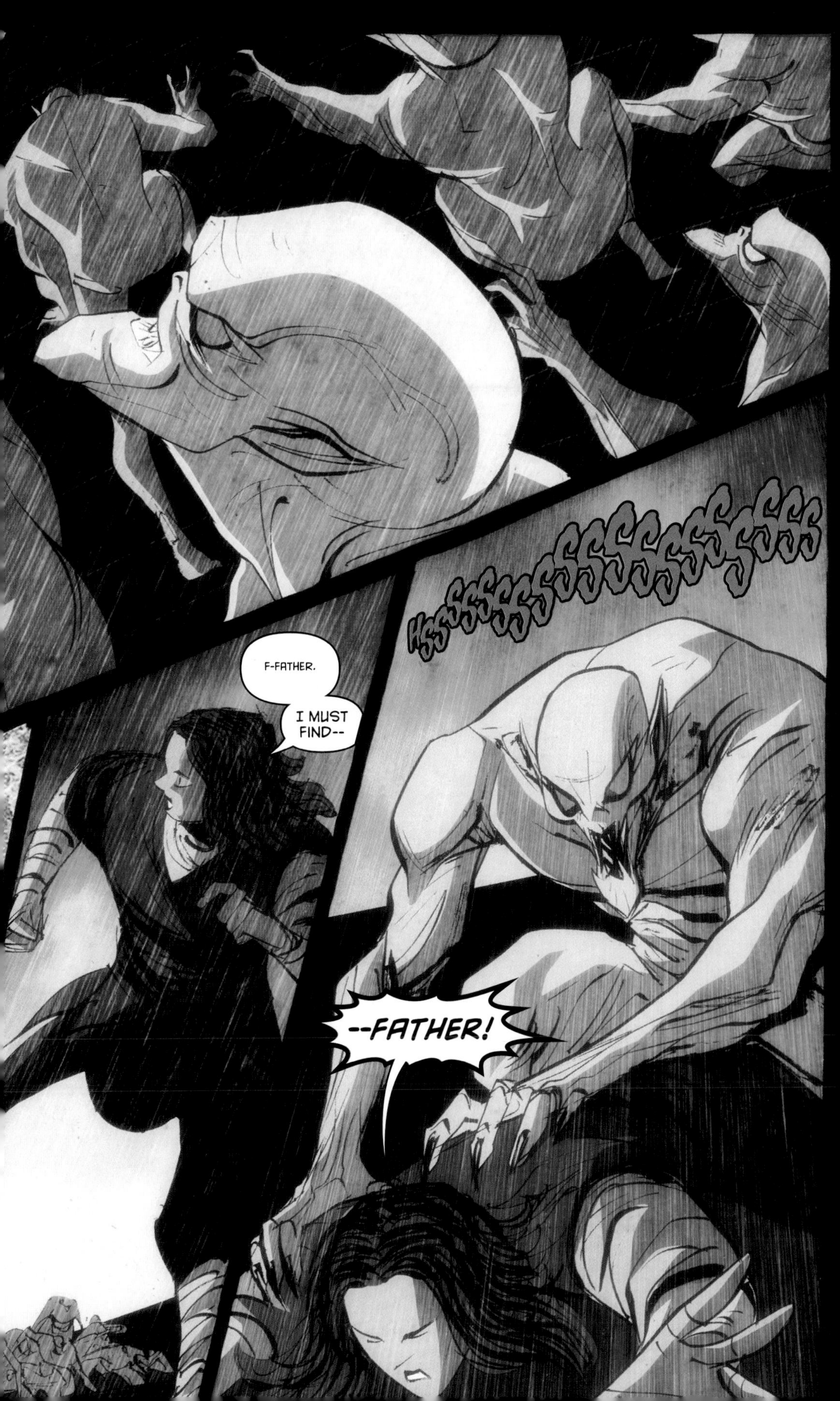
HSSSSSSSSSSSSSSSSSSSS
F-FATHER.
I MUST FIND--
--FATHER!

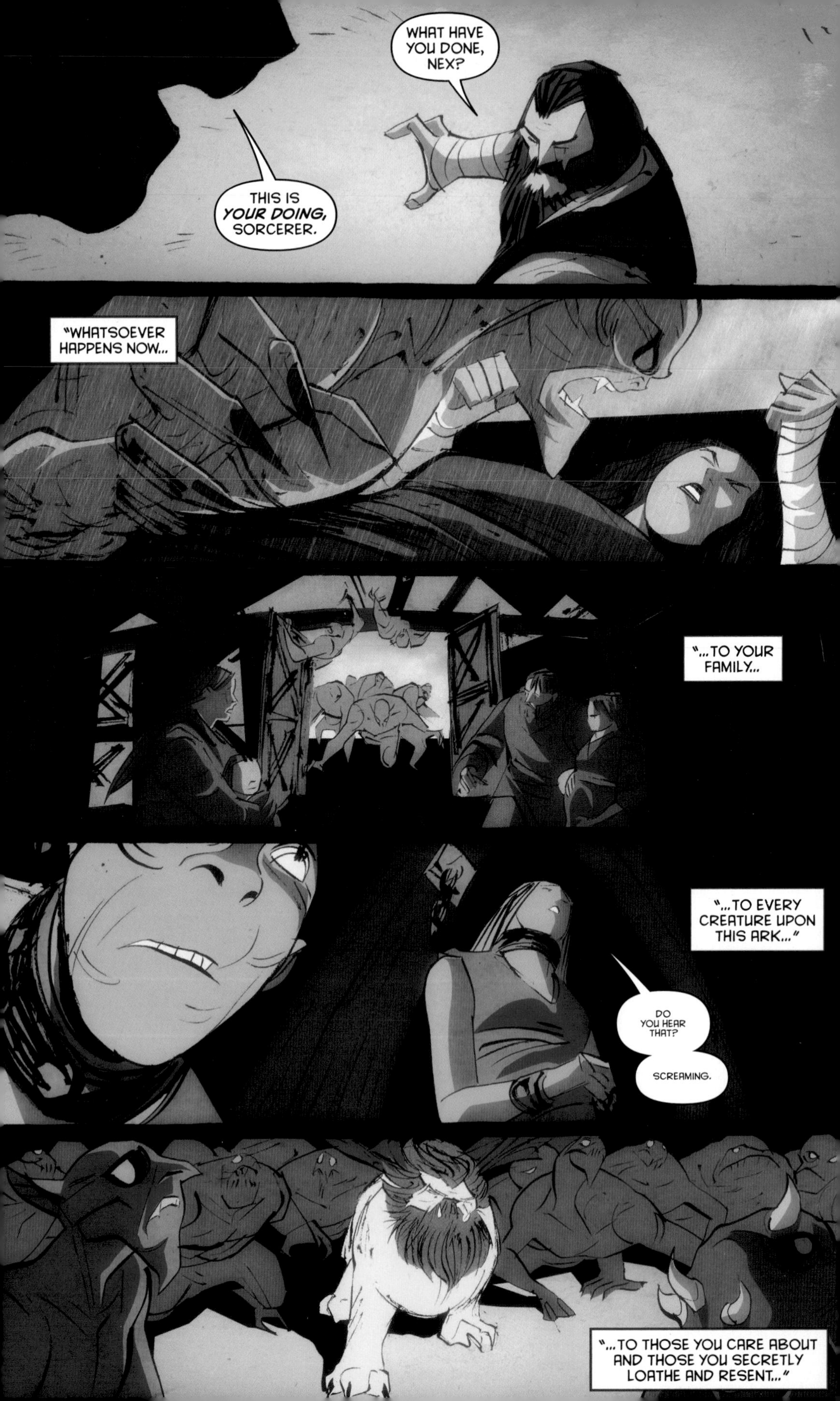

WHAT HAVE YOU DONE, NEX?
THIS IS YOUR DOING, SORCERER.
"WHATSOEVER HAPPENS NOW...
"...TO YOUR FAMILY...
"...TO EVERY CREATURE UPON THIS ARK..."
DO YOU HEAR THAT?
SCREAMING.
"...TO THOSE YOU CARE ABOUT AND THOSE YOU SECRETLY LOATHE AND RESENT..."

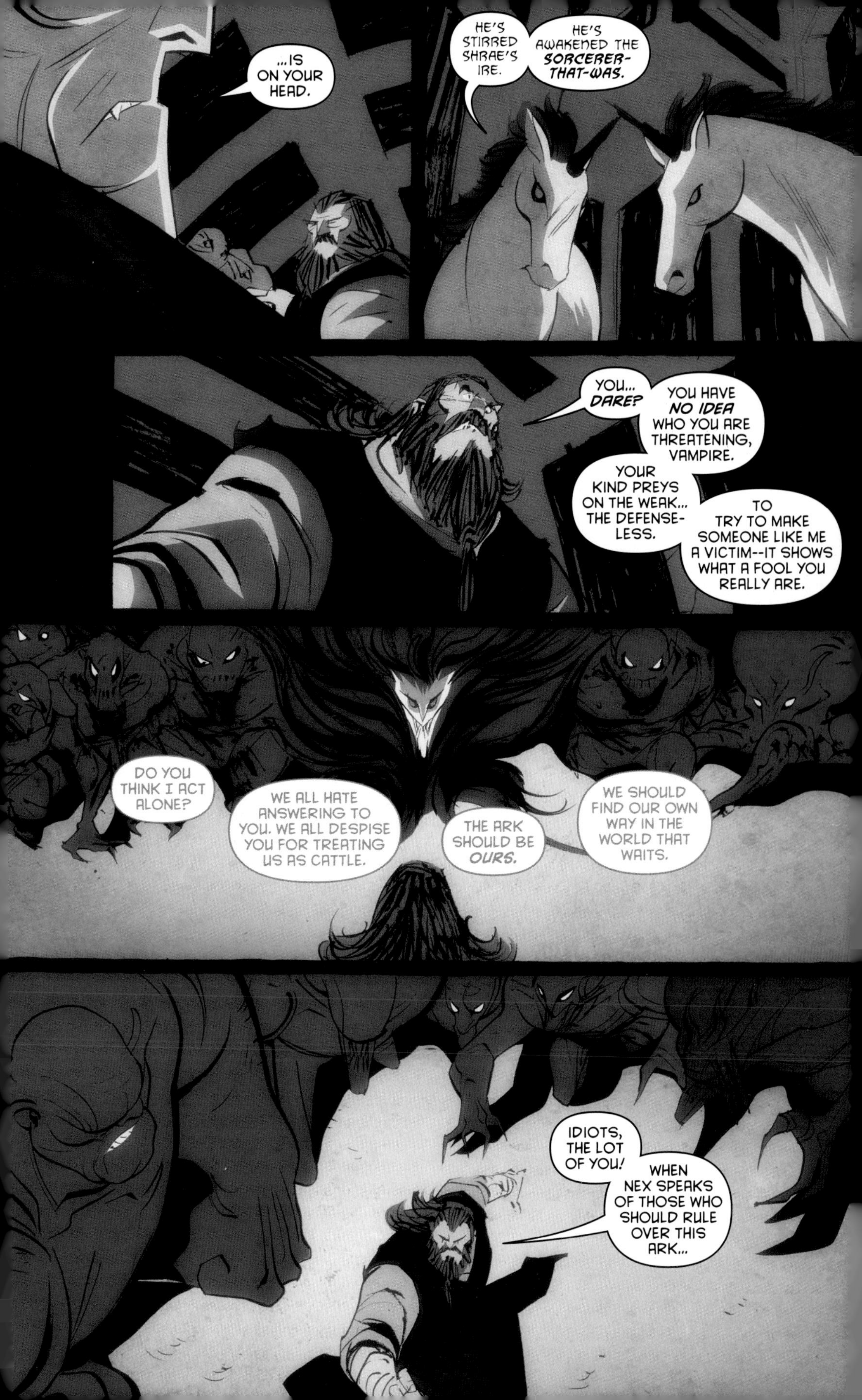
...IS ON YOUR HEAD.
HE'S STIRRED SHRAE'S IRE.
HE'S AWAKENED THE SORCERER-THAT-WAS.
YOU... DARE?
YOU HAVE NO IDEA WHO YOU ARE THREATENING, VAMPIRE.
YOUR KIND PREYS ON THE WEAK... THE DEFENSE-LESS.
TO TRY TO MAKE SOMEONE LIKE ME A VICTIM--IT SHOWS WHAT A FOOL YOU REALLY ARE.
DO YOU THINK I ACT ALONE?
WE ALL HATE ANSWERING TO YOU. WE ALL DESPISE YOU FOR TREATING US AS CATTLE.
THE ARK SHOULD BE OURS.
WE SHOULD FIND OUR OWN WAY IN THE WORLD THAT WAITS.
IDIOTS, THE LOT OF YOU!
WHEN NEX SPEAKS OF THOSE WHO SHOULD RULE OVER THIS ARK...

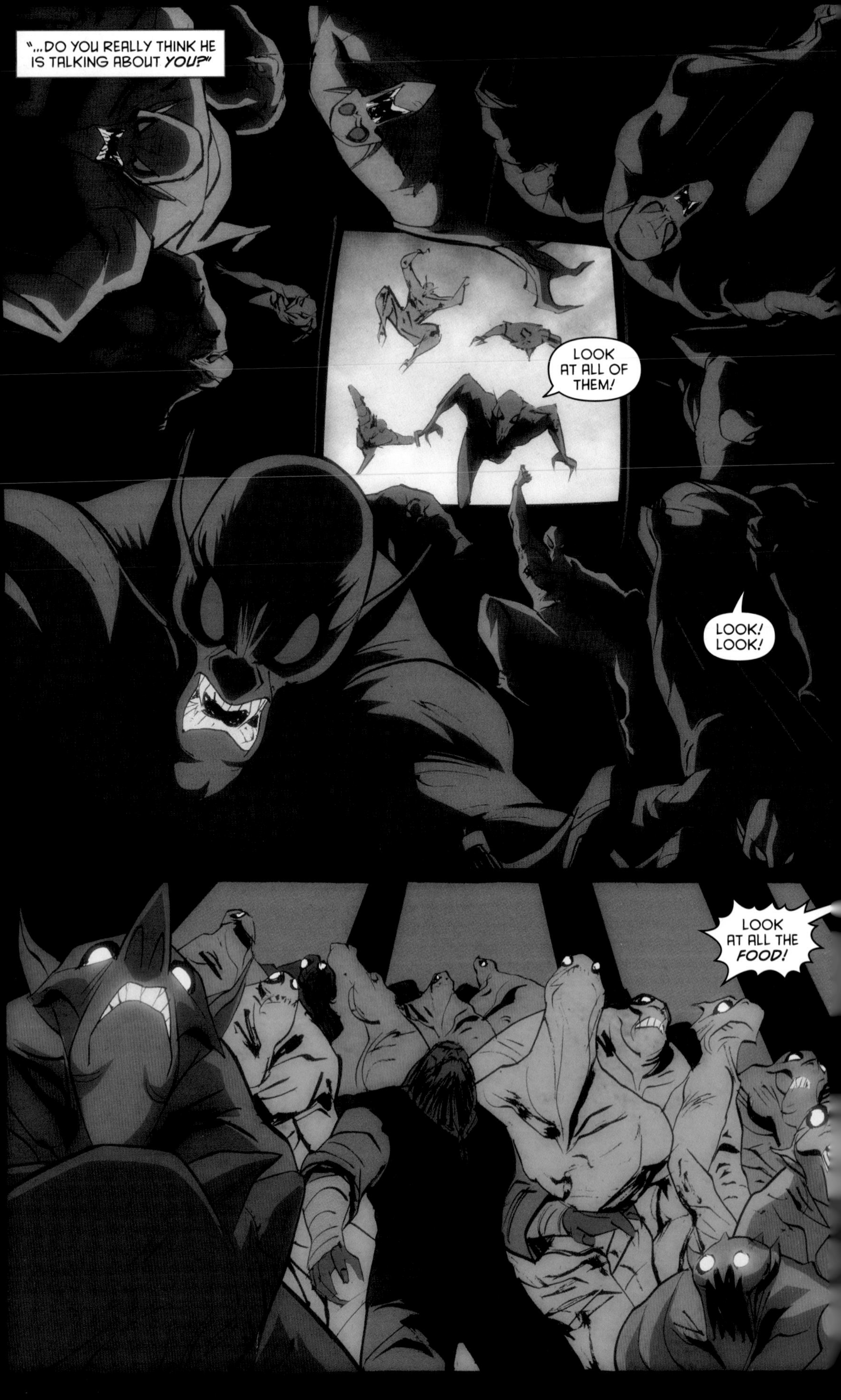
"...DO YOU REALLY THINK HE IS TALKING ABOUT *YOU?*"
LOOK AT ALL OF THEM!
LOOK! LOOK!
LOOK AT ALL THE *FOOD!*

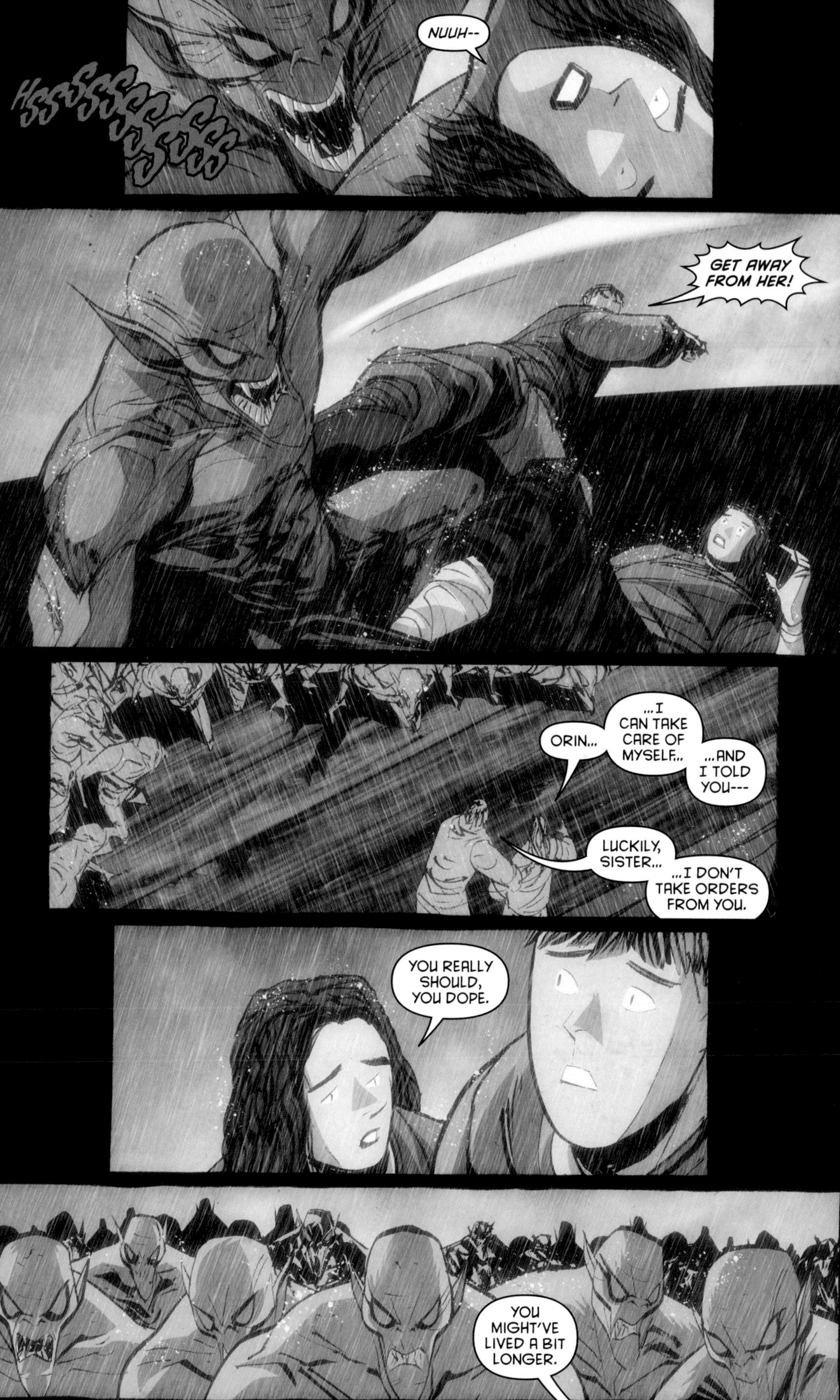
HSSSSSSSSSSS
NUUH--
GET AWAY FROM HER!
ORIN...
...I CAN TAKE CARE OF MYSELF...
...AND I TOLD YOU---
LUCKILY, SISTER...
...I DON'T TAKE ORDERS FROM YOU.
YOU REALLY SHOULD, YOU DOPE.
YOU MIGHT'VE LIVED A BIT LONGER.

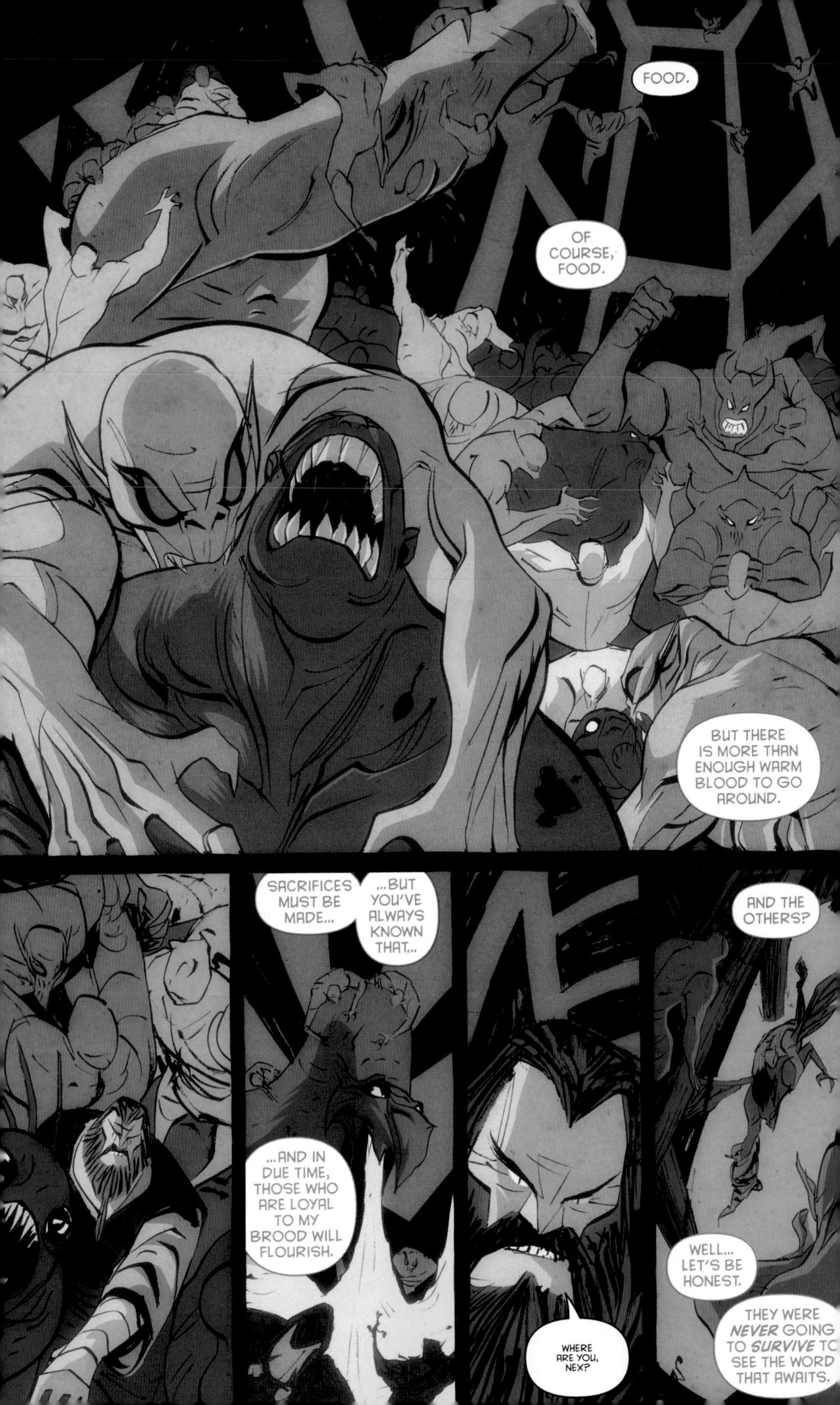

FOOD.
OF COURSE, FOOD.
BUT THERE IS MORE THAN ENOUGH WARM BLOOD TO GO AROUND.
SACRIFICES MUST BE MADE...
...BUT YOU'VE ALWAYS KNOWN THAT...
...AND IN DUE TIME, THOSE WHO ARE LOYAL TO MY BROOD WILL FLOURISH.
WHERE ARE YOU, NEX?
AND THE OTHERS?
WELL... LET'S BE HONEST.
THEY WERE *NEVER* GOING TO *SURVIVE* TO SEE THE WORD THAT AWAITS.

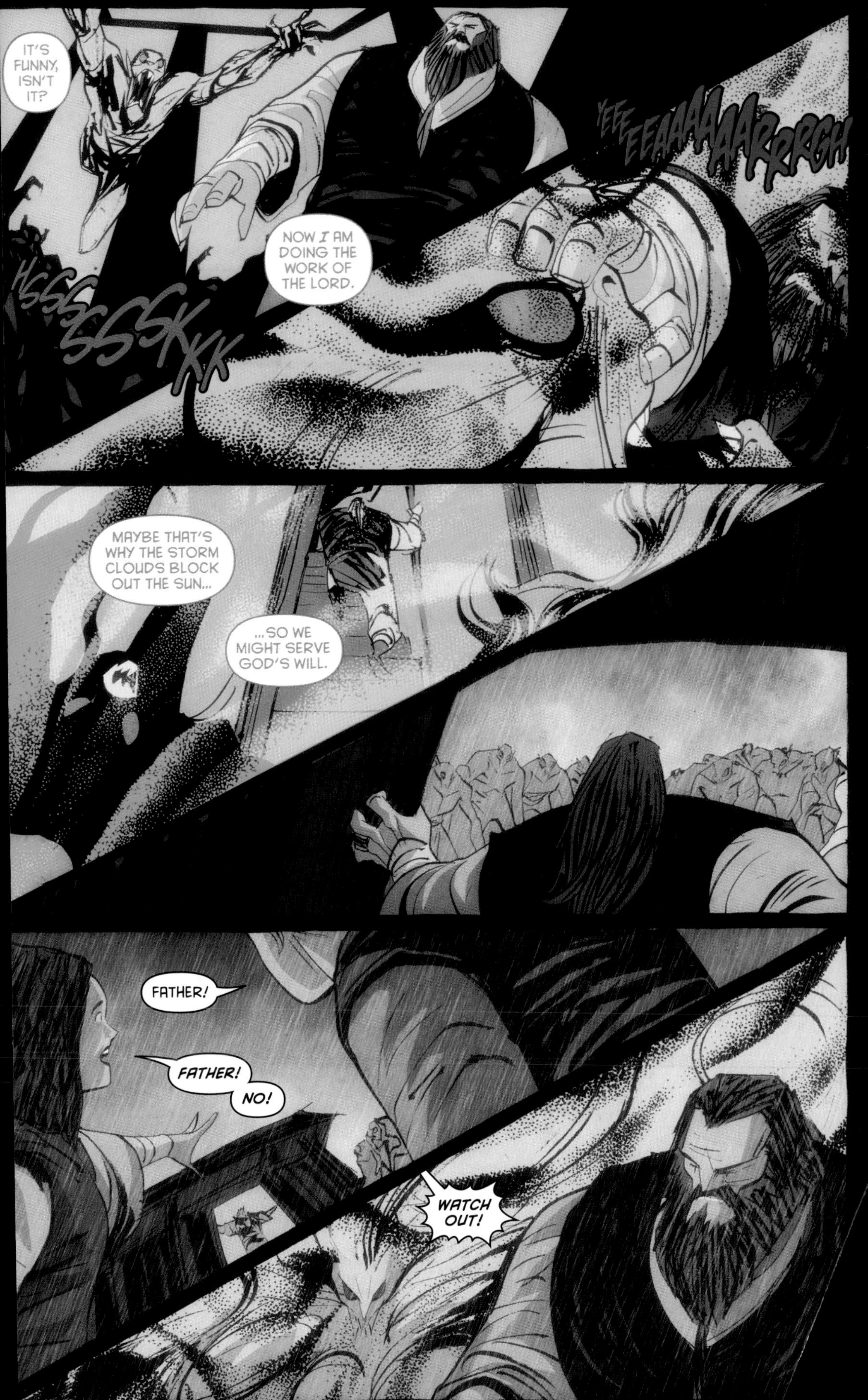
IT'S FUNNY, ISN'T IT?
YEEEEEAAAAAAARRRGH
NOW I AM DOING THE WORK OF THE LORD.
HSSSSSSSKKK
MAYBE THAT'S WHY THE STORM CLOUDS BLOCK OUT THE SUN...
...SO WE MIGHT SERVE GOD'S WILL.
FATHER!
FATHER!
NO!
WATCH OUT!

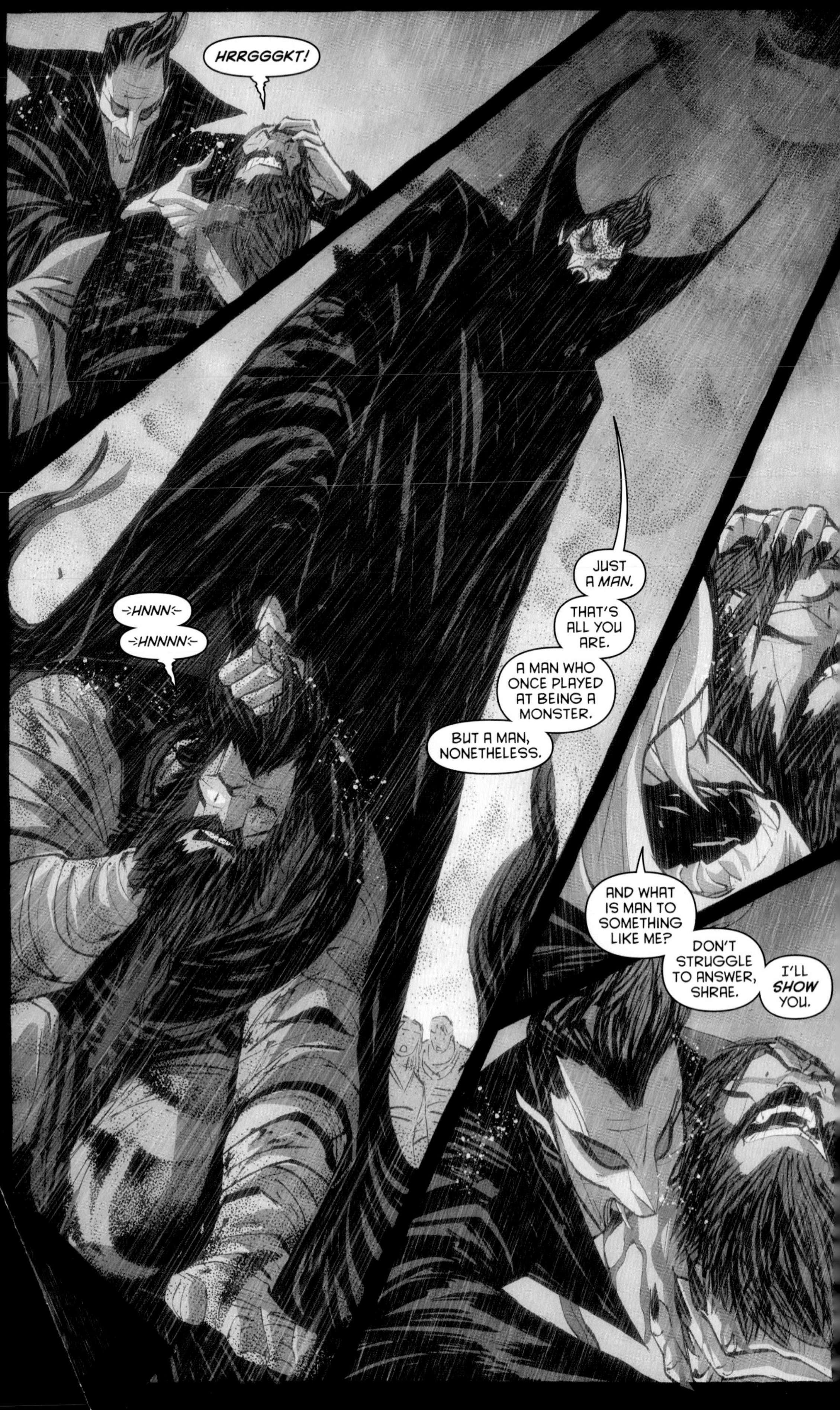
HRRGGGKT!
HNNN
HNNNN
JUST A MAN.
THAT'S ALL YOU ARE.
A MAN WHO ONCE PLAYED AT BEING A MONSTER.
BUT A MAN, NONETHELESS.
AND WHAT IS MAN TO SOMETHING LIKE ME?
DON'T STRUGGLE TO ANSWER, SHRAE.
I'LL SHOW YOU.

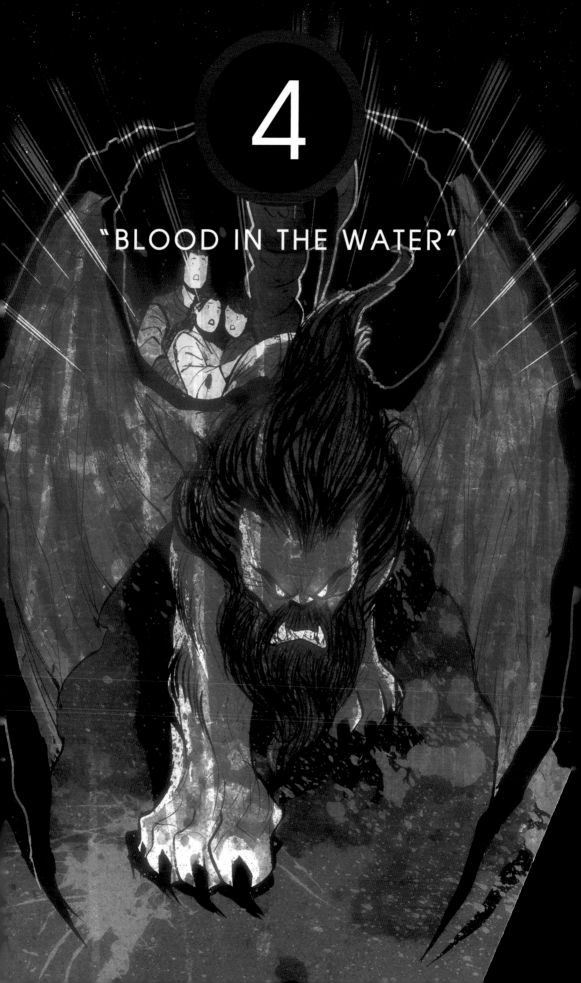

4

"BLOOD IN THE WATER"

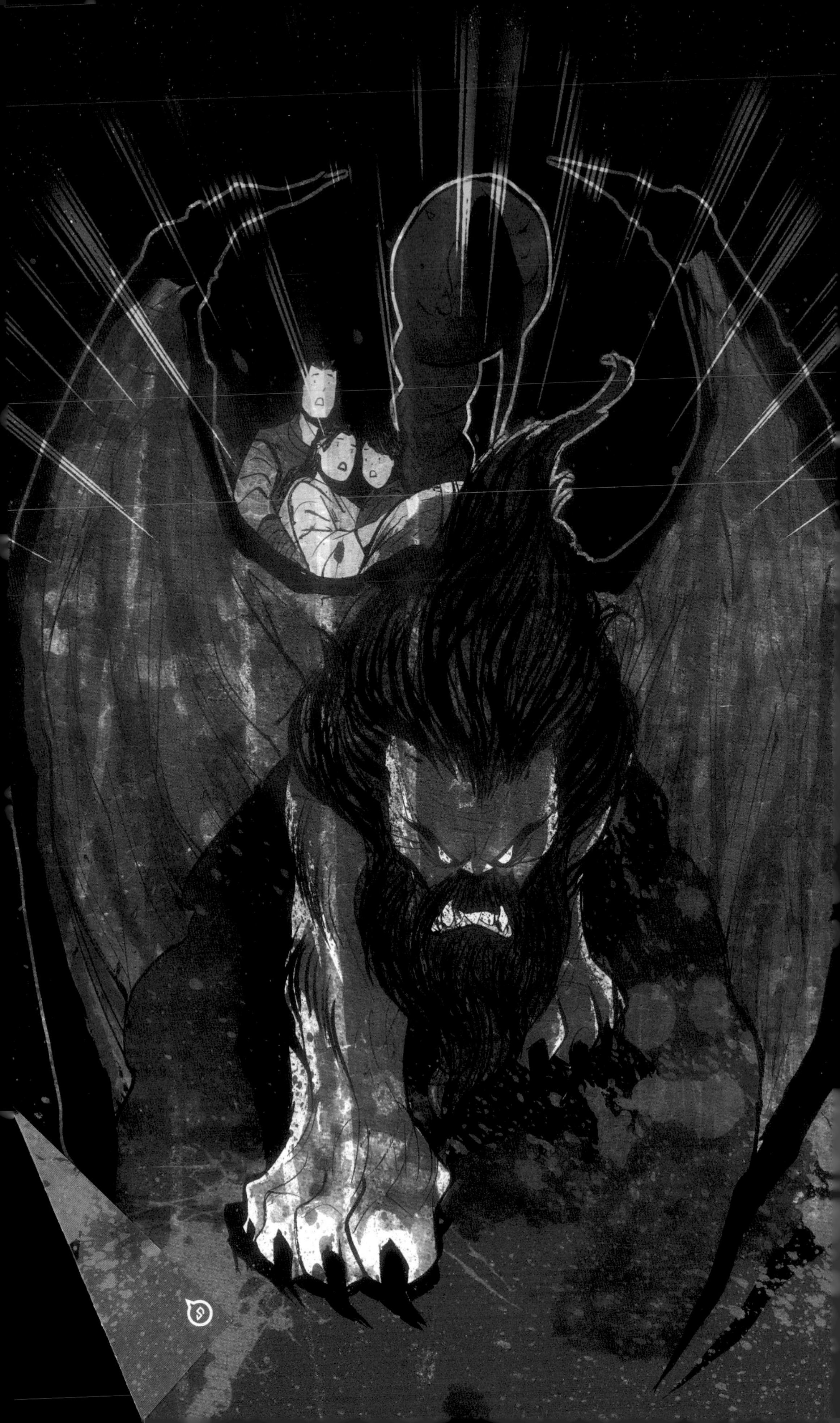

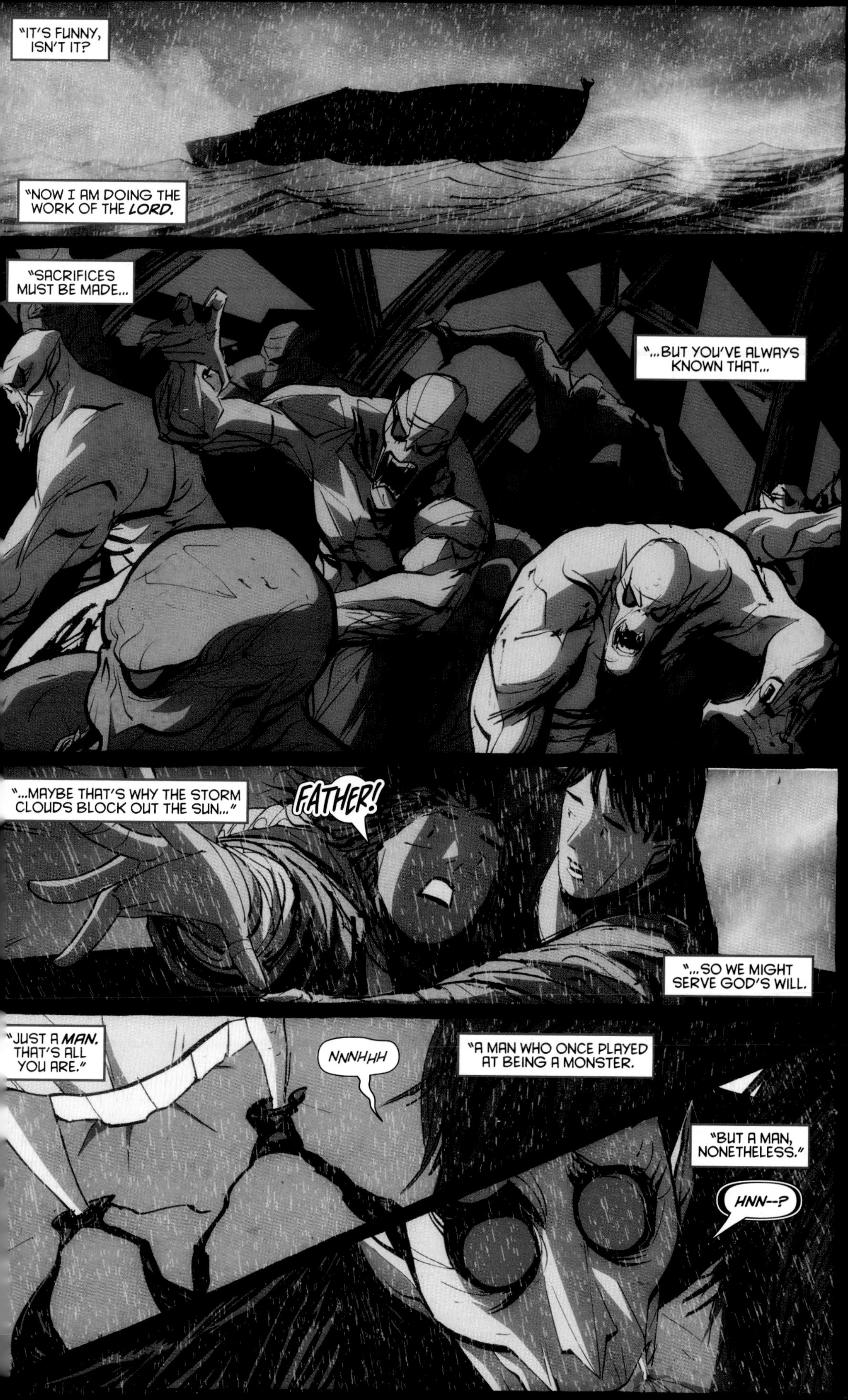
"IT'S FUNNY, ISN'T IT?
"NOW I AM DOING THE WORK OF THE *LORD.*
"SACRIFICES MUST BE MADE...
"...BUT YOU'VE ALWAYS KNOWN THAT...
"...MAYBE THAT'S WHY THE STORM CLOUDS BLOCK OUT THE SUN..."
FATHER!
"...SO WE MIGHT SERVE GOD'S WILL.
"JUST A *MAN.* THAT'S ALL YOU ARE."
NNNHHH
"A MAN WHO ONCE PLAYED AT BEING A MONSTER.
"BUT A MAN, NONETHELESS."
HNN--?

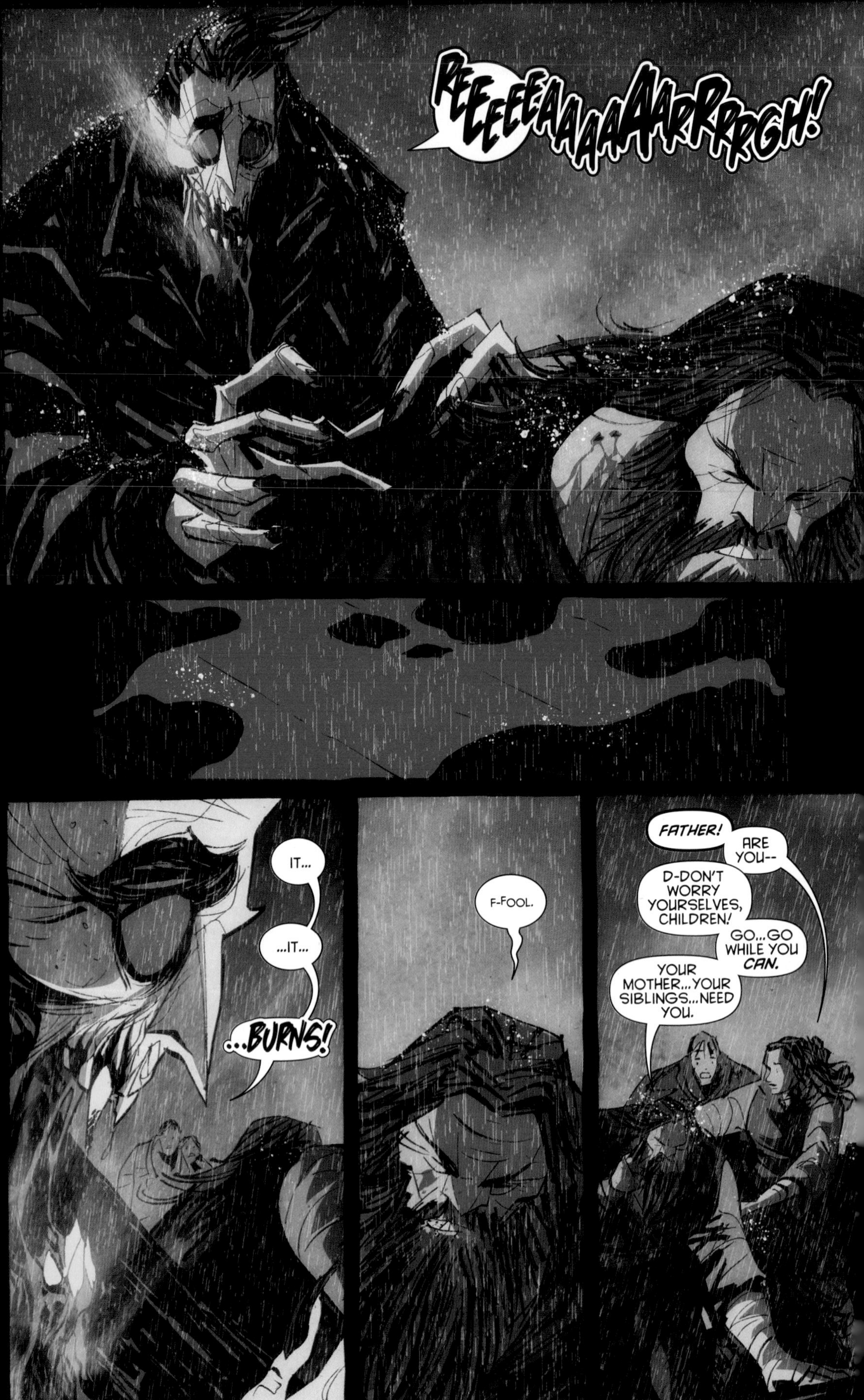
REEEEEEAAAAAAARRRRGH!
IT...
...IT...
...BURNS!
F-FOOL.
FATHER!
ARE YOU--
D-DON'T WORRY YOURSELVES, CHILDREN!
GO...GO WHILE YOU CAN.
YOUR MOTHER...YOUR SIBLINGS...NEED YOU.

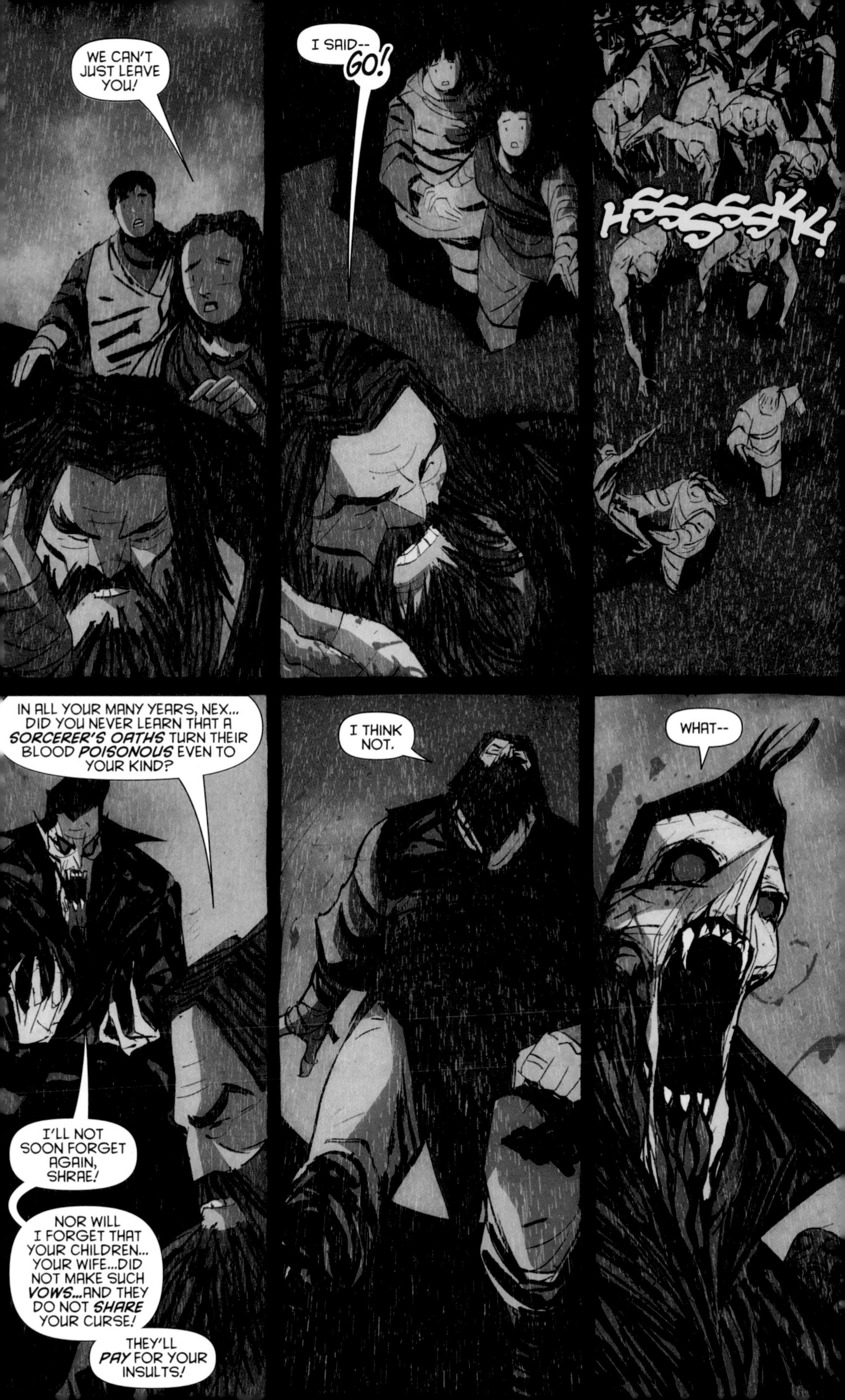
WE CAN'T JUST LEAVE YOU!
I SAID-- GO!
HSSSSSKK!
IN ALL YOUR MANY YEARS, NEX... DID YOU NEVER LEARN THAT A SORCERER'S OATHS TURN THEIR BLOOD POISONOUS EVEN TO YOUR KIND?
I'LL NOT SOON FORGET AGAIN, SHRAE!
NOR WILL I FORGET THAT YOUR CHILDREN... YOUR WIFE...DID NOT MAKE SUCH VOWS...AND THEY DO NOT SHARE YOUR CURSE!
THEY'LL PAY FOR YOUR INSULTS!
I THINK NOT.
WHAT--

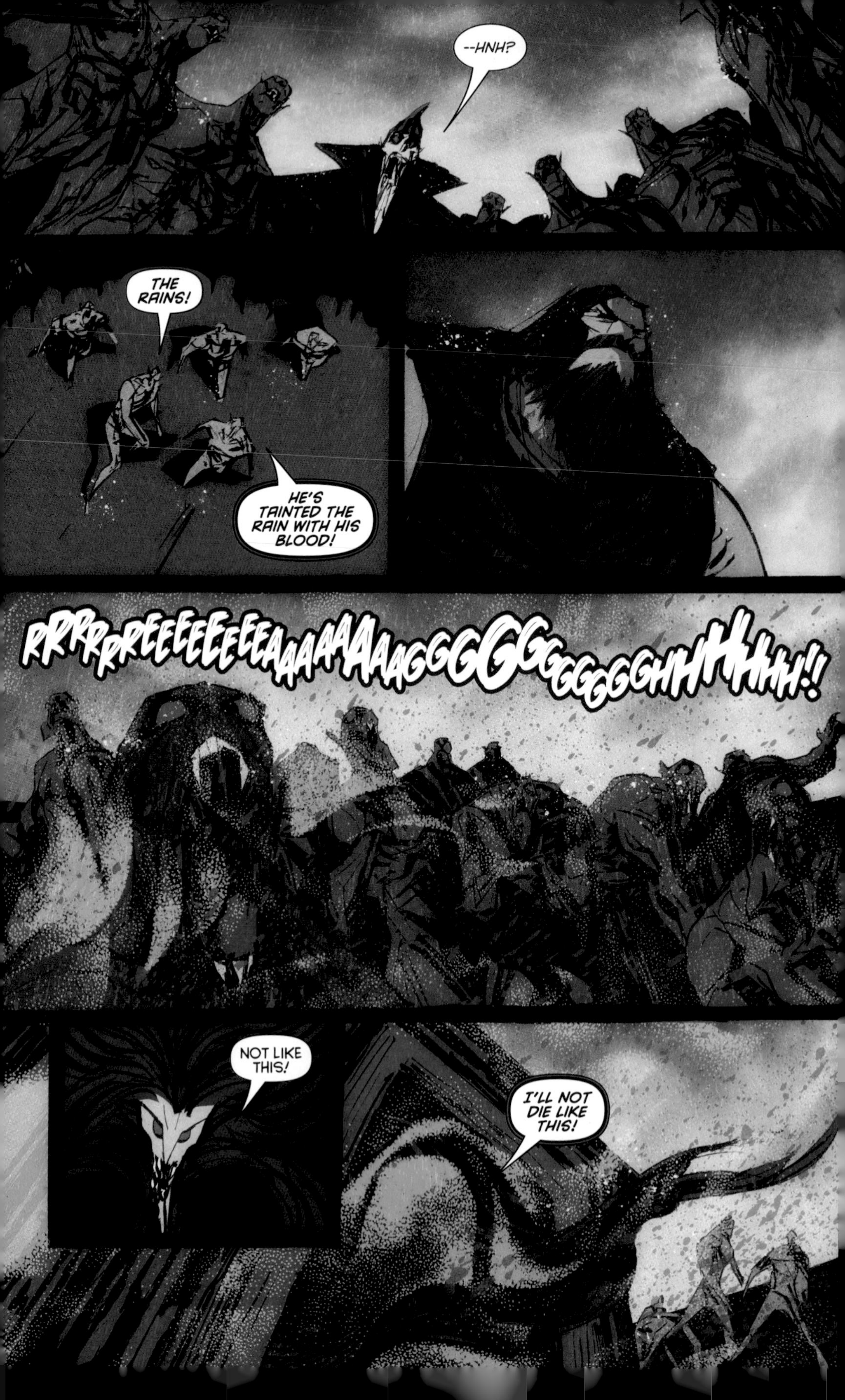
--HNH?
THE RAINS!
HE'S TAINTED THE RAIN WITH HIS BLOOD!
RRRRRREEEEEEEEEAAAAAAAAAAGGGGGGGGGGGHHHHHHH!!
NOT LIKE THIS!
I'LL NOT DIE LIKE THIS!

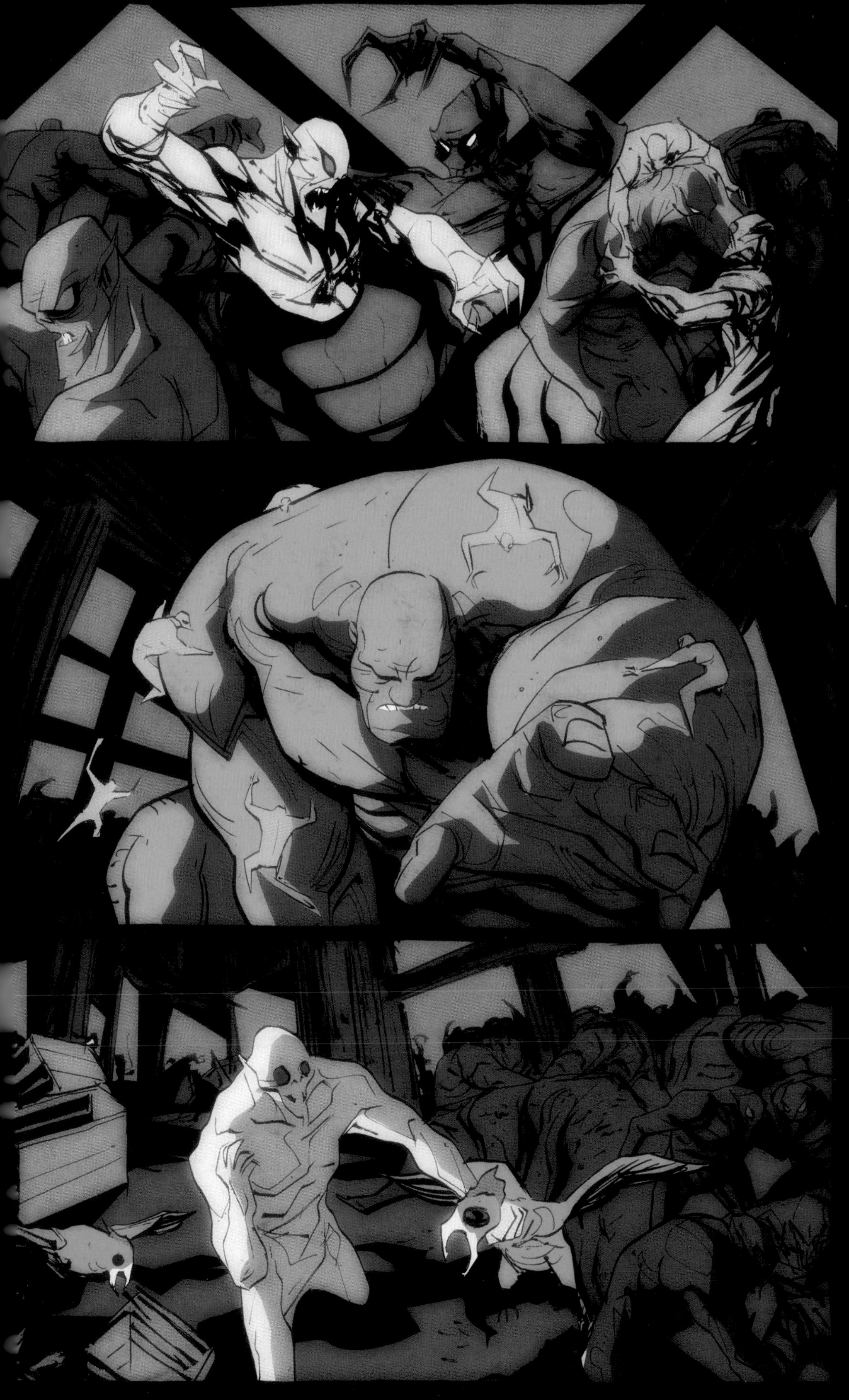

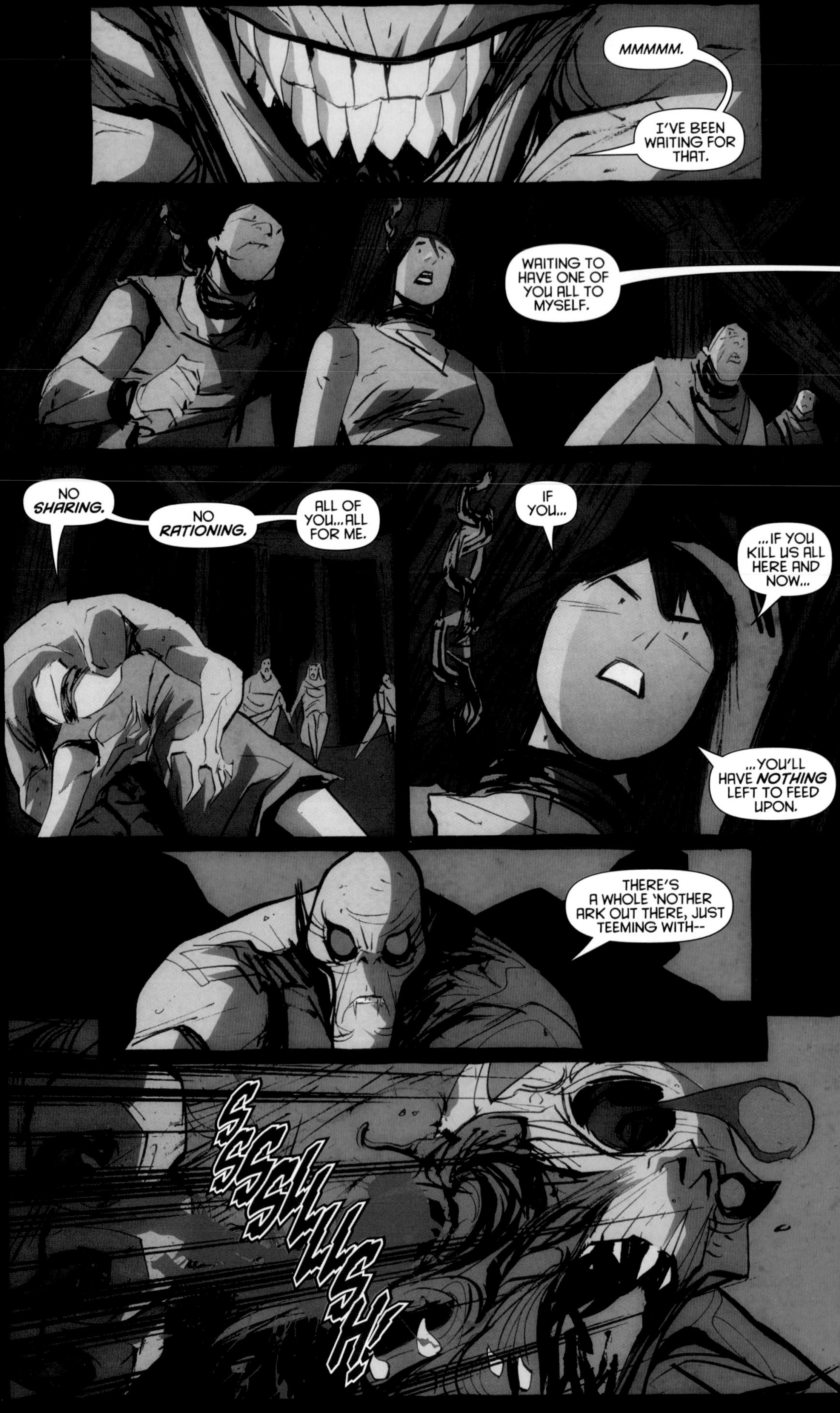
MMMMM.
I'VE BEEN WAITING FOR THAT.
WAITING TO HAVE ONE OF YOU ALL TO MYSELF.
NO SHARING.
NO RATIONING.
ALL OF YOU...ALL FOR ME.
IF YOU...
...IF YOU KILL US ALL HERE AND NOW...
...YOU'LL HAVE NOTHING LEFT TO FEED UPON.
THERE'S A WHOLE 'NOTHER ARK OUT THERE, JUST TEEMING WITH--
SSSHLLUSCH!

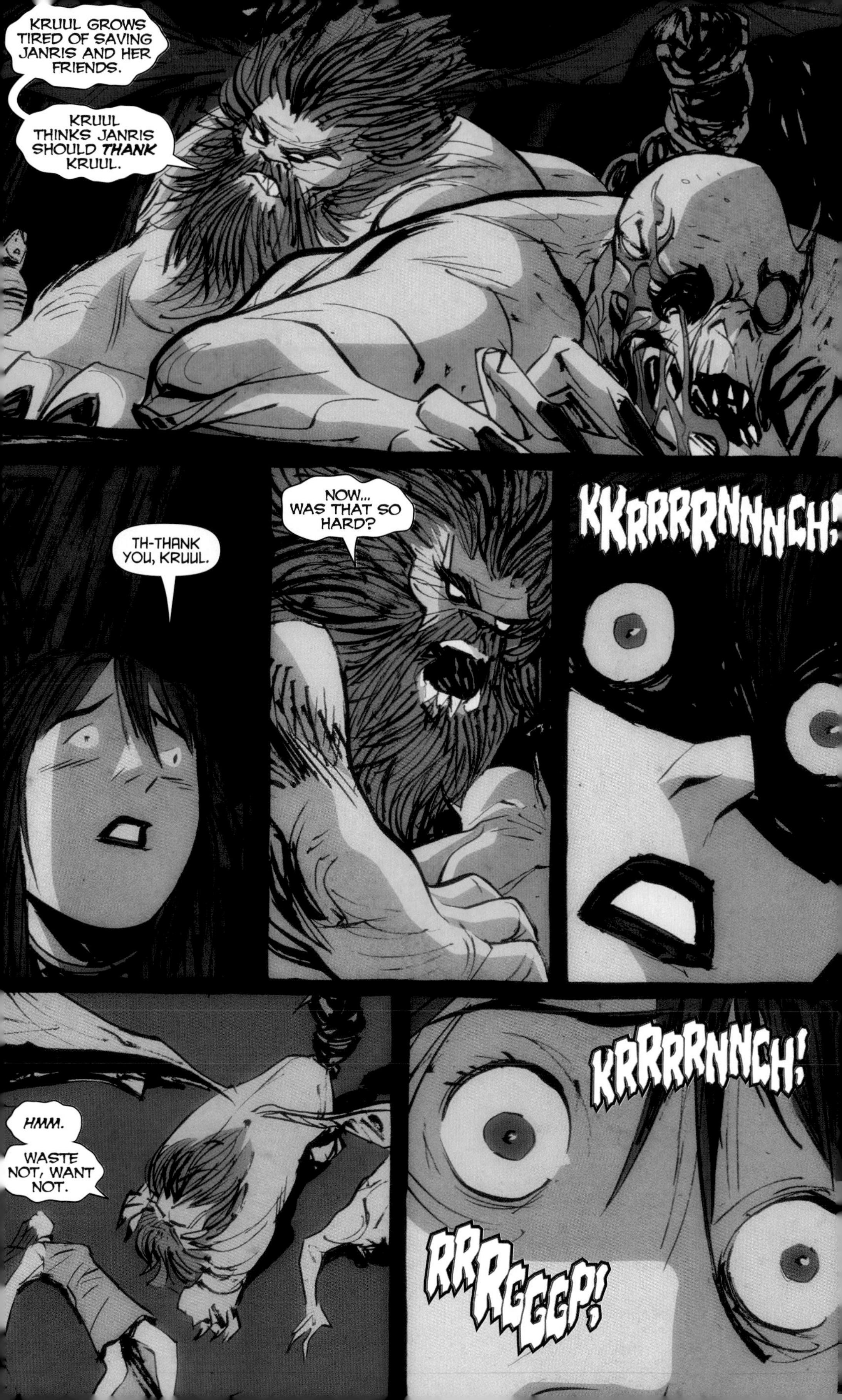
KRUUL GROWS TIRED OF SAVING JANRIS AND HER FRIENDS.
KRUUL THINKS JANRIS SHOULD *THANK* KRUUL.
TH-THANK YOU, KRUUL.
NOW... WAS THAT SO HARD?
KKRRRRNNNCH!
HMM.
WASTE NOT, WANT NOT.
KRRRRNNCH!
RRRGGGP!

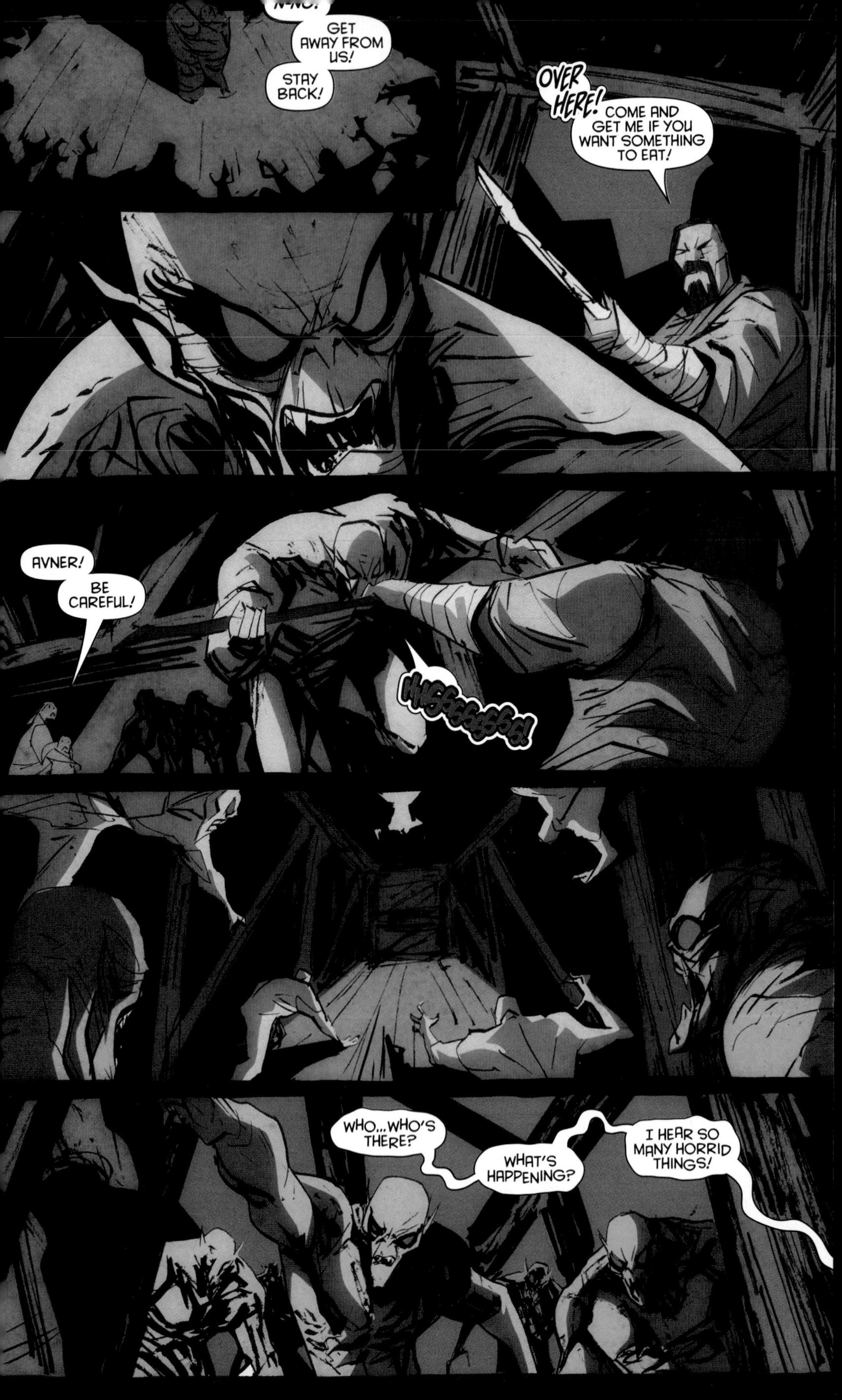
GET AWAY FROM US!
STAY BACK!
OVER HERE!
COME AND GET ME IF YOU WANT SOMETHING TO EAT!
AVNER!
BE CAREFUL!
WHO...WHO'S THERE?
WHAT'S HAPPENING?
I HEAR SO MANY HORRID THINGS!

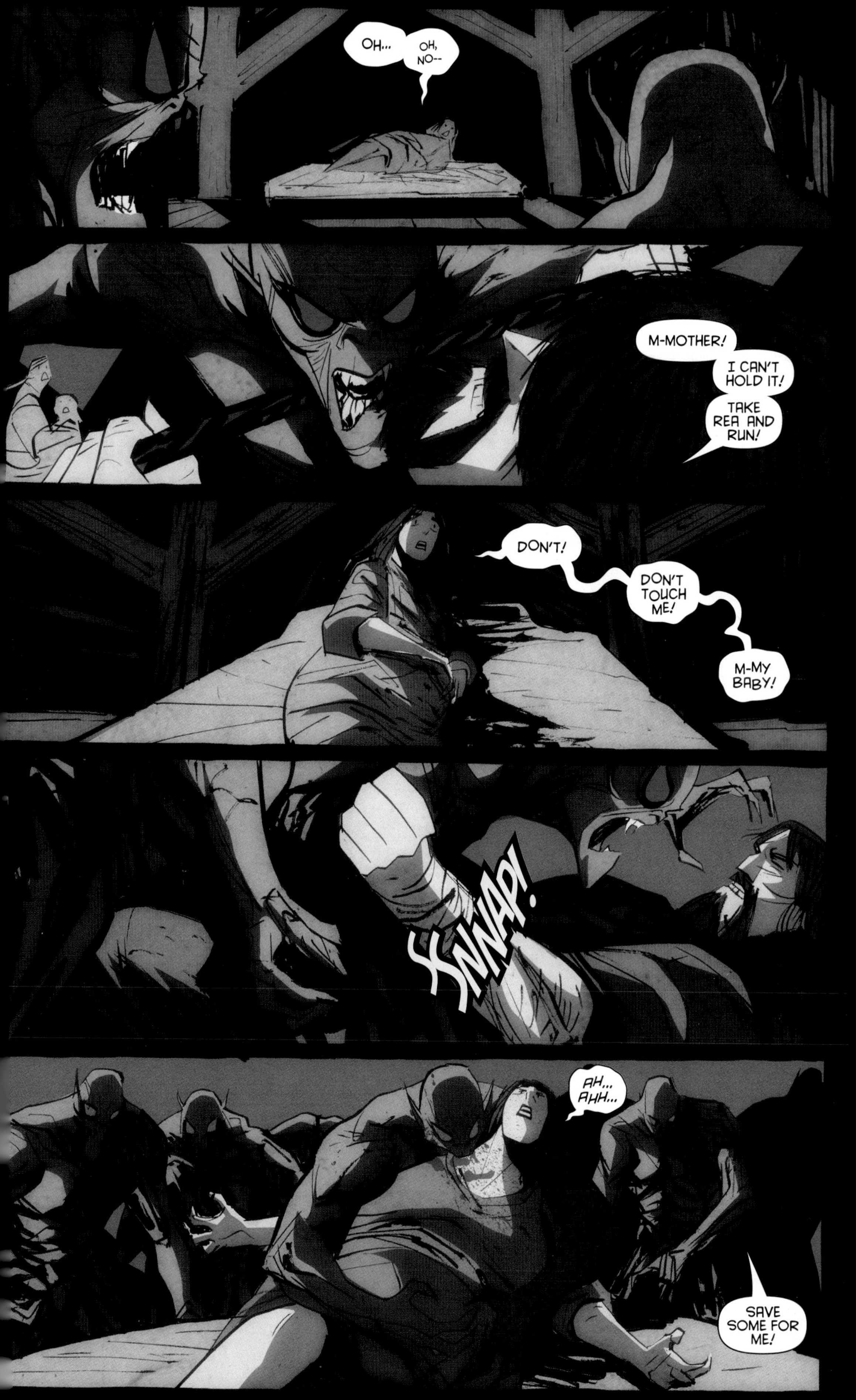
OH...
OH, NO--
M-MOTHER!
I CAN'T HOLD IT!
TAKE REA AND RUN!
DON'T!
DON'T TOUCH ME!
M-MY BABY!
SNNAP!
AH... AHH...
SAVE SOME FOR ME!

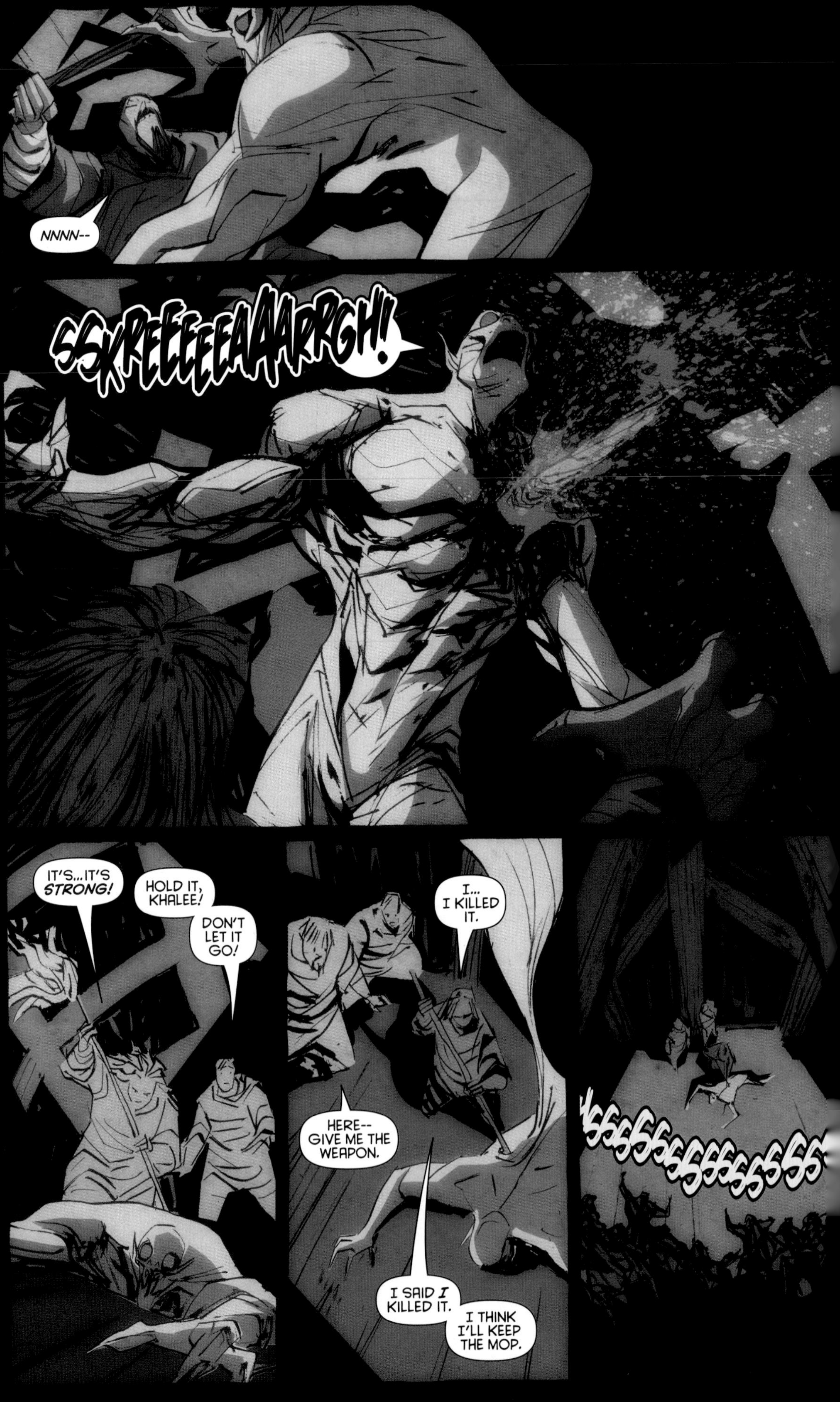
NNNN--
SSKREEEEEAAARRGH!!
IT'S...IT'S STRONG!
HOLD IT, KHALEE!
DON'T LET IT GO!
I... I KILLED IT.
HERE-- GIVE ME THE WEAPON.
I SAID I KILLED IT.
I THINK I'LL KEEP THE MOP.
HSSSSSSSSSSSSSSSS

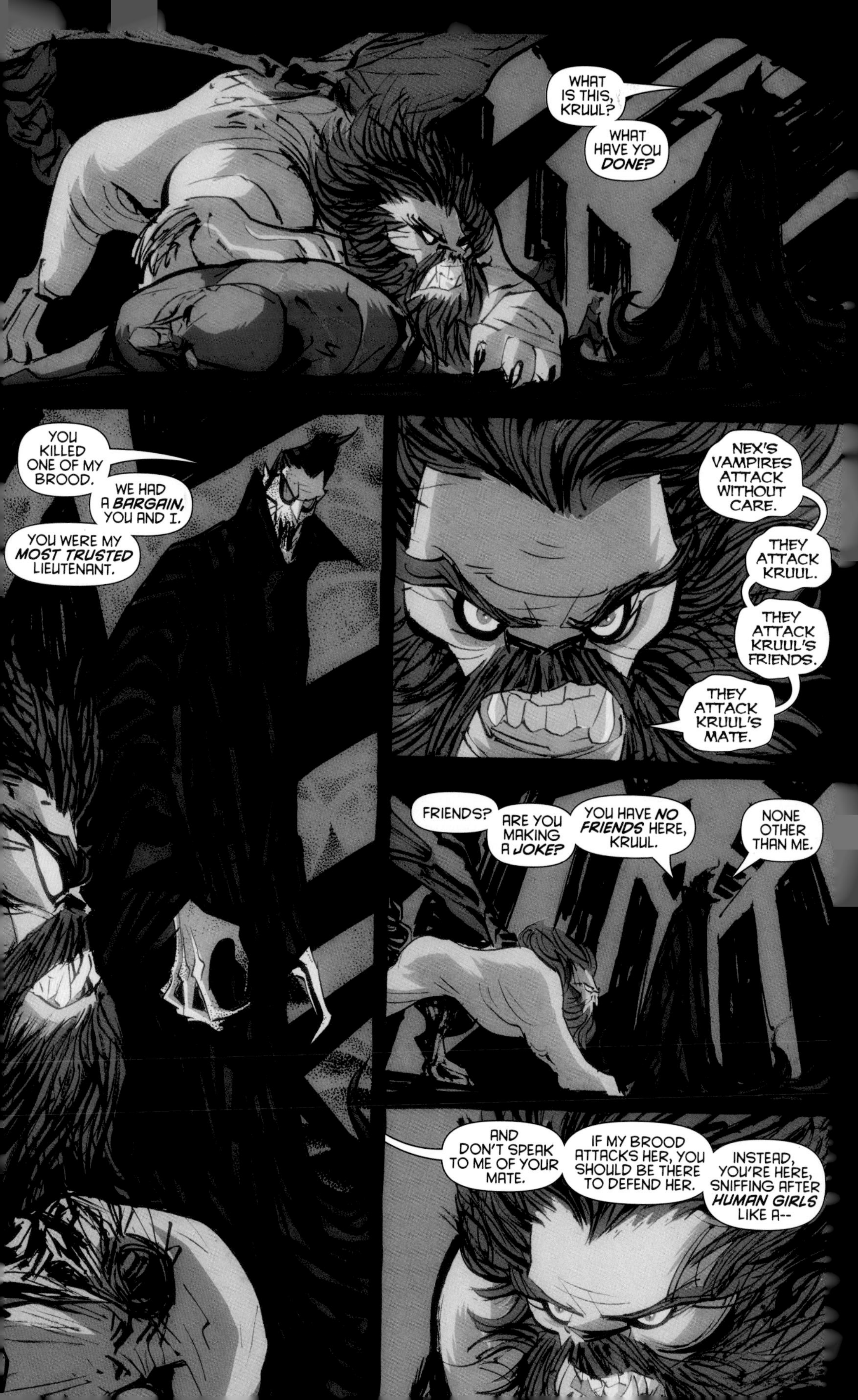
WHAT IS THIS, KRUUL?
WHAT HAVE YOU *DONE?*
YOU KILLED ONE OF MY BROOD.
WE HAD A *BARGAIN,* YOU AND I.
YOU WERE MY *MOST TRUSTED* LIEUTENANT.
NEX'S VAMPIRES ATTACK WITHOUT CARE.
THEY ATTACK KRUUL.
THEY ATTACK KRUUL'S FRIENDS.
THEY ATTACK KRUUL'S MATE.
FRIENDS?
ARE YOU MAKING A *JOKE?*
YOU HAVE *NO FRIENDS* HERE, KRUUL.
NONE OTHER THAN ME.
AND DON'T SPEAK TO ME OF YOUR MATE.
IF MY BROOD ATTACKS HER, YOU SHOULD BE THERE TO DEFEND HER.
INSTEAD, YOU'RE HERE, SNIFFING AFTER *HUMAN GIRLS* LIKE A--

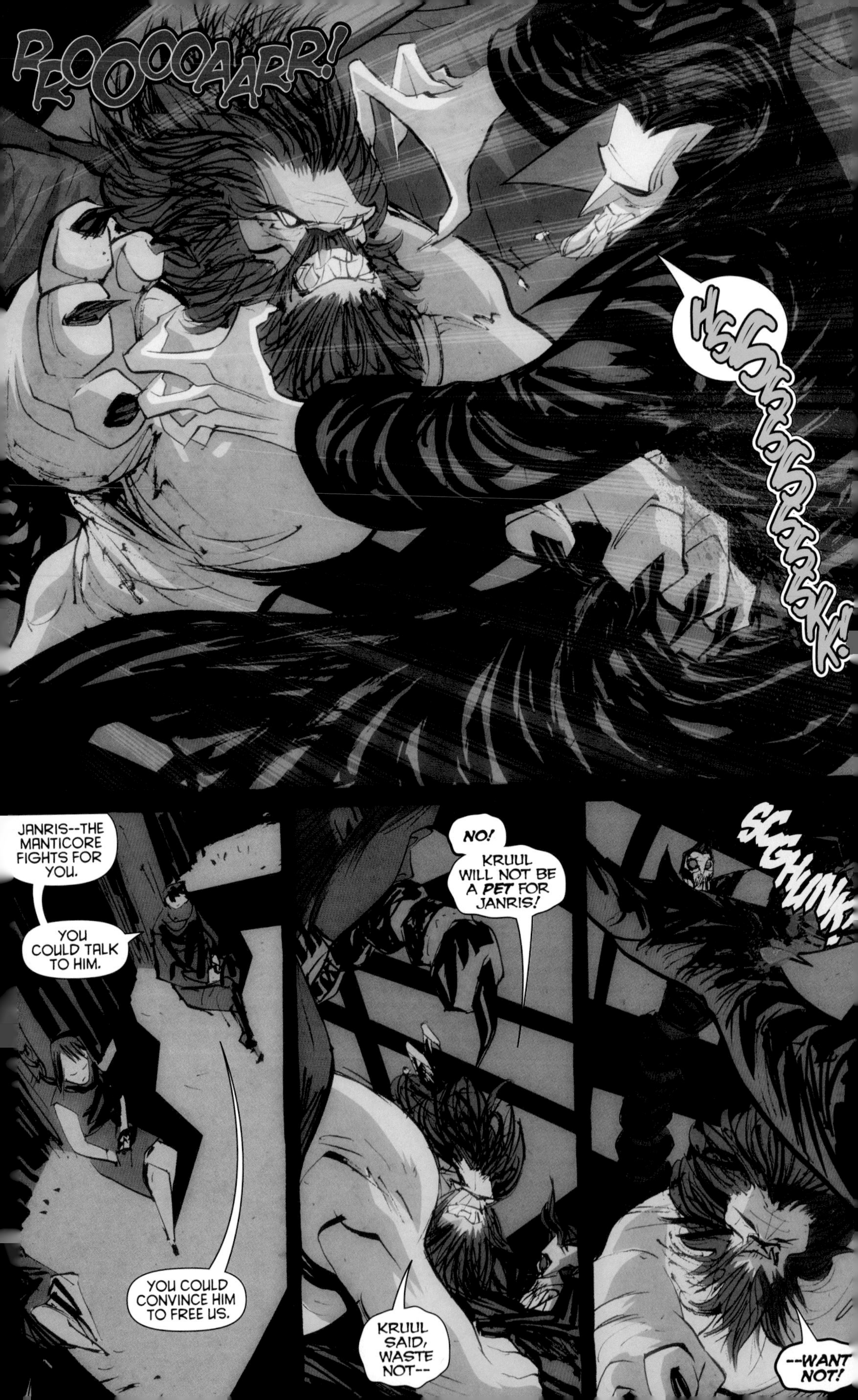

RROOOOOAARRR!
HSSSSSSSSSSK!
JANRIS--THE MANTICORE FIGHTS FOR YOU.
YOU COULD TALK TO HIM.
YOU COULD CONVINCE HIM TO FREE US.
NO!
KRUUL WILL NOT BE A PET FOR JANRIS!
KRUUL SAID, WASTE NOT--
SCHUNK!
--WANT NOT!

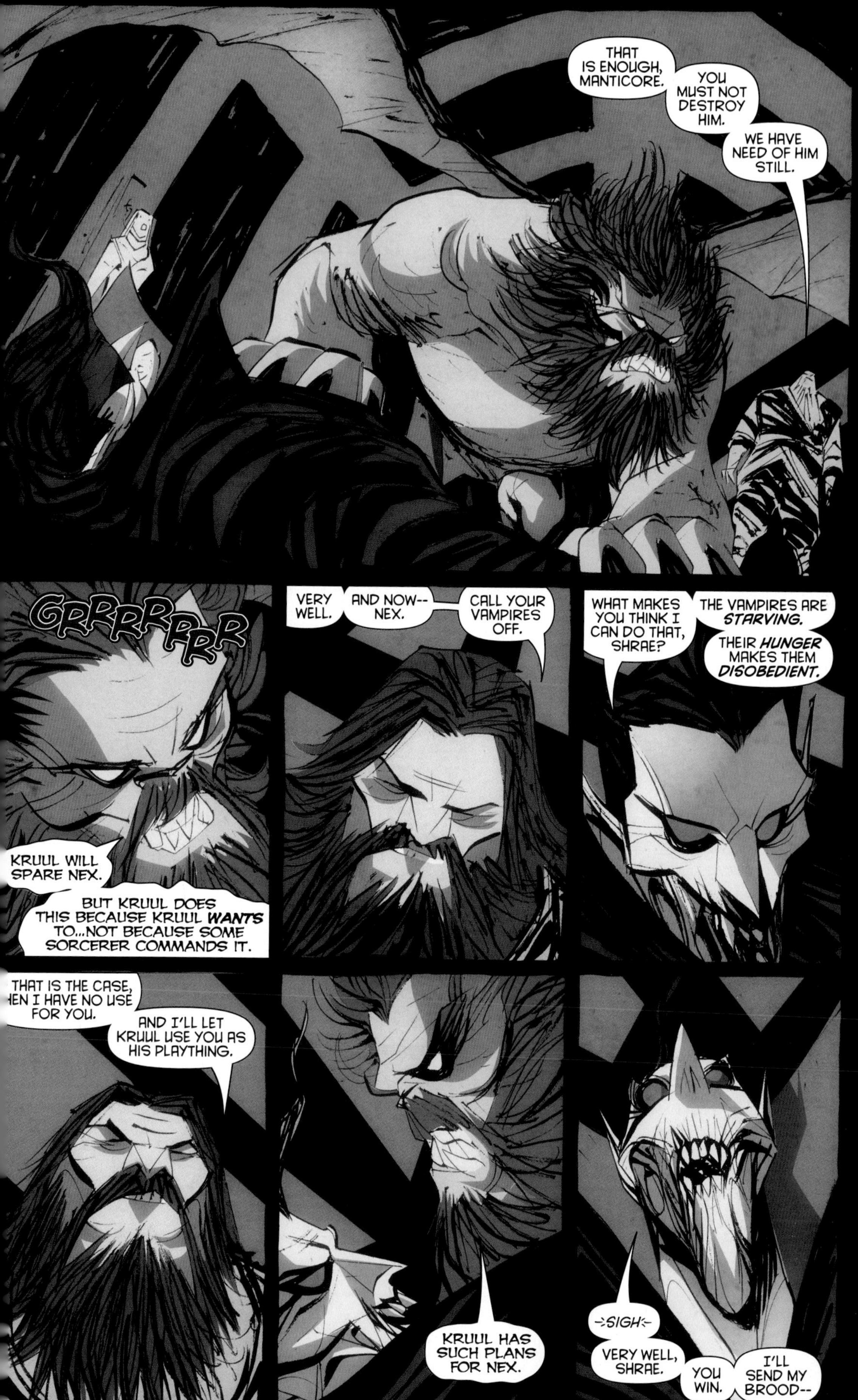
THAT IS ENOUGH, MANTICORE.
YOU MUST NOT DESTROY HIM.
WE HAVE NEED OF HIM STILL.
GRRRRRRR
KRUUL WILL SPARE NEX.
BUT KRUUL DOES THIS BECAUSE KRUUL **WANTS** TO...NOT BECAUSE SOME SORCERER COMMANDS IT.
VERY WELL.
AND NOW-- NEX.
CALL YOUR VAMPIRES OFF.
WHAT MAKES YOU THINK I CAN DO THAT, SHRAE?
THE VAMPIRES ARE ***STARVING.***
THEIR ***HUNGER*** MAKES THEM ***DISOBEDIENT.***
THAT IS THE CASE, HEN I HAVE NO USE FOR YOU.
AND I'LL LET KRUUL USE YOU AS HIS PLAYTHING.
KRUUL HAS SUCH PLANS FOR NEX.
SIGH
VERY WELL, SHRAE.
YOU WIN.
I'LL SEND MY BROOD--

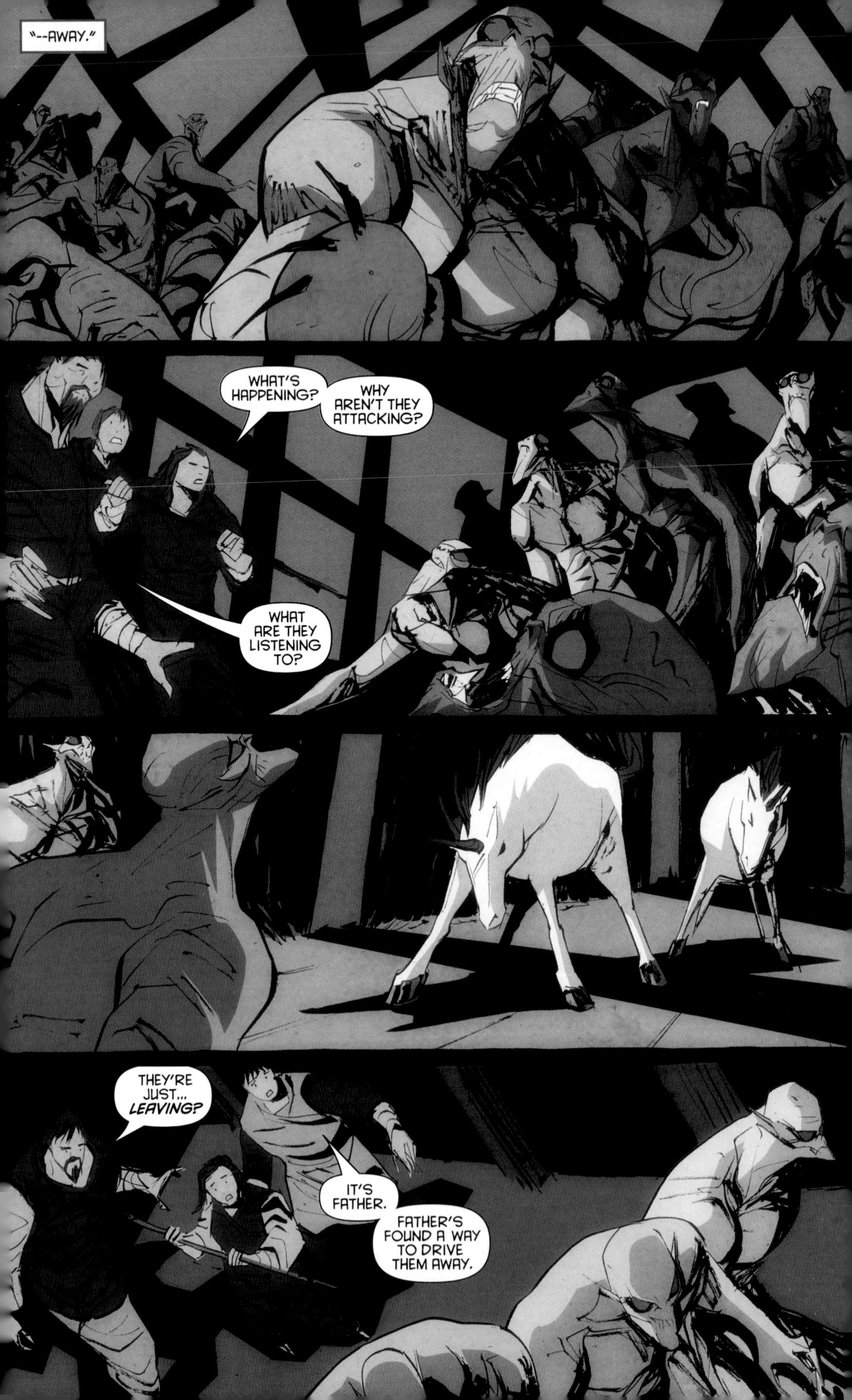
"--AWAY."
WHAT'S HAPPENING?
WHY AREN'T THEY ATTACKING?
WHAT ARE THEY LISTENING TO?
THEY'RE JUST... *LEAVING?*
IT'S FATHER.
FATHER'S FOUND A WAY TO DRIVE THEM AWAY.

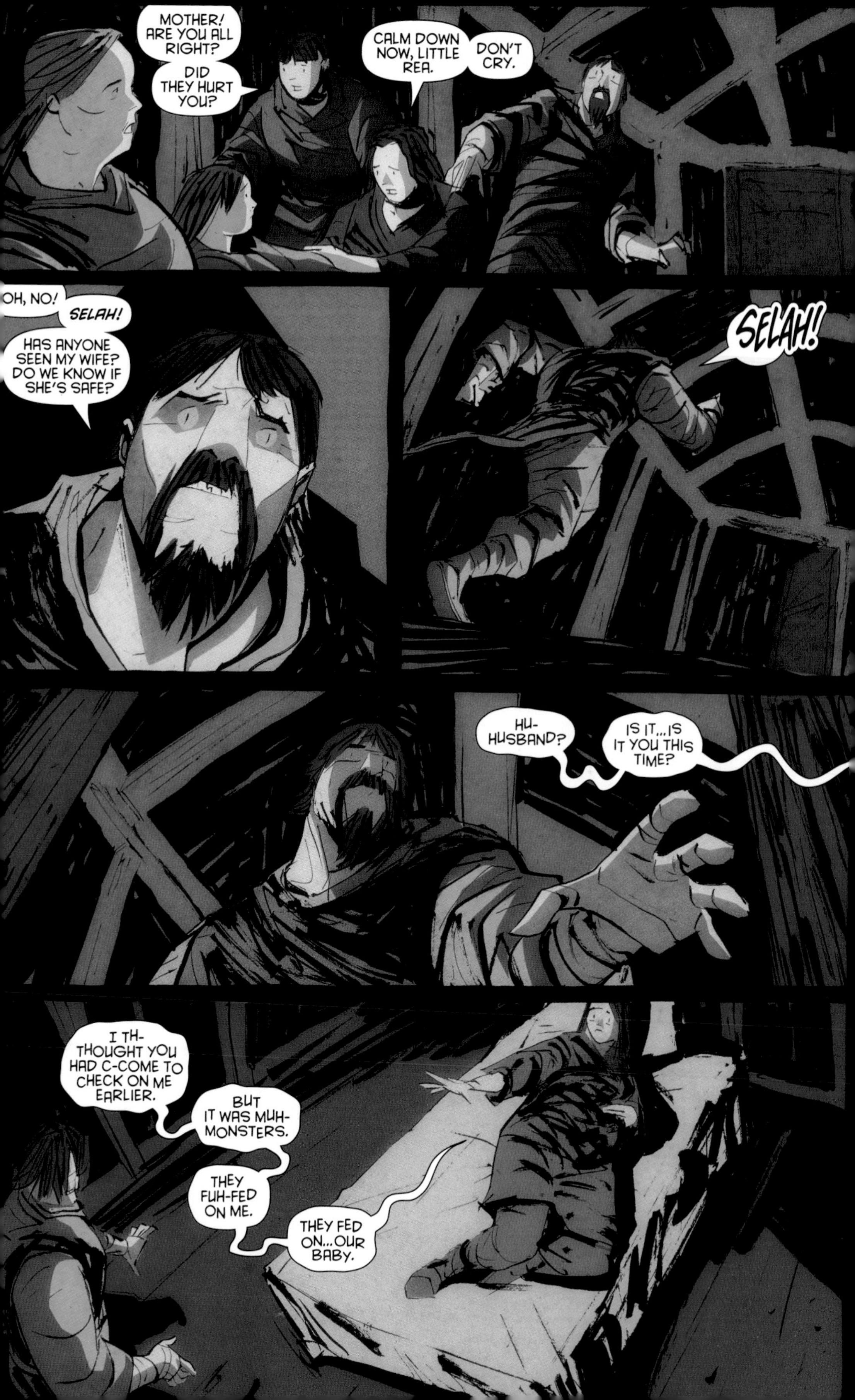
MOTHER! ARE YOU ALL RIGHT?
DID THEY HURT YOU?
CALM DOWN NOW, LITTLE REA.
DON'T CRY.
OH, NO!
SELAH!
HAS ANYONE SEEN MY WIFE? DO WE KNOW IF SHE'S SAFE?
SELAH!
HU- HUSBAND?
IS IT... IS IT YOU THIS TIME?
I TH- THOUGHT YOU HAD C-COME TO CHECK ON ME EARLIER.
BUT IT WAS MUH- MONSTERS.
THEY FUH-FED ON ME.
THEY FED ON... OUR BABY.

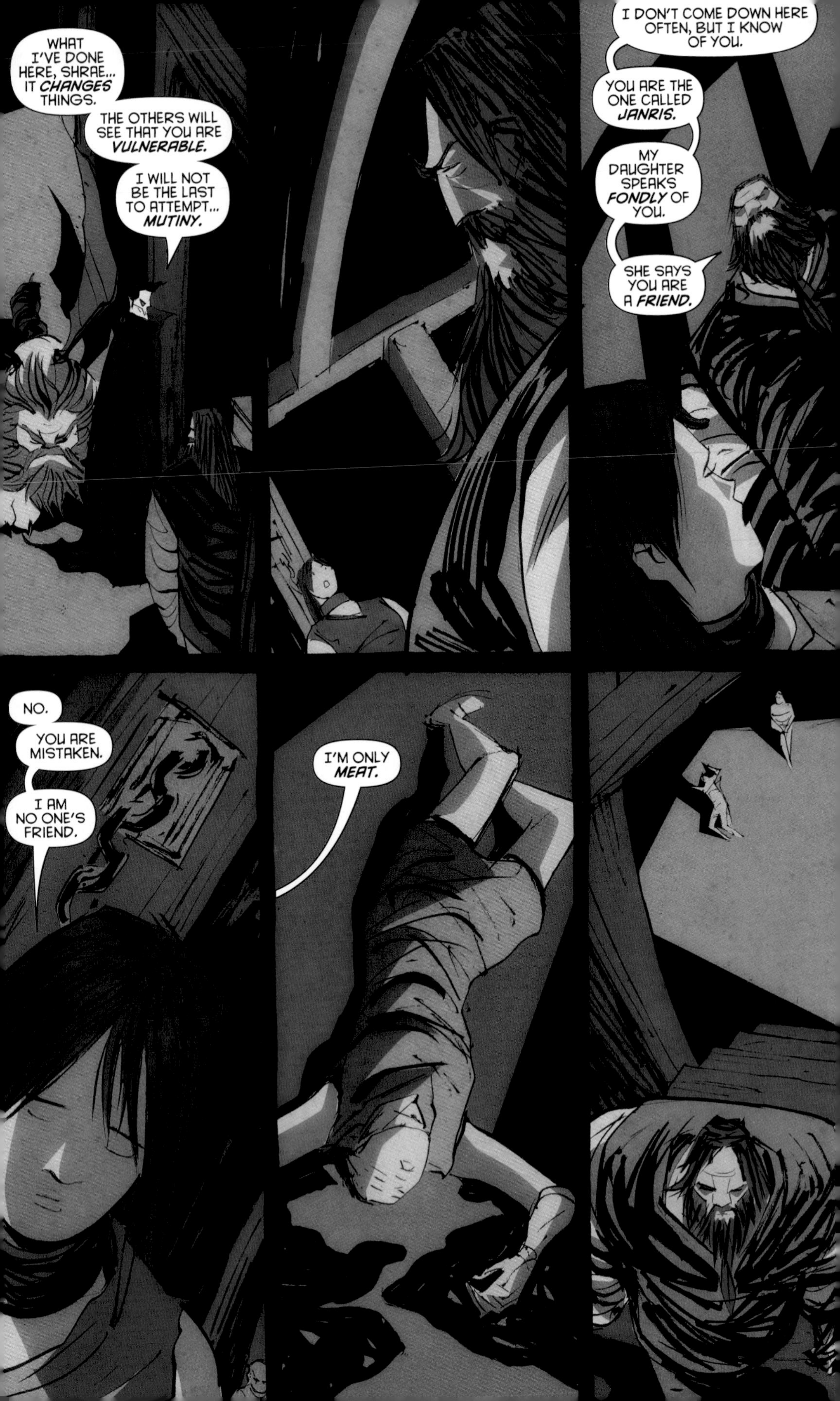

WHAT I'VE DONE HERE, SHRAE... IT *CHANGES* THINGS.
THE OTHERS WILL SEE THAT YOU ARE *VULNERABLE.*
I WILL NOT BE THE LAST TO ATTEMPT... *MUTINY.*
I DON'T COME DOWN HERE OFTEN, BUT I KNOW OF YOU.
YOU ARE THE ONE CALLED *JANRIS.*
MY DAUGHTER SPEAKS *FONDLY* OF YOU.
SHE SAYS YOU ARE A *FRIEND.*
NO.
YOU ARE MISTAKEN.
I AM NO ONE'S FRIEND.
I'M ONLY *MEAT.*

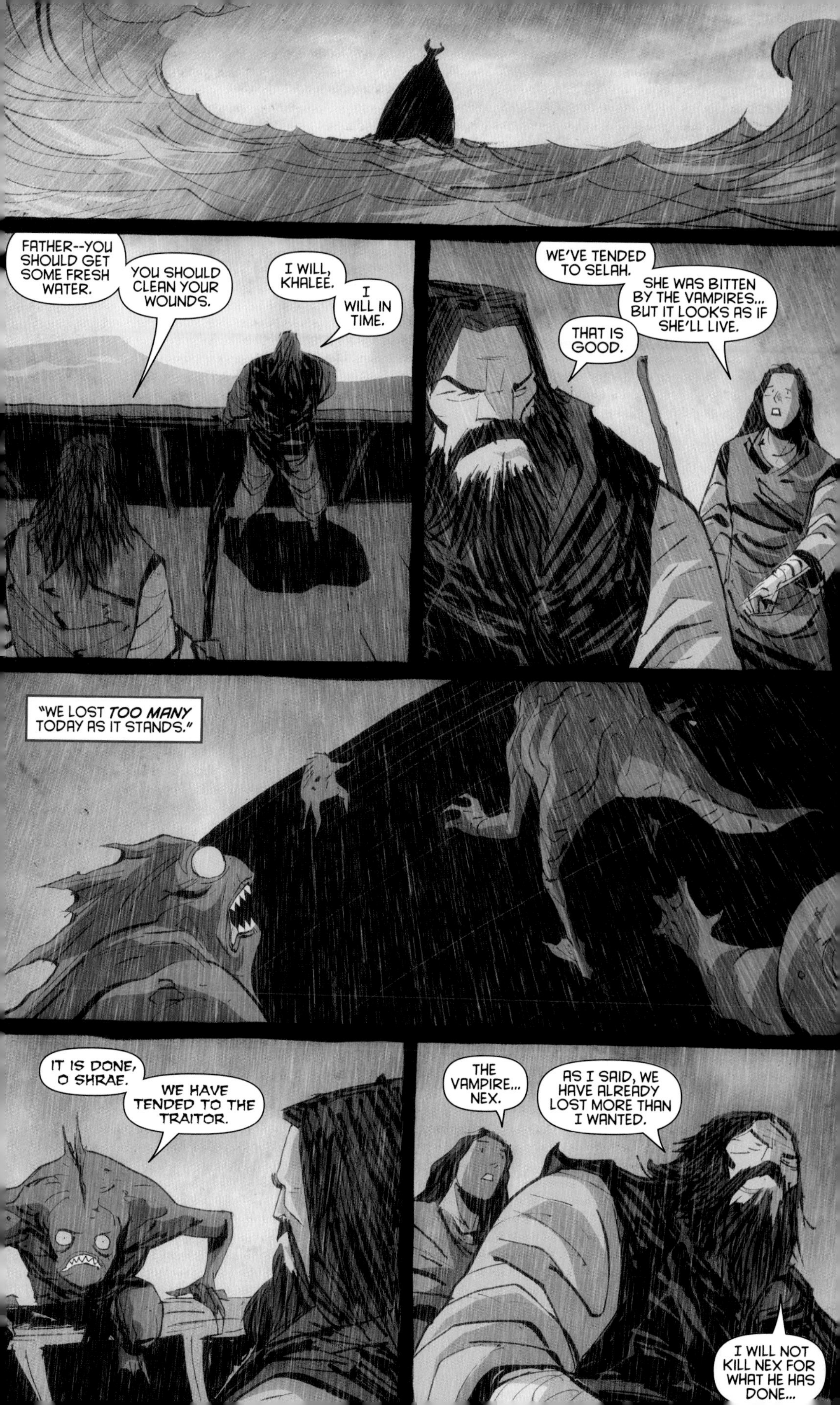
FATHER--YOU SHOULD GET SOME FRESH WATER.
YOU SHOULD CLEAN YOUR WOUNDS.
I WILL, KHALEE.
I WILL IN TIME.
WE'VE TENDED TO SELAH.
SHE WAS BITTEN BY THE VAMPIRES... BUT IT LOOKS AS IF SHE'LL LIVE.
THAT IS GOOD.
"WE LOST TOO MANY TODAY AS IT STANDS."
IT IS DONE, O SHRAE.
WE HAVE TENDED TO THE TRAITOR.
THE VAMPIRE... NEX.
AS I SAID, WE HAVE ALREADY LOST MORE THAN I WANTED.
I WILL NOT KILL NEX FOR WHAT HE HAS DONE...

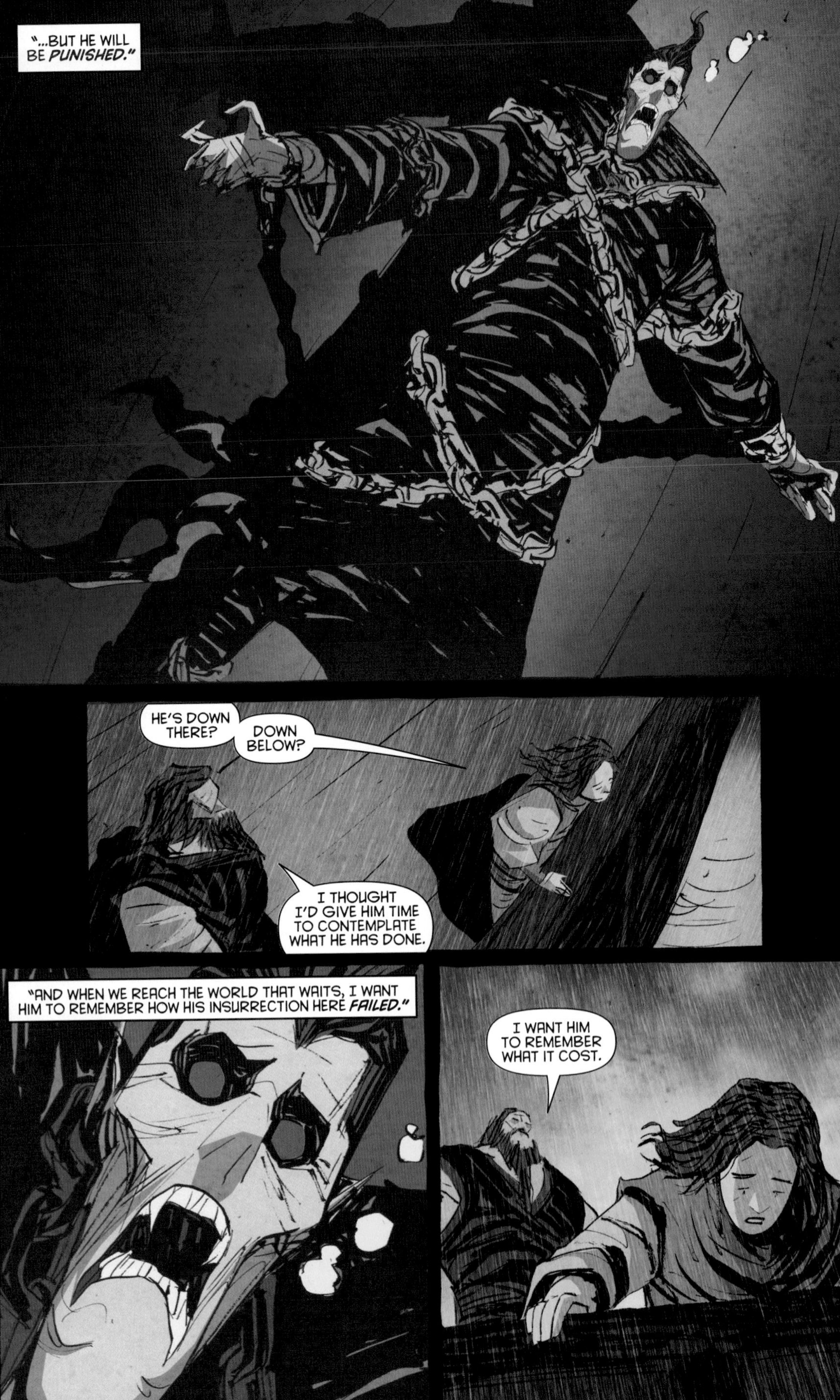
"...BUT HE WILL BE *PUNISHED.*"
HE'S DOWN THERE?
DOWN BELOW?
I THOUGHT I'D GIVE HIM TIME TO CONTEMPLATE WHAT HE HAS DONE.
"AND WHEN WE REACH THE WORLD THAT WAITS, I WANT HIM TO REMEMBER HOW HIS INSURRECTION HERE *FAILED.*"
I WANT HIM TO REMEMBER WHAT IT COST.

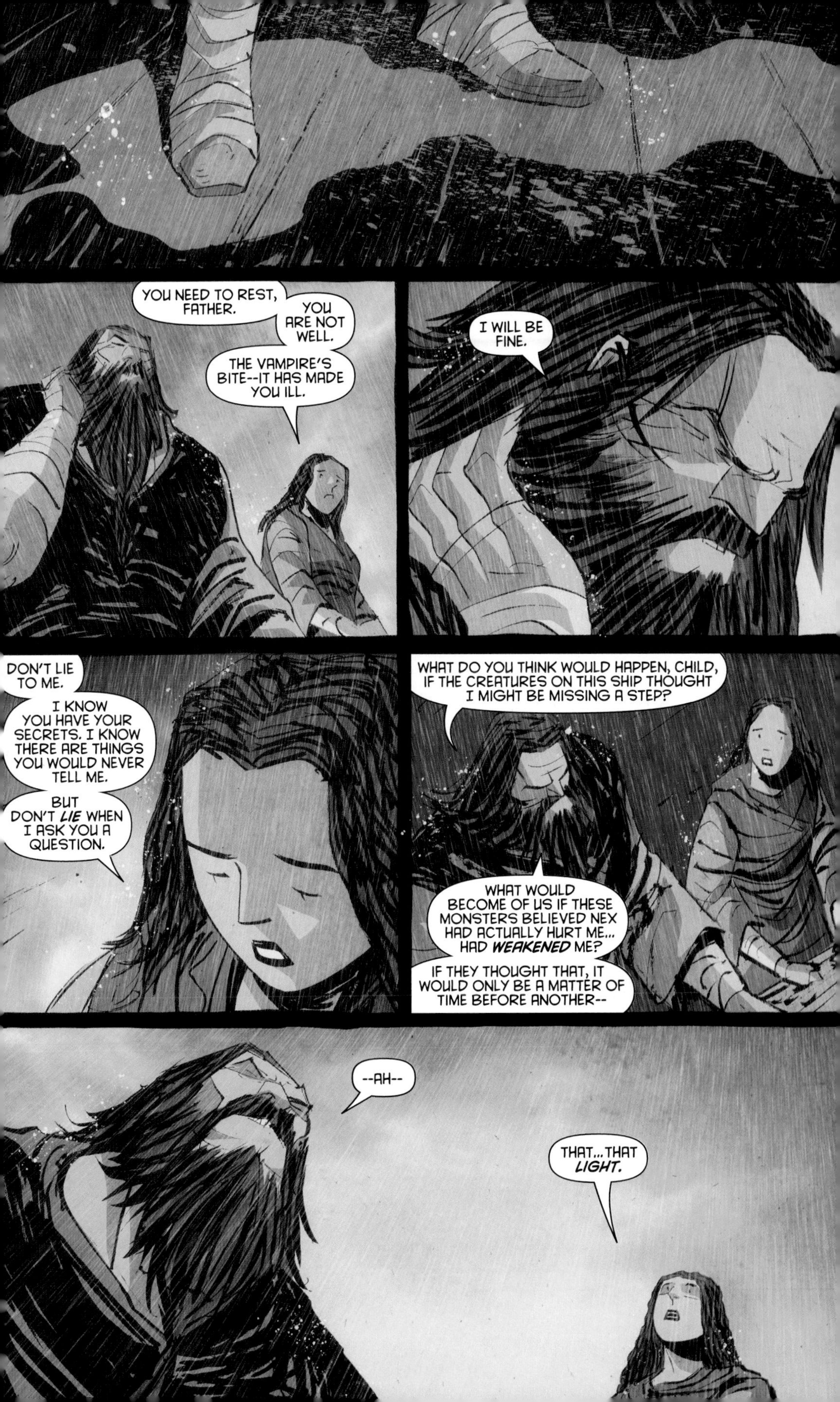

YOU NEED TO REST, FATHER.
YOU ARE NOT WELL.
THE VAMPIRE'S BITE--IT HAS MADE YOU ILL.
I WILL BE FINE.
DON'T LIE TO ME.
I KNOW YOU HAVE YOUR SECRETS. I KNOW THERE ARE THINGS YOU WOULD NEVER TELL ME.
BUT DON'T *LIE* WHEN I ASK YOU A QUESTION.
WHAT DO YOU THINK WOULD HAPPEN, CHILD, IF THE CREATURES ON THIS SHIP THOUGHT I MIGHT BE MISSING A STEP?
WHAT WOULD BECOME OF US IF THESE MONSTERS BELIEVED NEX HAD ACTUALLY HURT ME... HAD *WEAKENED* ME?
IF THEY THOUGHT THAT, IT WOULD ONLY BE A MATTER OF TIME BEFORE ANOTHER--
--AH--
THAT... THAT *LIGHT.*

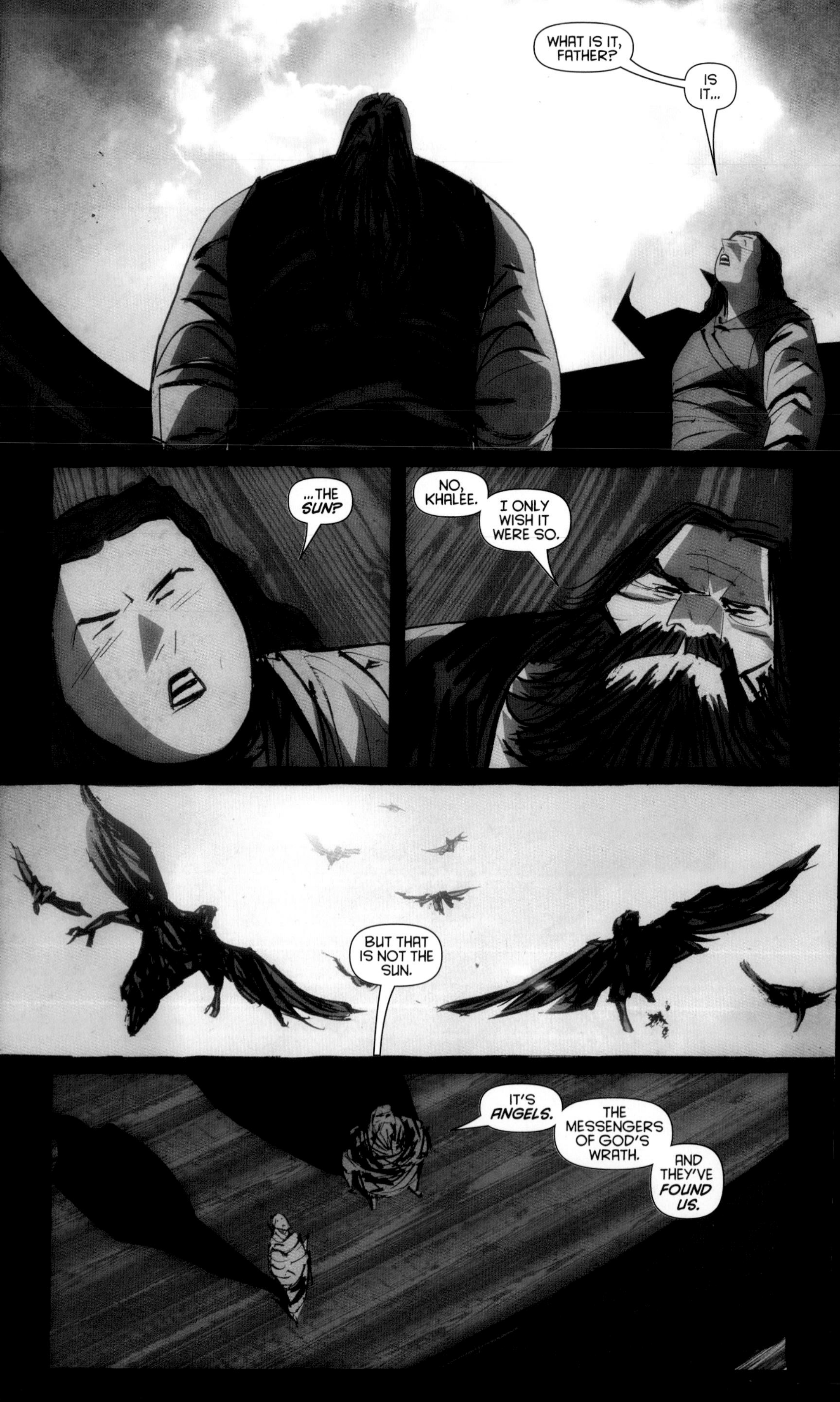
WHAT IS IT, FATHER?
IS IT...
...THE SUN?
NO, KHALEE.
I ONLY WISH IT WERE SO.
BUT THAT IS NOT THE SUN.
IT'S ANGELS.
THE MESSENGERS OF GOD'S WRATH.
AND THEY'VE FOUND US.

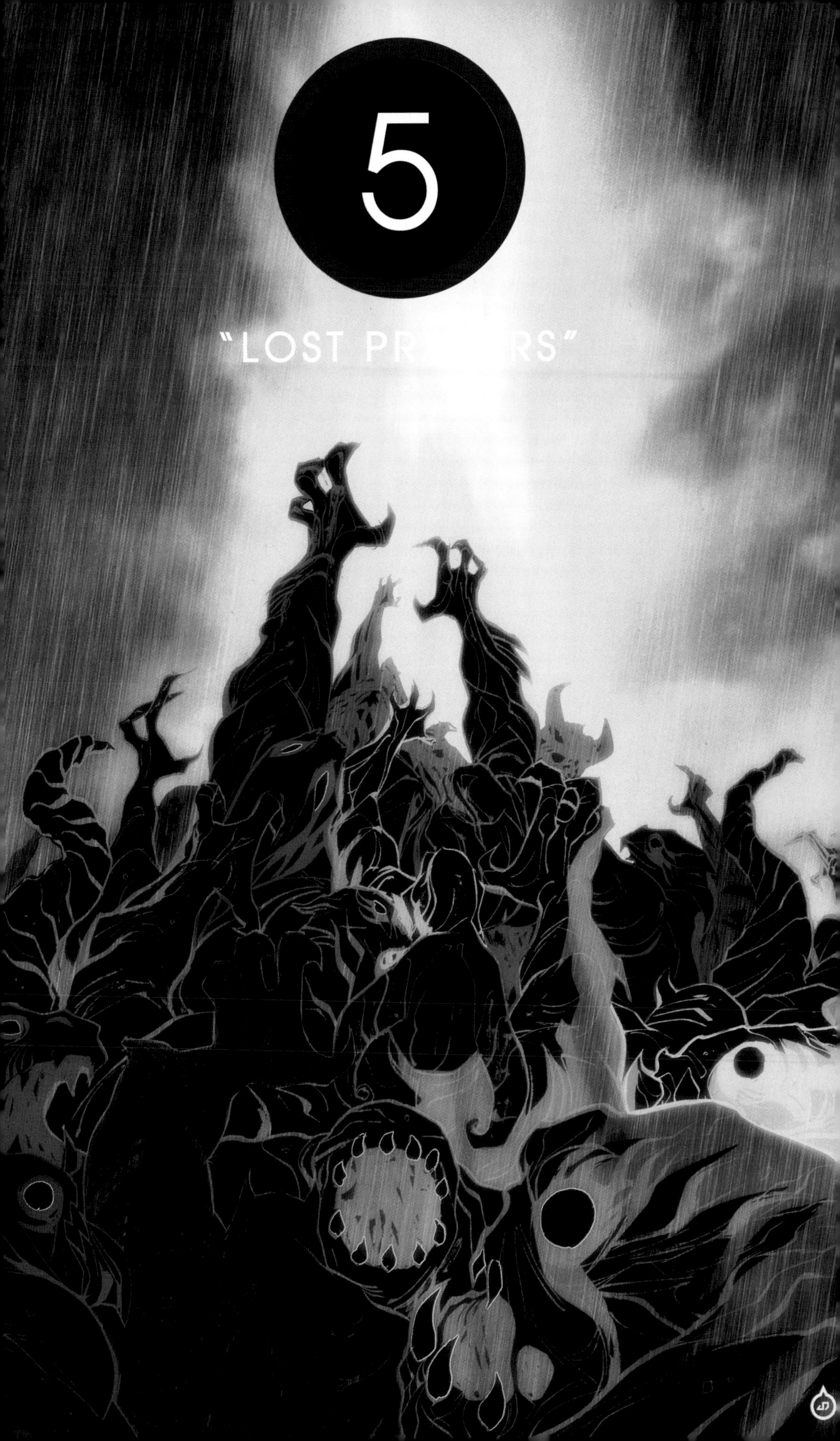
5
“LOST PR RS”

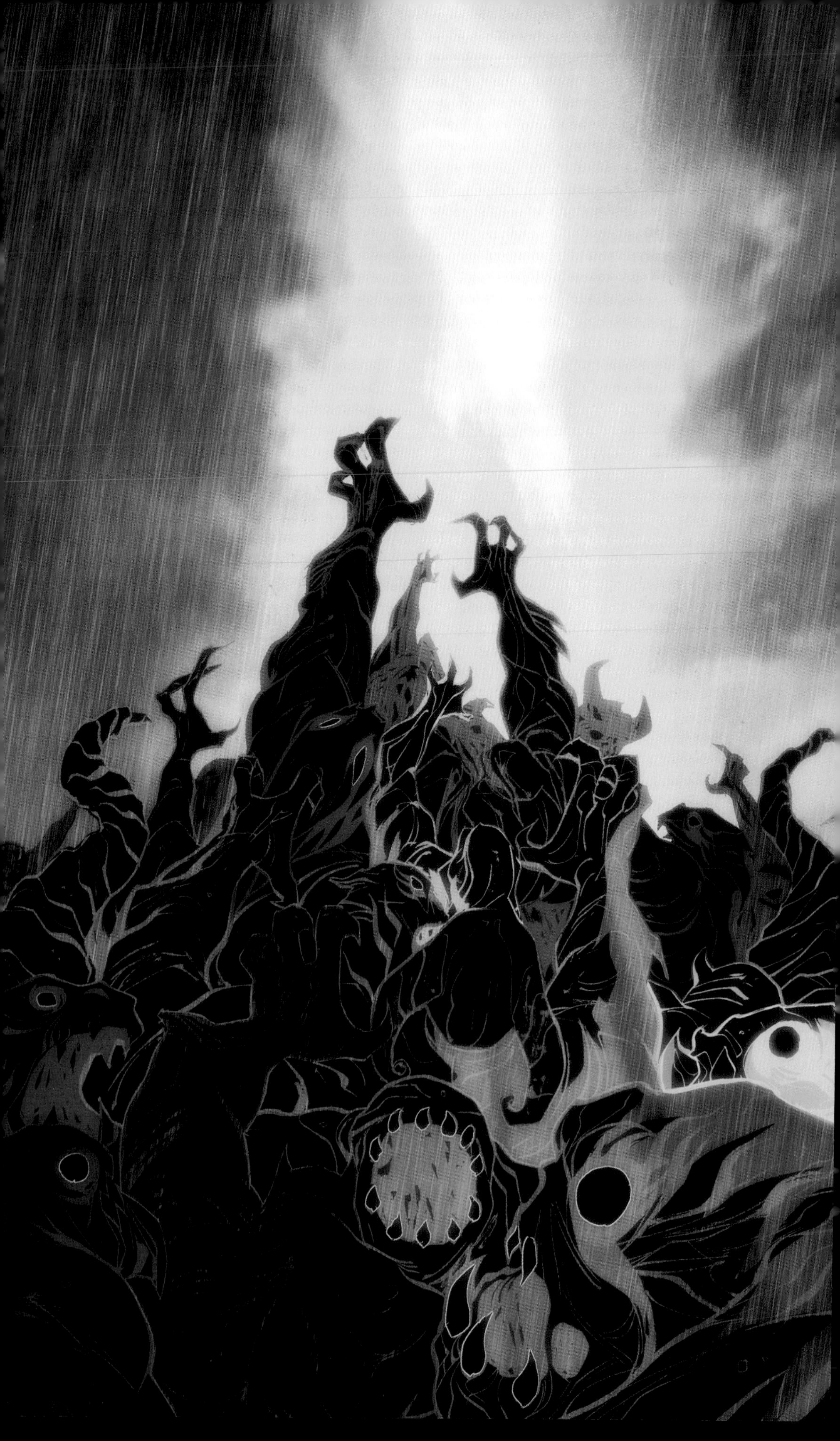

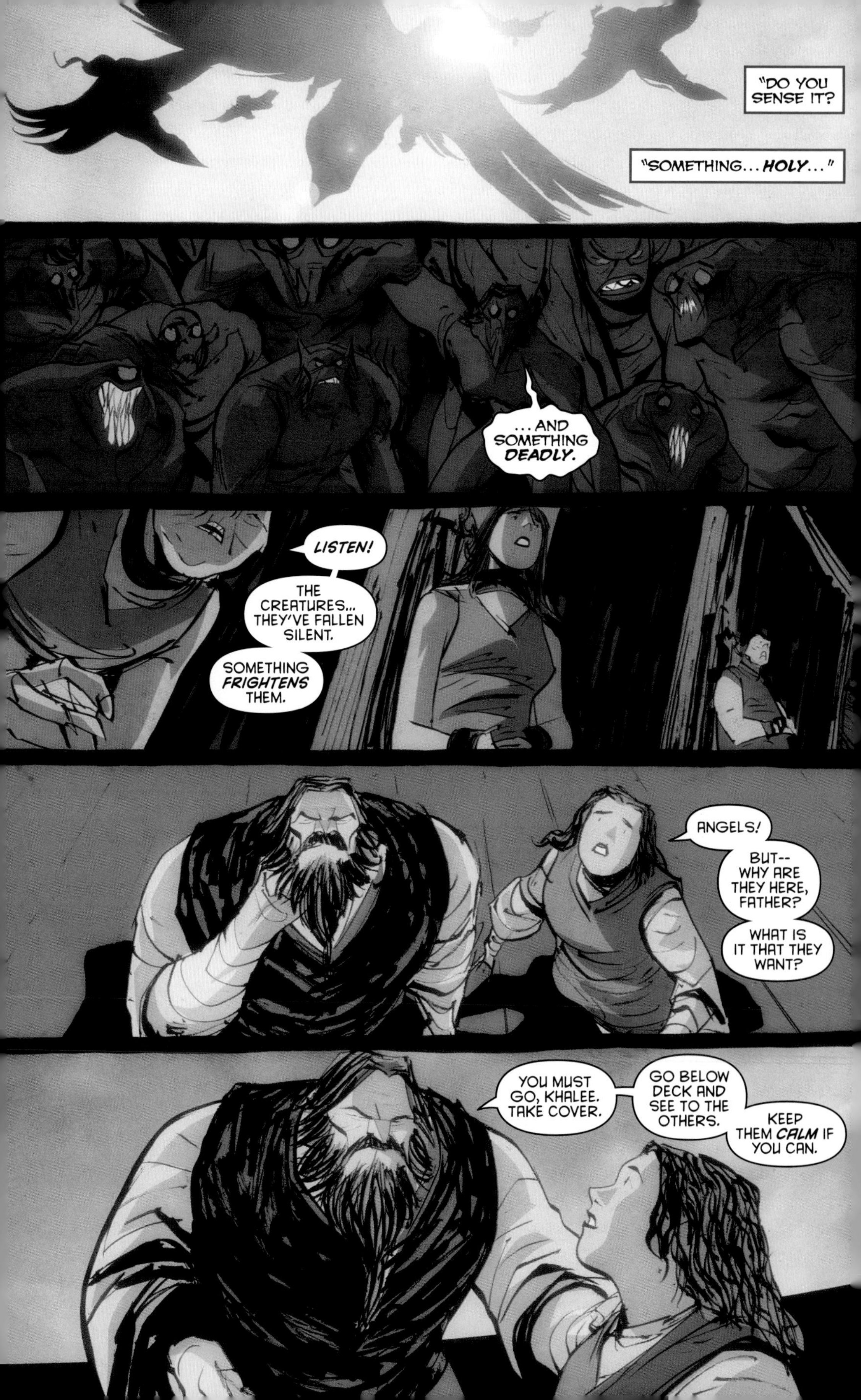
"DO YOU SENSE IT?
"SOMETHING... HOLY..."
...AND SOMETHING DEADLY.
LISTEN!
THE CREATURES... THEY'VE FALLEN SILENT.
SOMETHING FRIGHTENS THEM.
ANGELS!
BUT-- WHY ARE THEY HERE, FATHER?
WHAT IS IT THAT THEY WANT?
YOU MUST GO, KHALEE. TAKE COVER.
GO BELOW DECK AND SEE TO THE OTHERS.
KEEP THEM CALM IF YOU CAN.

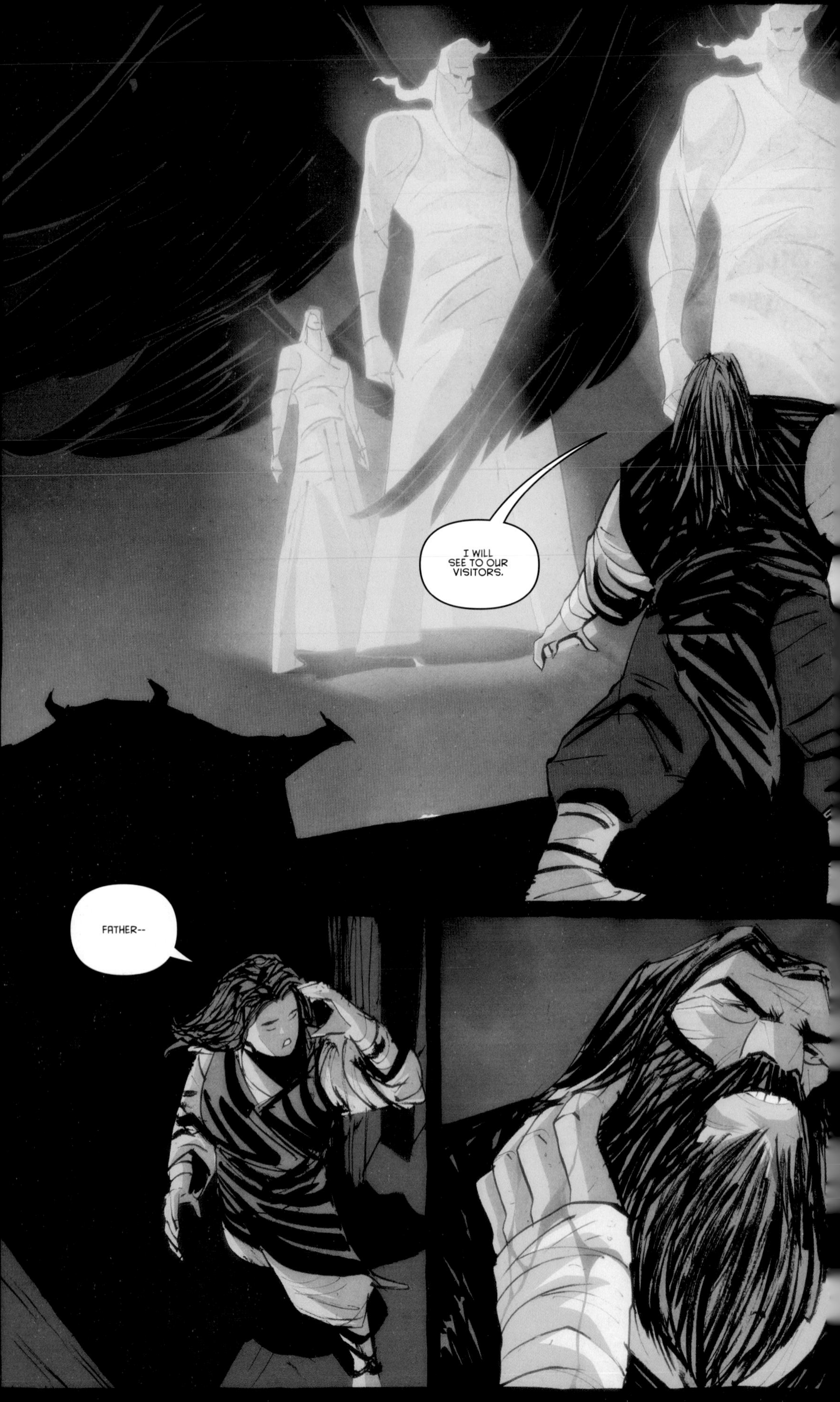
I WILL SEE TO OUR VISITORS.
FATHER--

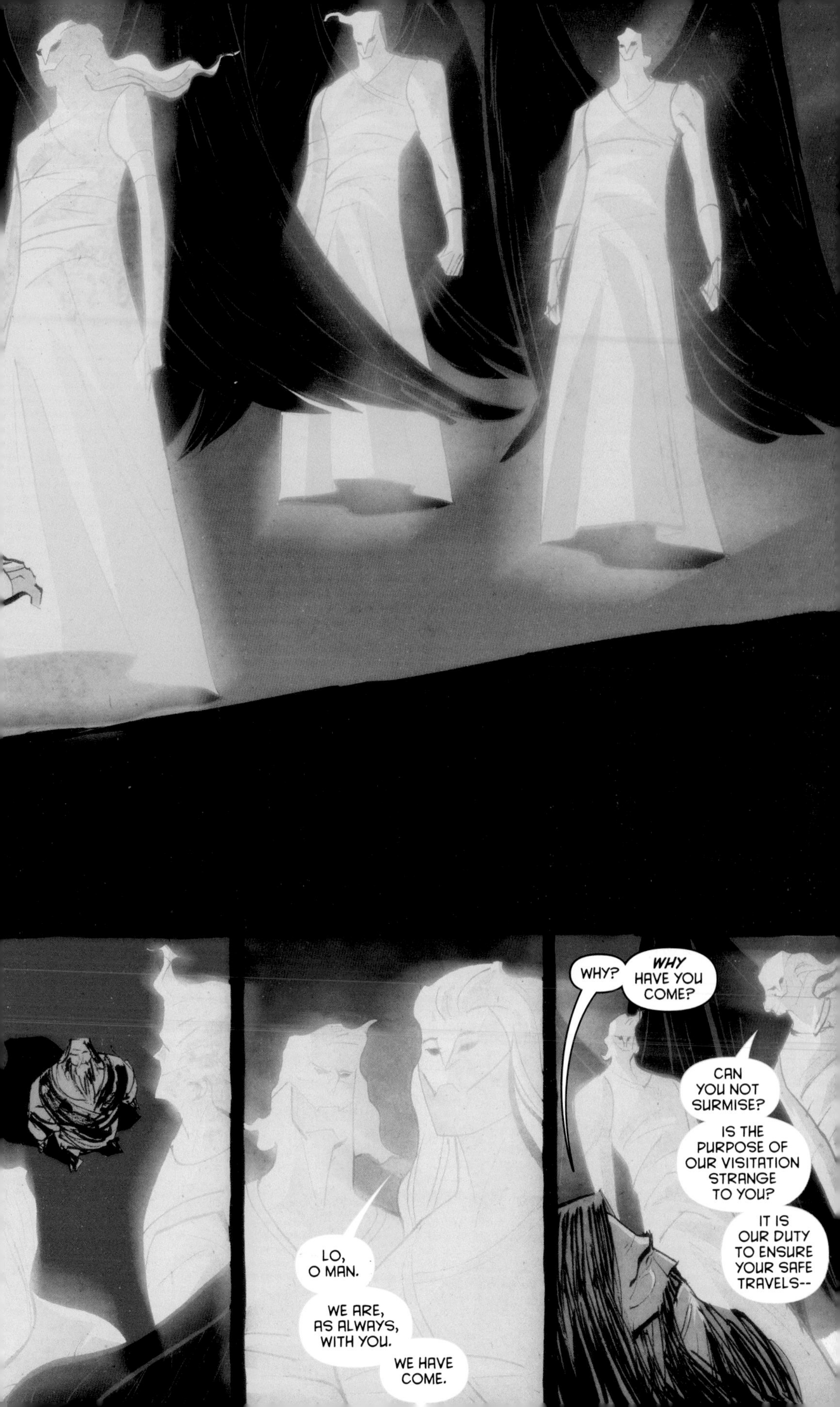
LO,
O MAN.
WE ARE,
AS ALWAYS,
WITH YOU.
WE HAVE
COME.
WHY?
WHY
HAVE YOU
COME?
CAN
YOU NOT
SURMISE?
IS THE
PURPOSE OF
OUR VISITATION
STRANGE
TO YOU?
IT IS
OUR DUTY
TO ENSURE
YOUR SAFE
TRAVELS--

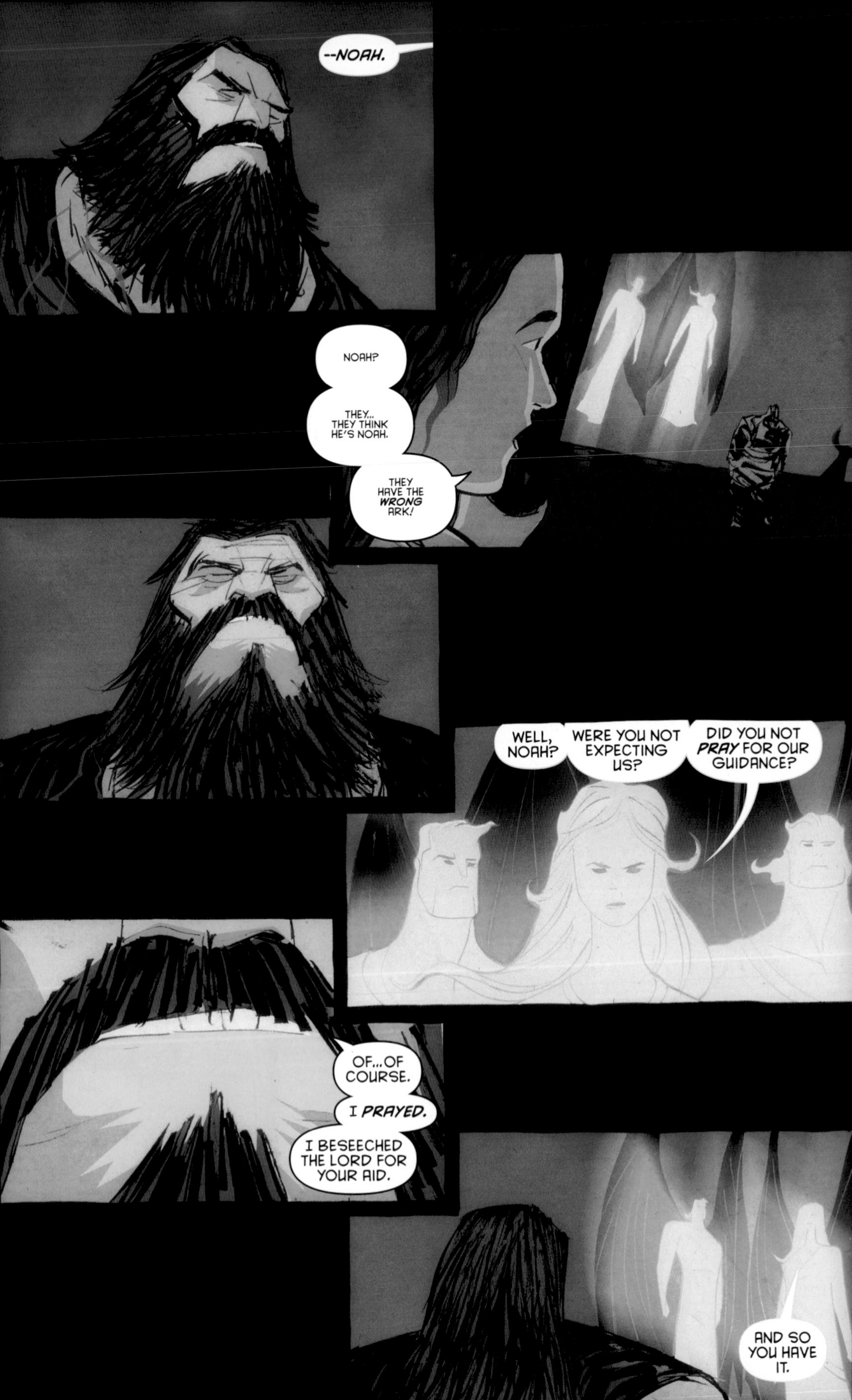
--NOAH.
NOAH?
THEY... THEY THINK HE'S NOAH.
THEY HAVE THE WRONG ARK!
WELL, NOAH?
WERE YOU NOT EXPECTING US?
DID YOU NOT PRAY FOR OUR GUIDANCE?
OF... OF COURSE.
I PRAYED.
I BESEECHED THE LORD FOR YOUR AID.
AND SO YOU HAVE IT.

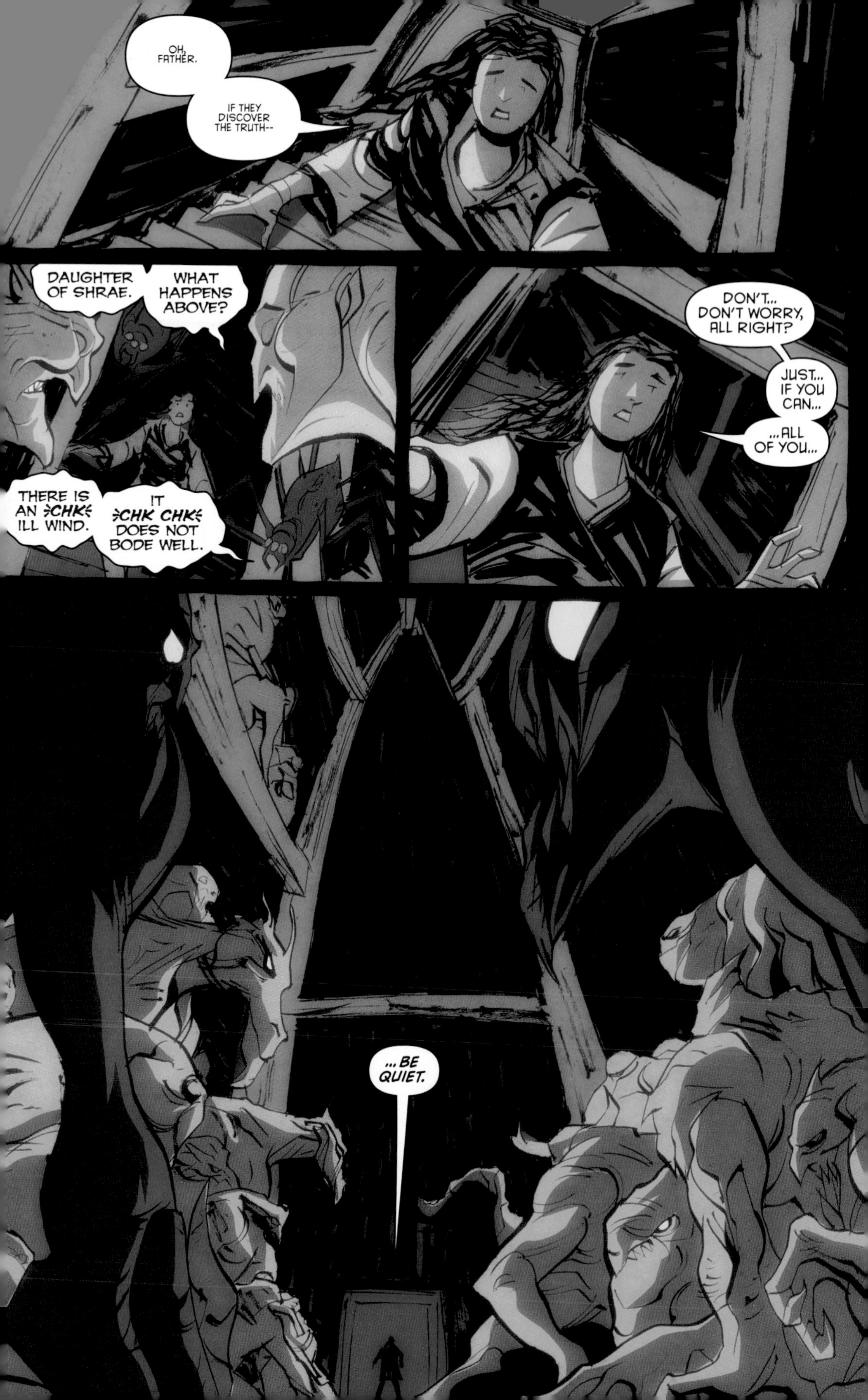
OH, FATHER.
IF THEY DISCOVER THE TRUTH--
DAUGHTER OF SHRAE.
WHAT HAPPENS ABOVE?
THERE IS AN *CHK* ILL WIND.
IT *CHK CHK* DOES NOT BODE WELL.
DON'T... DON'T WORRY, ALL RIGHT?
JUST... IF YOU CAN...
...ALL OF YOU...
...BE QUIET.

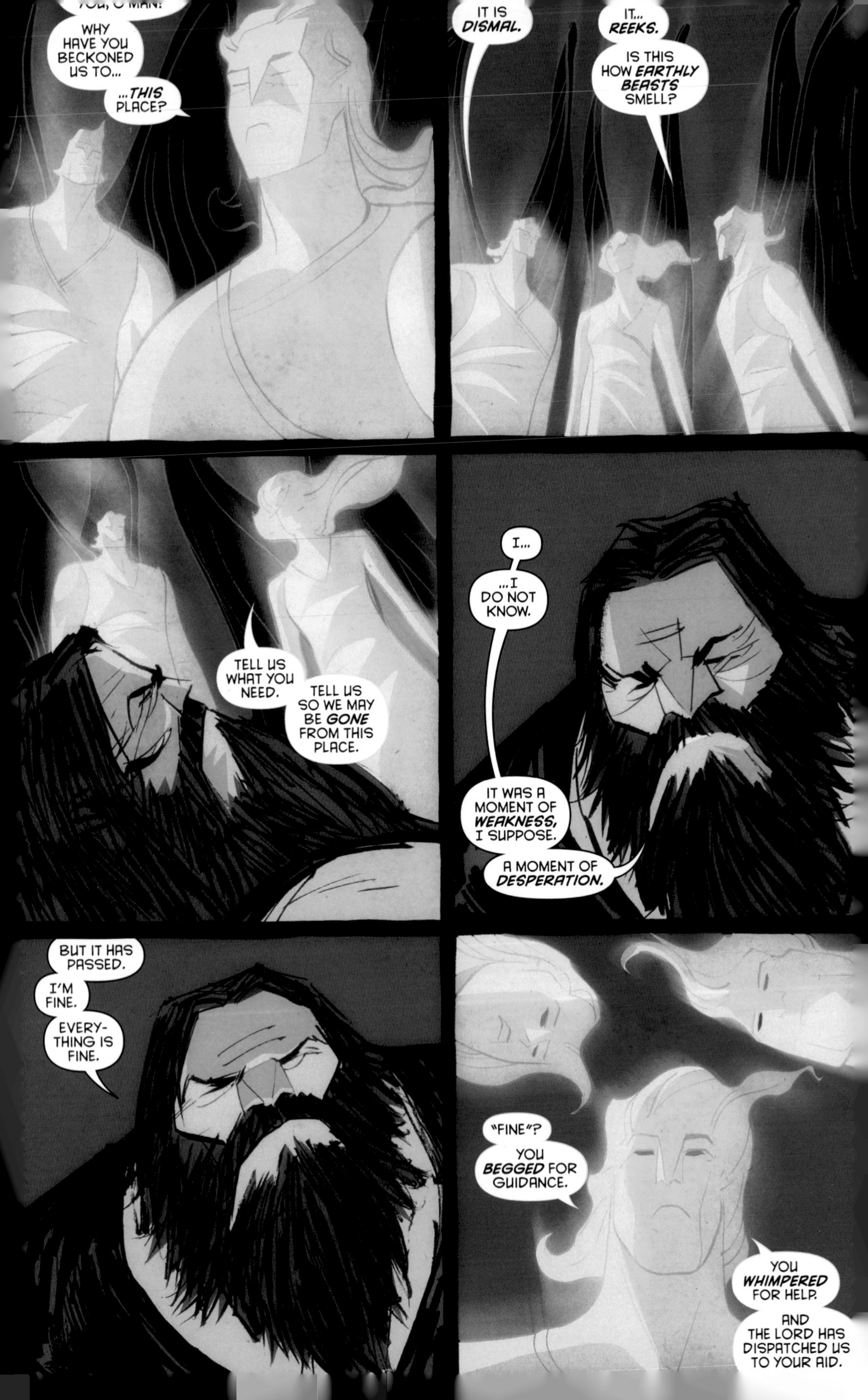
WHY HAVE YOU BECKONED US TO...
...THIS PLACE?
IT IS DISMAL.
IT... REEKS.
IS THIS HOW EARTHLY BEASTS SMELL?
TELL US WHAT YOU NEED.
TELL US SO WE MAY BE GONE FROM THIS PLACE.
I...
...I DO NOT KNOW.
IT WAS A MOMENT OF WEAKNESS, I SUPPOSE.
A MOMENT OF DESPERATION.
BUT IT HAS PASSED.
I'M FINE.
EVERY-THING IS FINE.
"FINE"?
YOU BEGGED FOR GUIDANCE.
YOU WHIMPERED FOR HELP.
AND THE LORD HAS DISPATCHED US TO YOUR AID.

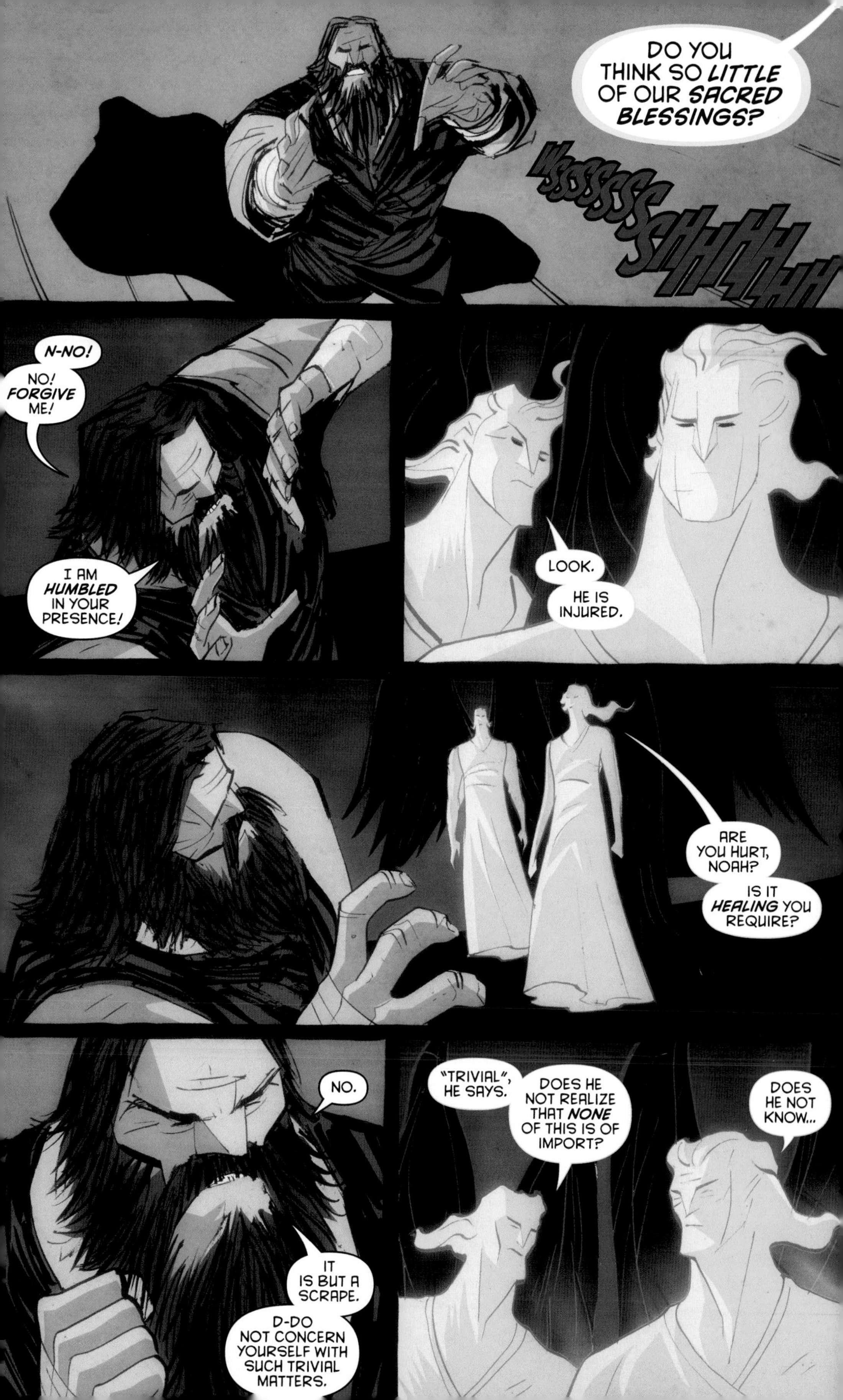
DO YOU THINK SO LITTLE OF OUR SACRED BLESSINGS?
WSSSSSSSHHHHHHH
N-NO!
NO! FORGIVE ME!
I AM HUMBLED IN YOUR PRESENCE!
LOOK.
HE IS INJURED.
ARE YOU HURT, NOAH?
IS IT HEALING YOU REQUIRE?
NO.
IT IS BUT A SCRAPE.
D-DO NOT CONCERN YOURSELF WITH SUCH TRIVIAL MATTERS.
"TRIVIAL", HE SAYS.
DOES HE NOT REALIZE THAT NONE OF THIS IS OF IMPORT?
DOES HE NOT KNOW...

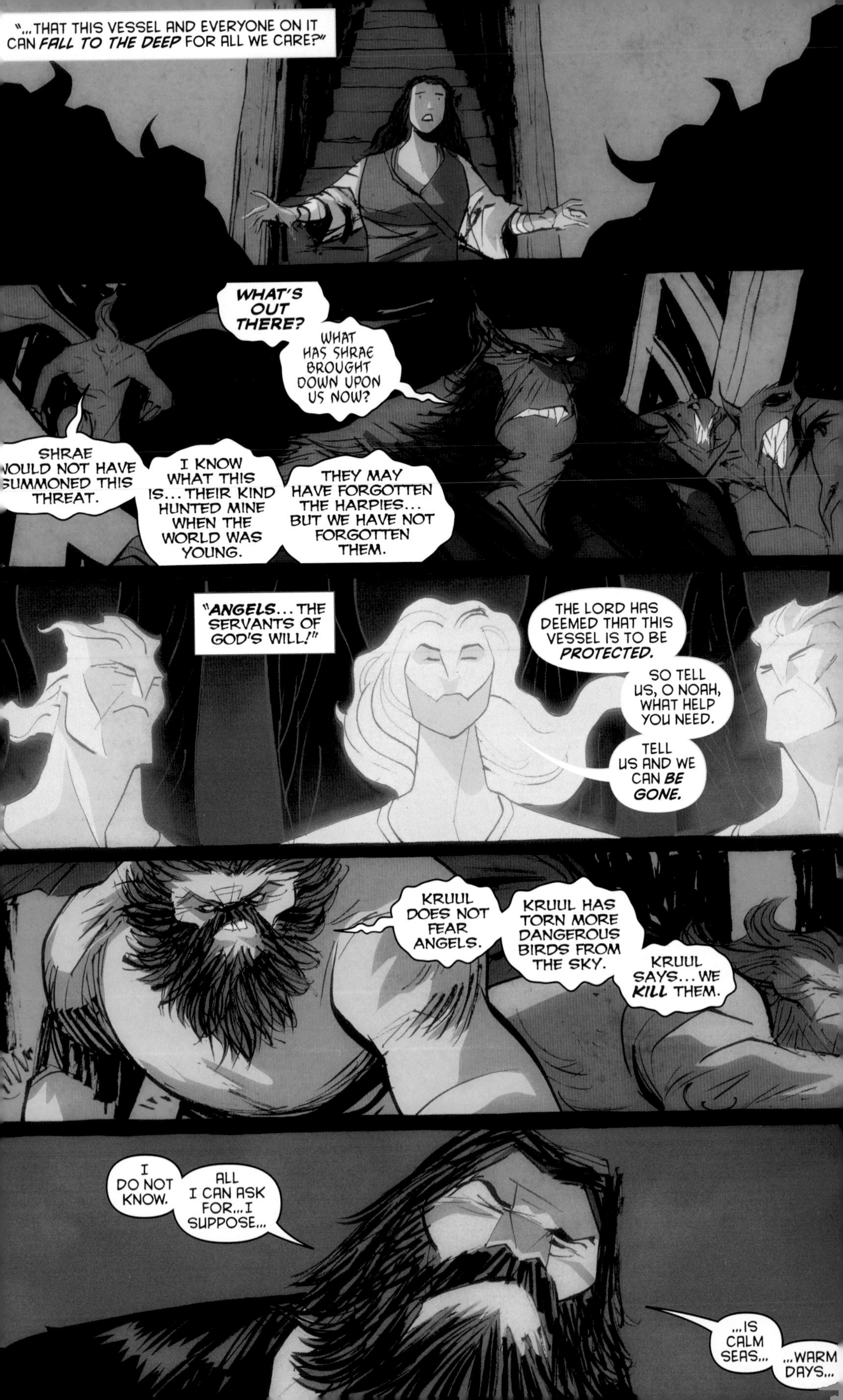
"...THAT THIS VESSEL AND EVERYONE ON IT CAN FALL TO THE DEEP FOR ALL WE CARE?"
WHAT'S OUT THERE?
WHAT HAS SHRAE BROUGHT DOWN UPON US NOW?
SHRAE WOULD NOT HAVE SUMMONED THIS THREAT.
I KNOW WHAT THIS IS... THEIR KIND HUNTED MINE WHEN THE WORLD WAS YOUNG.
THEY MAY HAVE FORGOTTEN THE HARPIES... BUT WE HAVE NOT FORGOTTEN THEM.
"ANGELS... THE SERVANTS OF GOD'S WILL!"
THE LORD HAS DEEMED THAT THIS VESSEL IS TO BE PROTECTED.
SO TELL US, O NOAH, WHAT HELP YOU NEED.
TELL US AND WE CAN BE GONE.
KRUUL DOES NOT FEAR ANGELS.
KRUUL HAS TORN MORE DANGEROUS BIRDS FROM THE SKY.
KRUUL SAYS... WE KILL THEM.
I DO NOT KNOW.
ALL I CAN ASK FOR...I SUPPOSE...
...IS CALM SEAS...
...WARM DAYS...

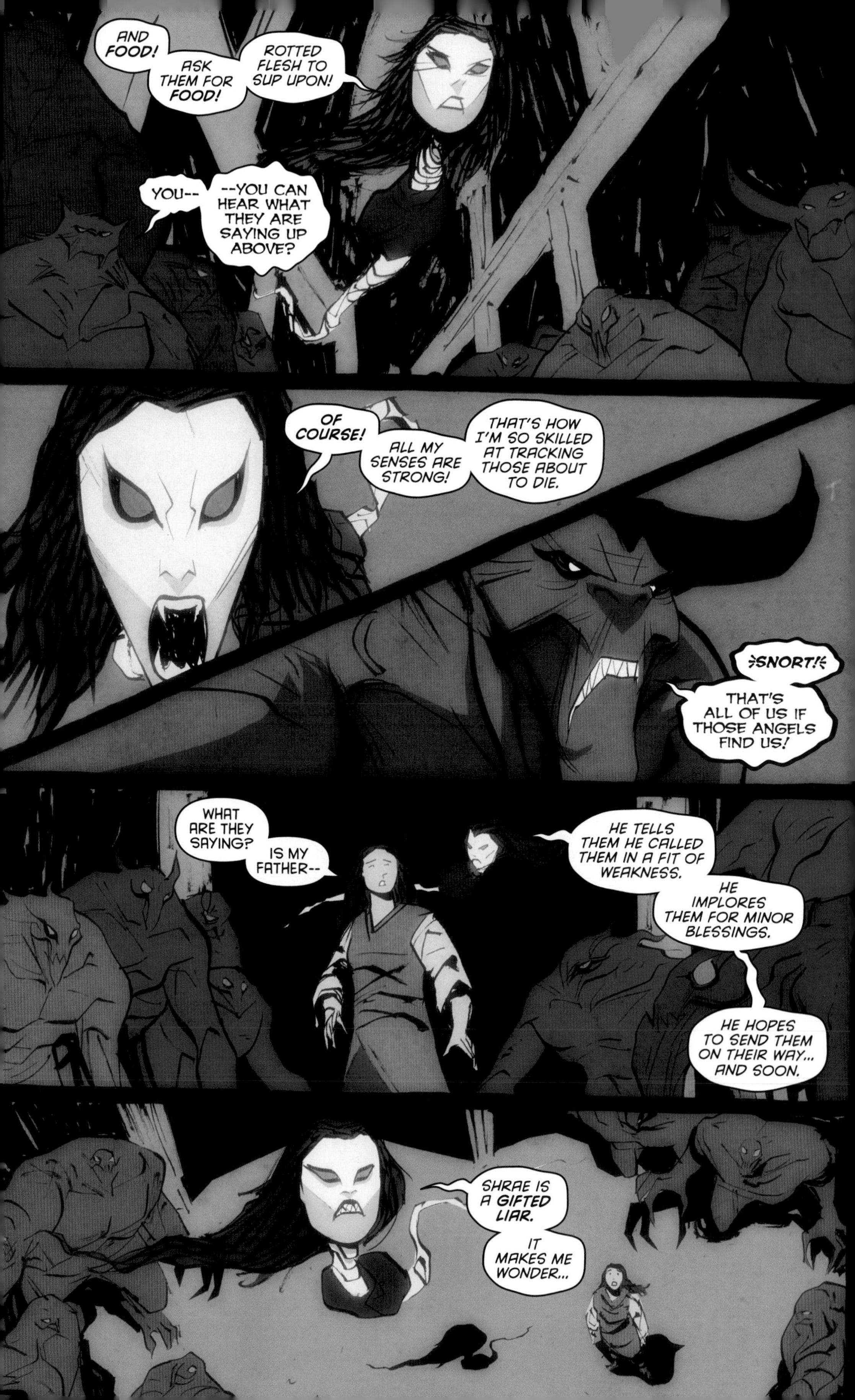
AND FOOD!
ASK THEM FOR FOOD!
ROTTED FLESH TO SUP UPON!
YOU--
--YOU CAN HEAR WHAT THEY ARE SAYING UP ABOVE?
OF COURSE!
ALL MY SENSES ARE STRONG!
THAT'S HOW I'M SO SKILLED AT TRACKING THOSE ABOUT TO DIE.
SNORT!
THAT'S ALL OF US IF THOSE ANGELS FIND US!
WHAT ARE THEY SAYING?
IS MY FATHER--
HE TELLS THEM HE CALLED THEM IN A FIT OF WEAKNESS.
HE IMPLORES THEM FOR MINOR BLESSINGS.
HE HOPES TO SEND THEM ON THEIR WAY... AND SOON.
SHRAE IS A GIFTED LIAR.
IT MAKES ME WONDER...

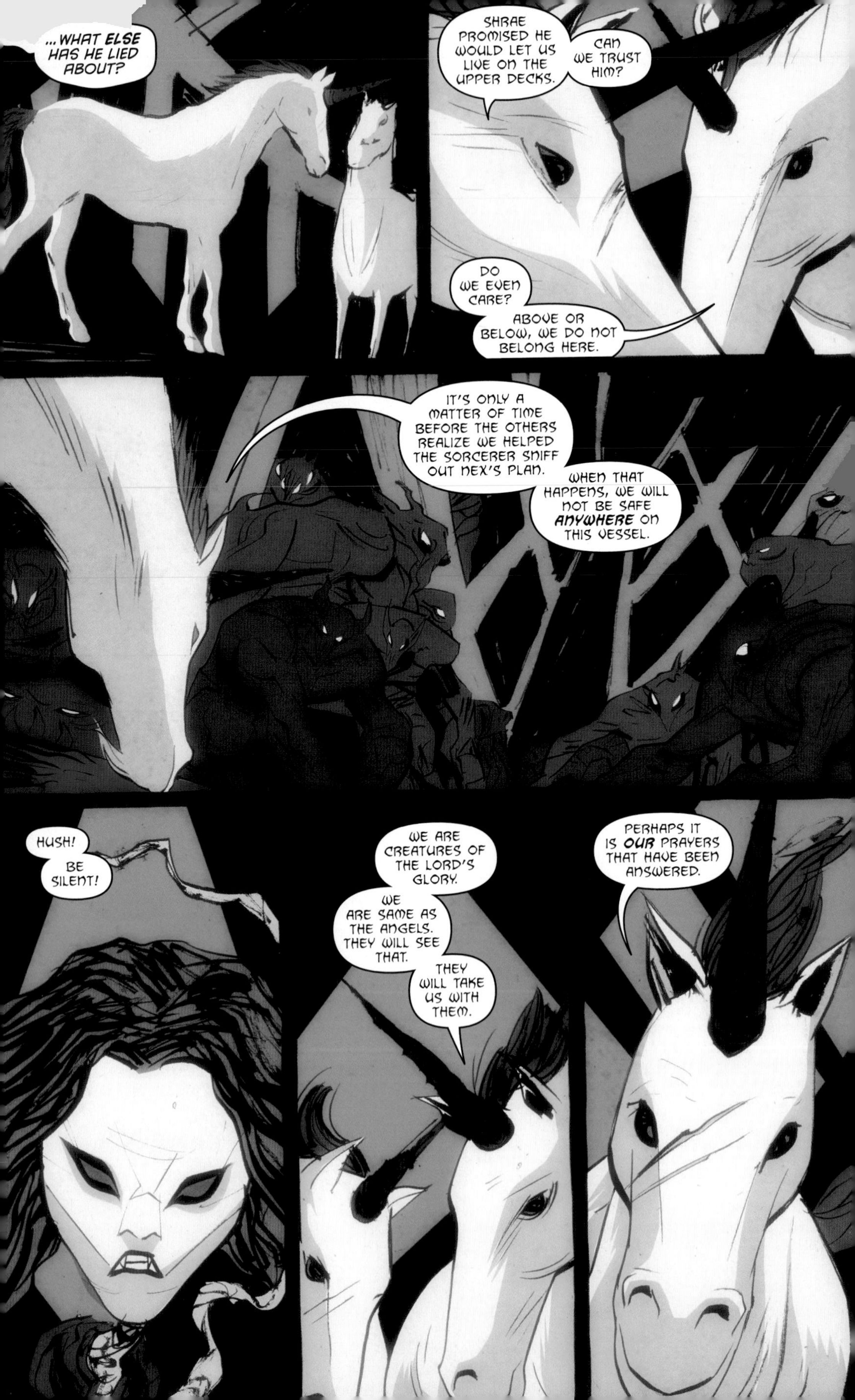

...WHAT ELSE HAS HE LIED ABOUT?
SHRAE PROMISED HE WOULD LET US LIVE ON THE UPPER DECKS.
CAN WE TRUST HIM?
DO WE EVEN CARE?
ABOVE OR BELOW, WE DO NOT BELONG HERE.
IT'S ONLY A MATTER OF TIME BEFORE THE OTHERS REALIZE WE HELPED THE SORCERER SNIFF OUT NEX'S PLAN.
WHEN THAT HAPPENS, WE WILL NOT BE SAFE ANYWHERE ON THIS VESSEL.
HUSH!
BE SILENT!
WE ARE CREATURES OF THE LORD'S GLORY.
WE ARE SAME AS THE ANGELS. THEY WILL SEE THAT.
THEY WILL TAKE US WITH THEM.
PERHAPS IT IS OUR PRAYERS THAT HAVE BEEN ANSWERED.

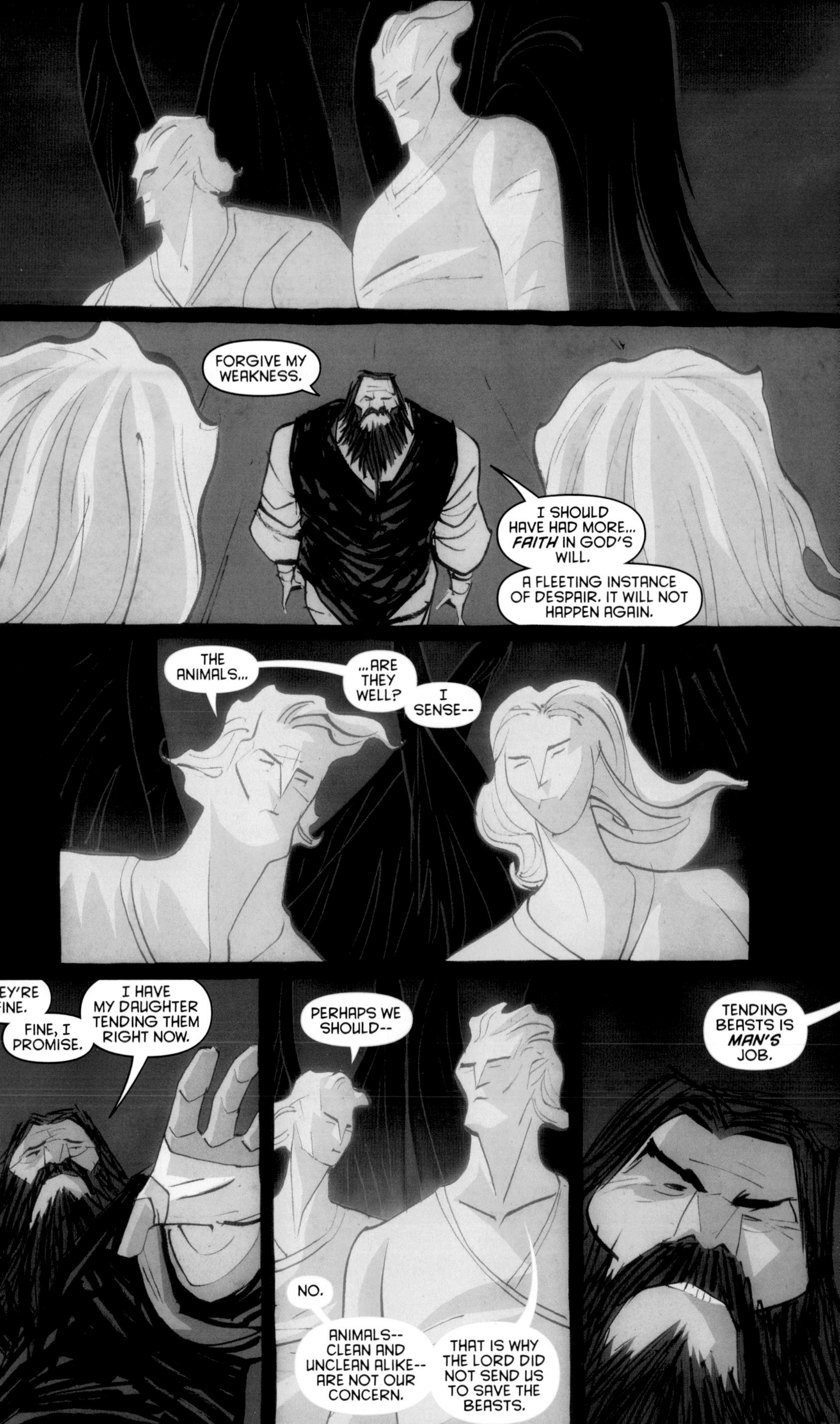
FORGIVE MY WEAKNESS.
I SHOULD HAVE HAD MORE... *FAITH* IN GOD'S WILL.
A FLEETING INSTANCE OF DESPAIR. IT WILL NOT HAPPEN AGAIN.
THE ANIMALS...
...ARE THEY WELL?
I SENSE--
EY'RE FINE.
FINE, I PROMISE.
I HAVE MY DAUGHTER TENDING THEM RIGHT NOW.
PERHAPS WE SHOULD--
NO.
ANIMALS-- CLEAN AND UNCLEAN ALIKE-- ARE NOT OUR CONCERN.
THAT IS WHY THE LORD DID NOT SEND US TO SAVE THE BEASTS.
TENDING BEASTS IS *MAN'S* JOB.

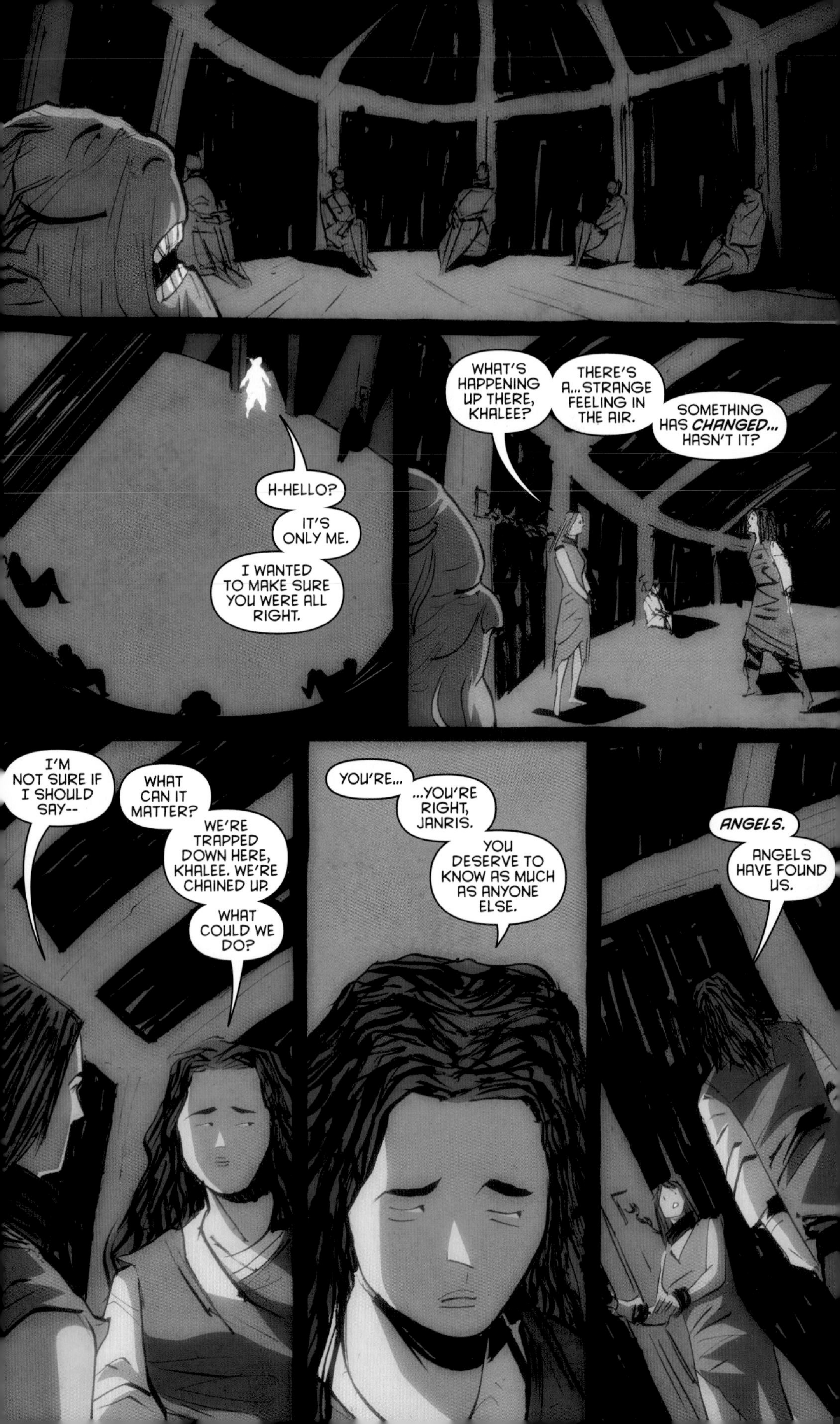
H-HELLO?
IT'S ONLY ME.
I WANTED TO MAKE SURE YOU WERE ALL RIGHT.
WHAT'S HAPPENING UP THERE, KHALEE?
THERE'S A... STRANGE FEELING IN THE AIR.
SOMETHING HAS *CHANGED...* HASN'T IT?
I'M NOT SURE IF I SHOULD SAY--
WHAT CAN IT MATTER?
WE'RE TRAPPED DOWN HERE, KHALEE. WE'RE CHAINED UP.
WHAT COULD WE DO?
YOU'RE...
...YOU'RE RIGHT, JANRIS.
YOU DESERVE TO KNOW AS MUCH AS ANYONE ELSE.
ANGELS.
ANGELS HAVE FOUND US.

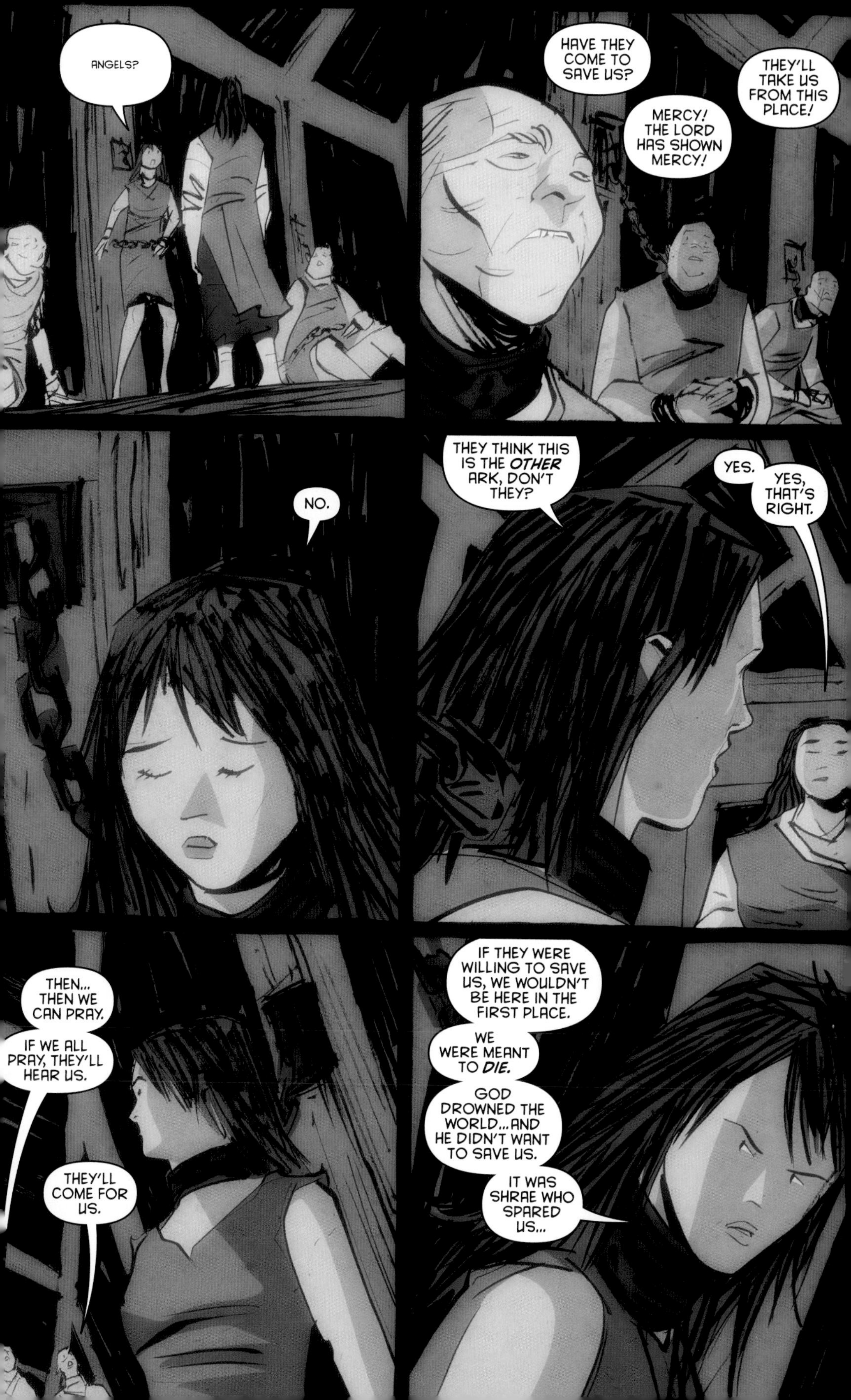
ANGELS?
HAVE THEY COME TO SAVE US?
MERCY! THE LORD HAS SHOWN MERCY!
THEY'LL TAKE US FROM THIS PLACE!
NO.
THEY THINK THIS IS THE *OTHER* ARK, DON'T THEY?
YES.
YES, THAT'S RIGHT.
THEN... THEN WE CAN PRAY.
IF WE ALL PRAY, THEY'LL HEAR US.
THEY'LL COME FOR US.
IF THEY WERE WILLING TO SAVE US, WE WOULDN'T BE HERE IN THE FIRST PLACE.
WE WERE MEANT TO *DIE.*
GOD DROWNED THE WORLD...AND HE DIDN'T WANT TO SAVE US.
IT WAS SHRAE WHO SPARED US...

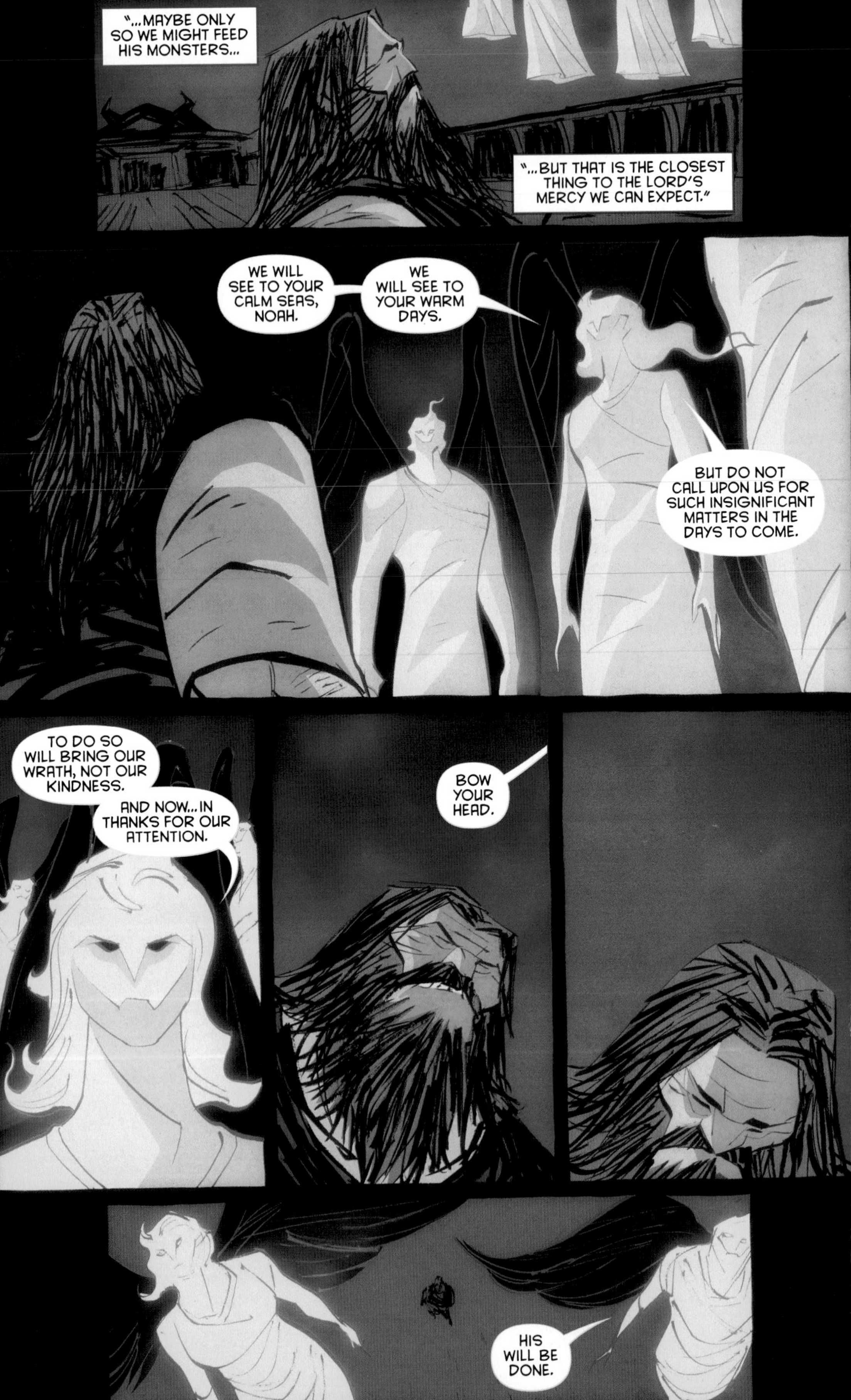
"...MAYBE ONLY SO WE MIGHT FEED HIS MONSTERS...
"...BUT THAT IS THE CLOSEST THING TO THE LORD'S MERCY WE CAN EXPECT."
WE WILL SEE TO YOUR CALM SEAS, NOAH.
WE WILL SEE TO YOUR WARM DAYS.
BUT DO NOT CALL UPON US FOR SUCH INSIGNIFICANT MATTERS IN THE DAYS TO COME.
TO DO SO WILL BRING OUR WRATH, NOT OUR KINDNESS.
AND NOW...IN THANKS FOR OUR ATTENTION.
BOW YOUR HEAD.
HIS WILL BE DONE.

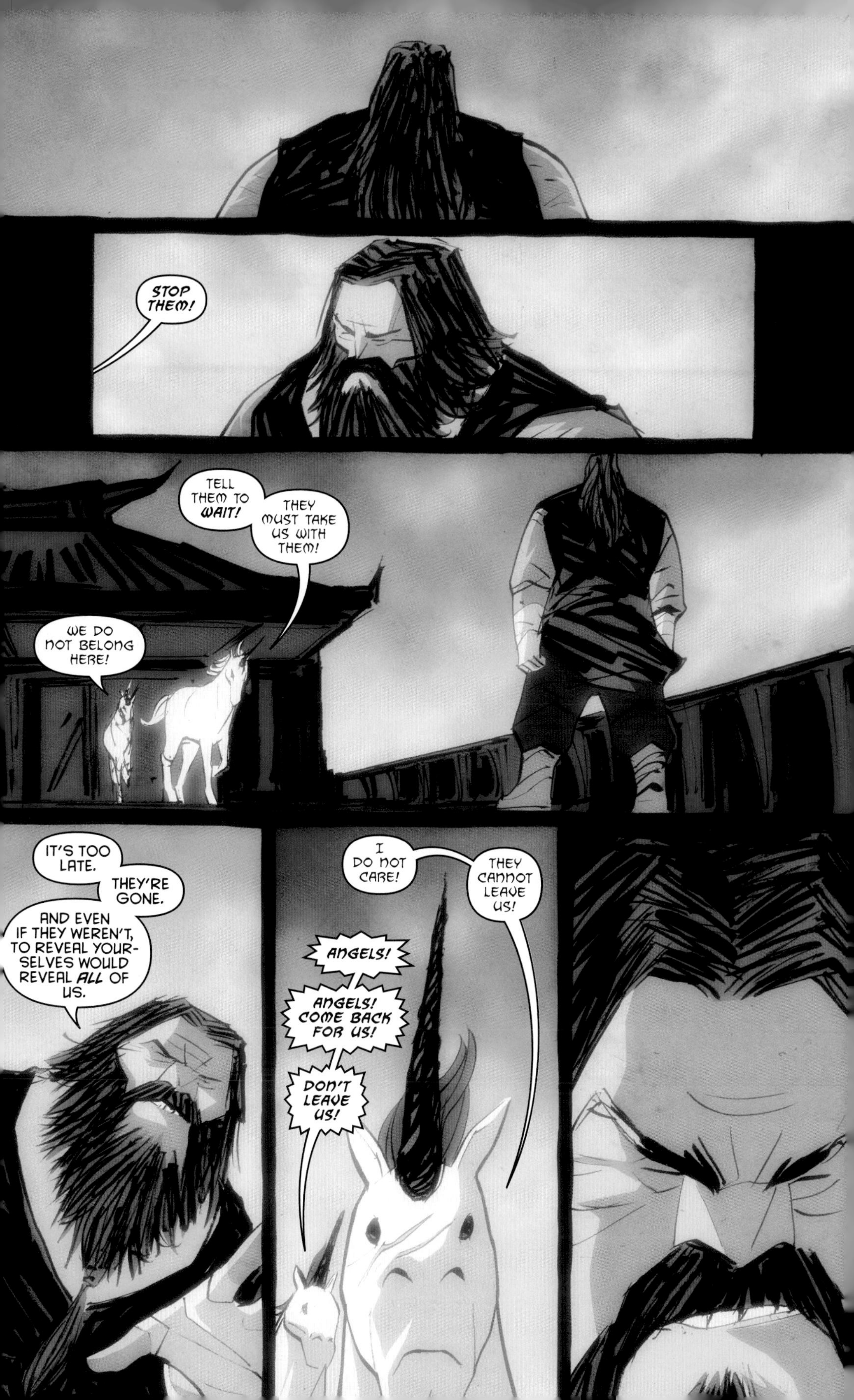
STOP THEM!
TELL THEM TO WAIT!
THEY MUST TAKE US WITH THEM!
WE DO NOT BELONG HERE!
IT'S TOO LATE.
THEY'RE GONE.
AND EVEN IF THEY WEREN'T, TO REVEAL YOUR-SELVES WOULD REVEAL ALL OF US.
I DO NOT CARE!
THEY CANNOT LEAVE US!
ANGELS!
ANGELS! COME BACK FOR US!
DON'T LEAVE US!

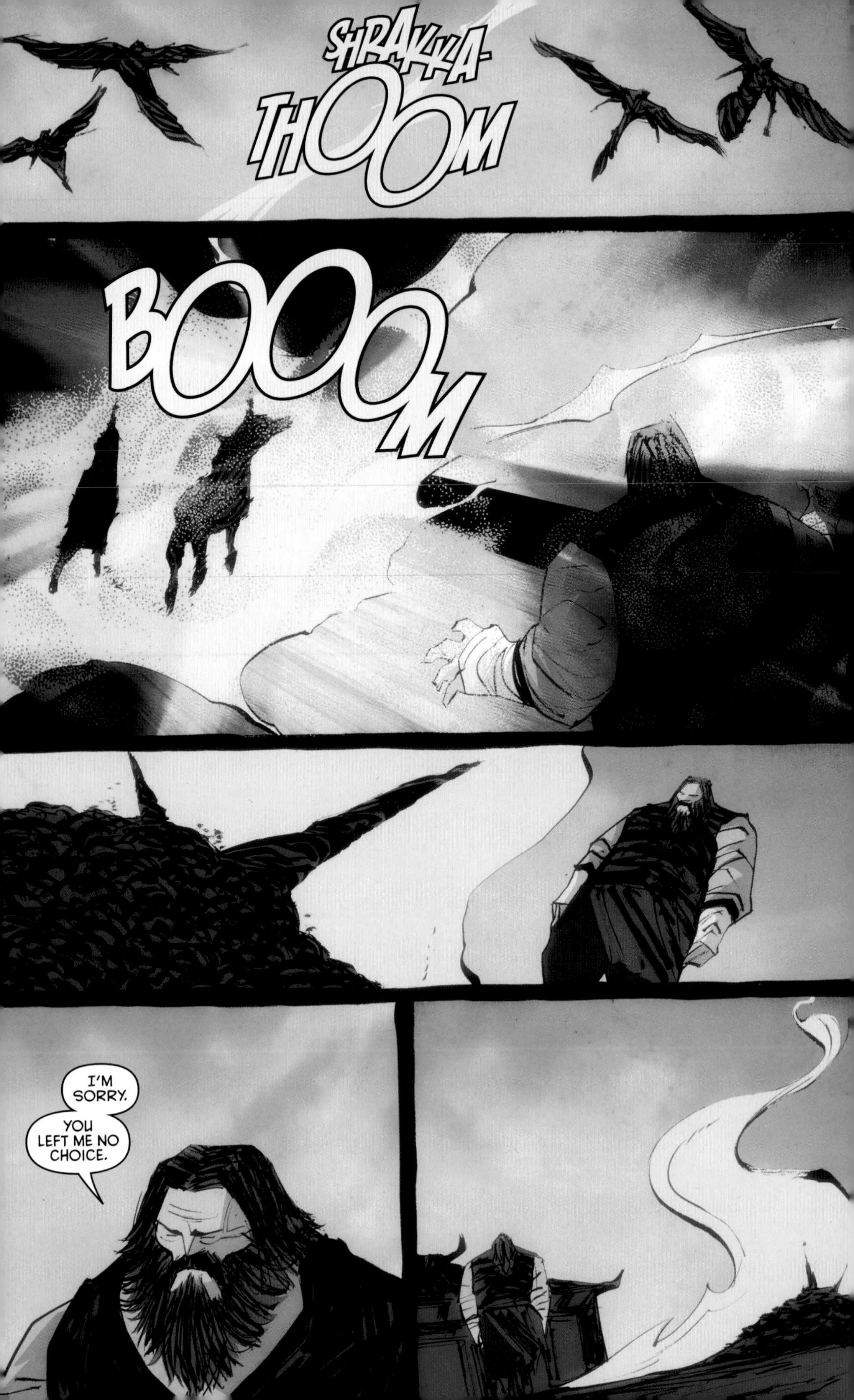
SHRAKKA-THOOOM
BOOOOM
I'M SORRY.
YOU LEFT ME NO CHOICE.

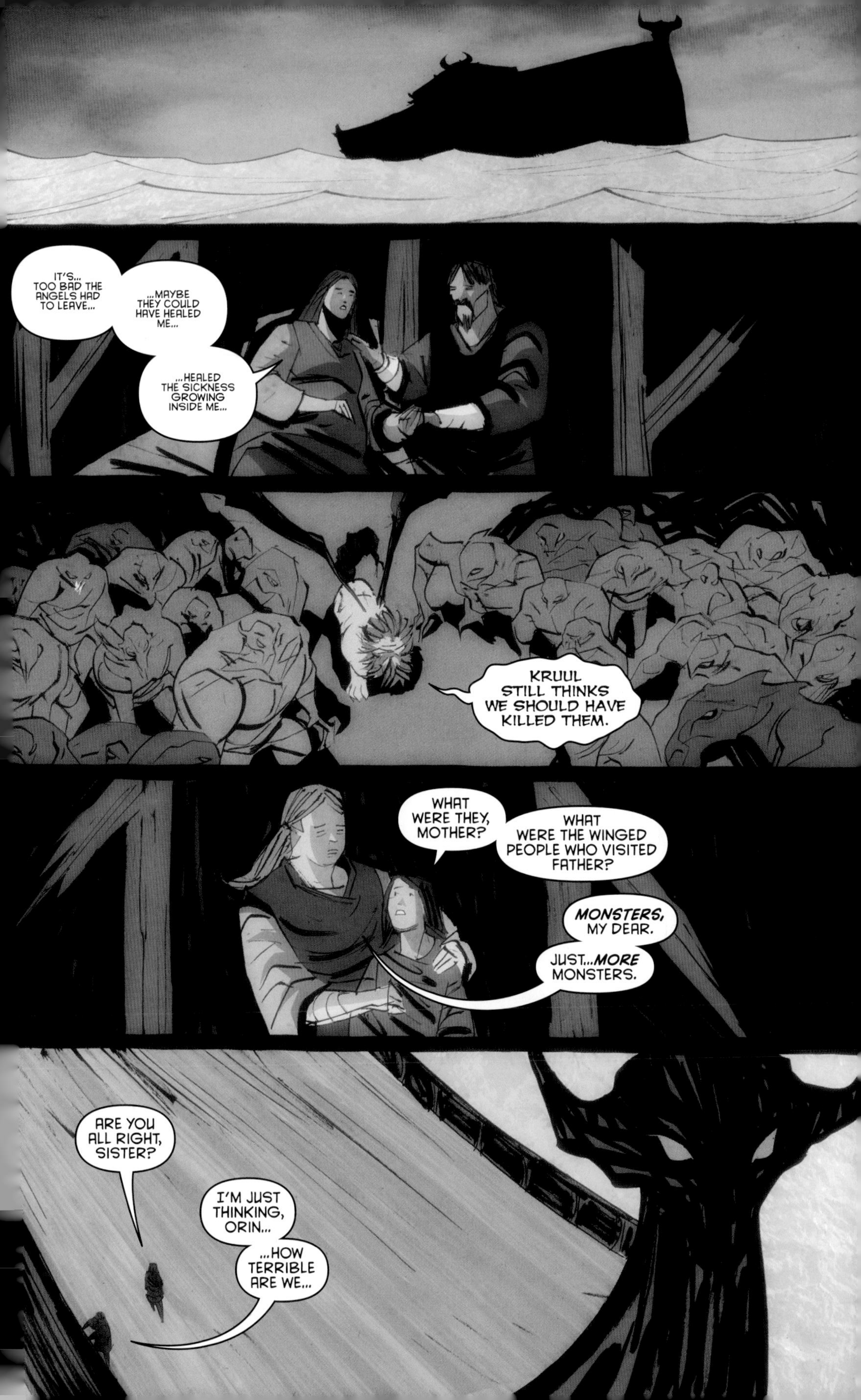
IT'S... TOO BAD THE ANGELS HAD TO LEAVE...
...MAYBE THEY COULD HAVE HEALED ME...
...HEALED THE SICKNESS GROWING INSIDE ME...
KRUUL STILL THINKS WE SHOULD HAVE KILLED THEM.
WHAT WERE THEY, MOTHER?
WHAT WERE THE WINGED PEOPLE WHO VISITED FATHER?
MONSTERS, MY DEAR.
JUST...MORE MONSTERS.
ARE YOU ALL RIGHT, SISTER?
I'M JUST THINKING, ORIN...
...HOW TERRIBLE ARE WE...

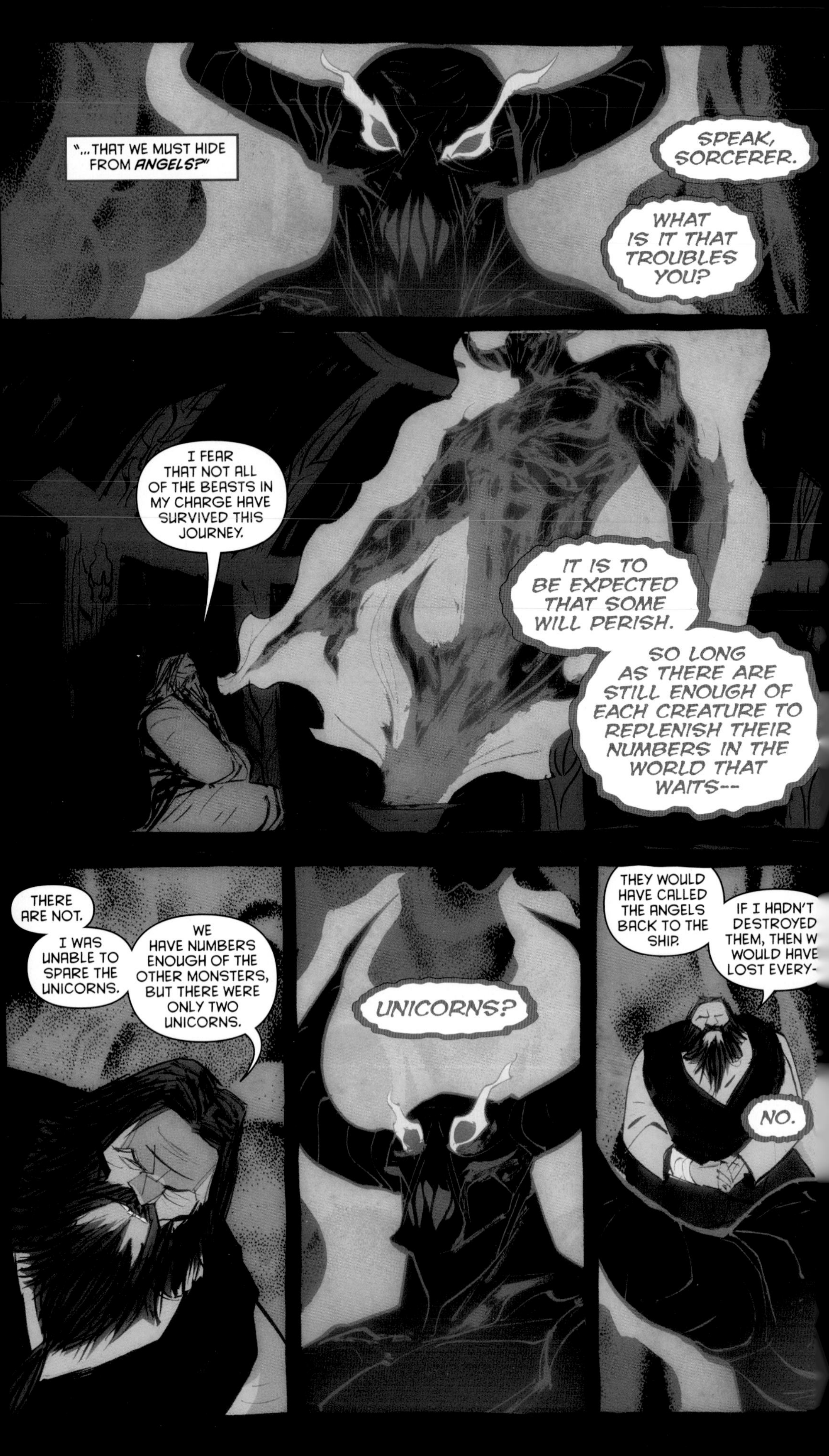
"...THAT WE MUST HIDE FROM ANGELS?"
SPEAK, SORCERER.
WHAT IS IT THAT TROUBLES YOU?
I FEAR THAT NOT ALL OF THE BEASTS IN MY CHARGE HAVE SURVIVED THIS JOURNEY.
IT IS TO BE EXPECTED THAT SOME WILL PERISH.
SO LONG AS THERE ARE STILL ENOUGH OF EACH CREATURE TO REPLENISH THEIR NUMBERS IN THE WORLD THAT WAITS--
THERE ARE NOT.
I WAS UNABLE TO SPARE THE UNICORNS.
WE HAVE NUMBERS ENOUGH OF THE OTHER MONSTERS, BUT THERE WERE ONLY TWO UNICORNS.
UNICORNS?
THEY WOULD HAVE CALLED THE ANGELS BACK TO THE SHIP.
IF I HADN'T DESTROYED THEM, THEN W WOULD HAVE LOST EVERY-
NO.

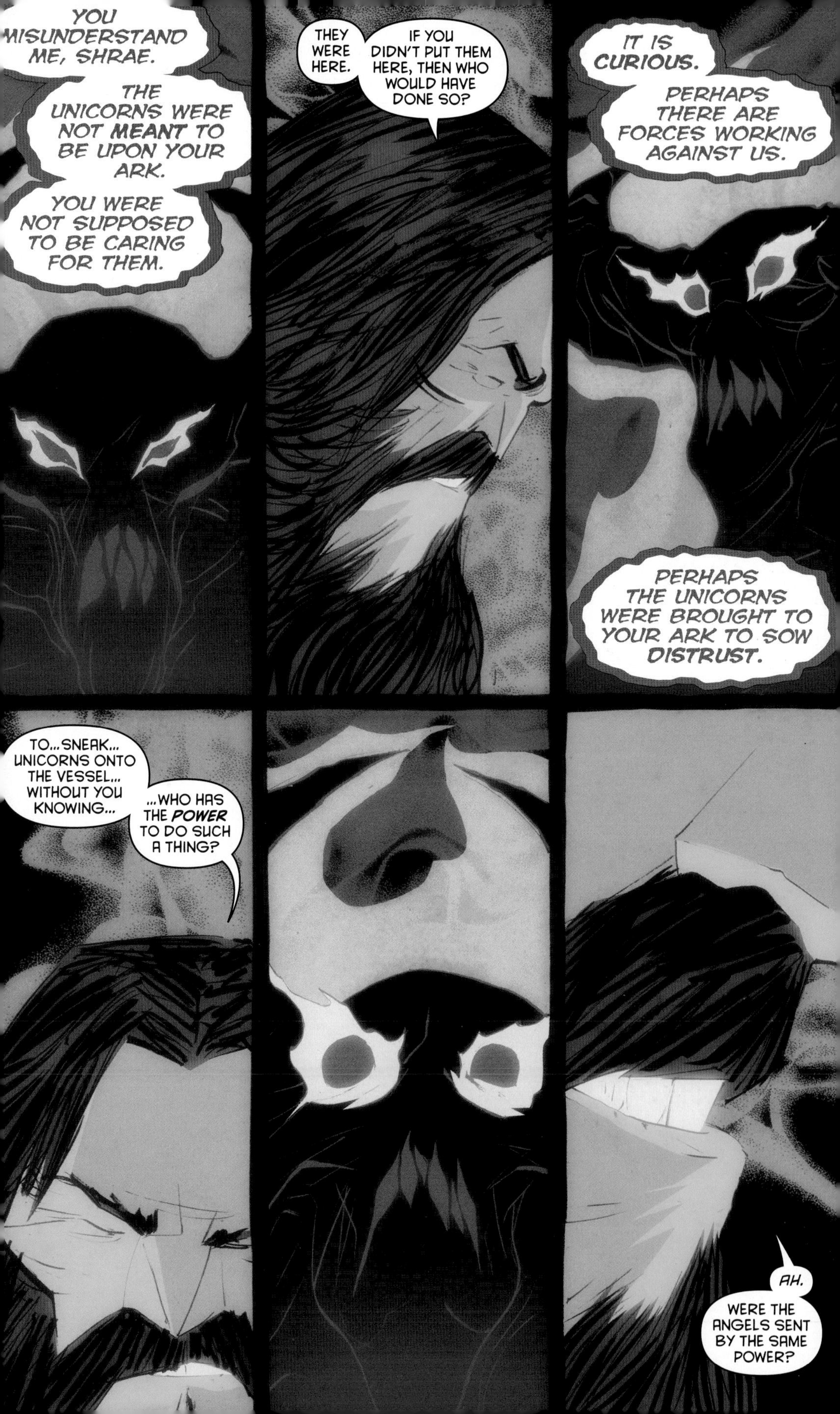
YOU MISUNDERSTAND ME, SHRAE.
THE UNICORNS WERE NOT MEANT TO BE UPON YOUR ARK.
YOU WERE NOT SUPPOSED TO BE CARING FOR THEM.
THEY WERE HERE.
IF YOU DIDN'T PUT THEM HERE, THEN WHO WOULD HAVE DONE SO?
IT IS CURIOUS.
PERHAPS THERE ARE FORCES WORKING AGAINST US.
PERHAPS THE UNICORNS WERE BROUGHT TO YOUR ARK TO SOW DISTRUST.
TO...SNEAK... UNICORNS ONTO THE VESSEL... WITHOUT YOU KNOWING...
...WHO HAS THE POWER TO DO SUCH A THING?
AH.
WERE THE ANGELS SENT BY THE SAME POWER?

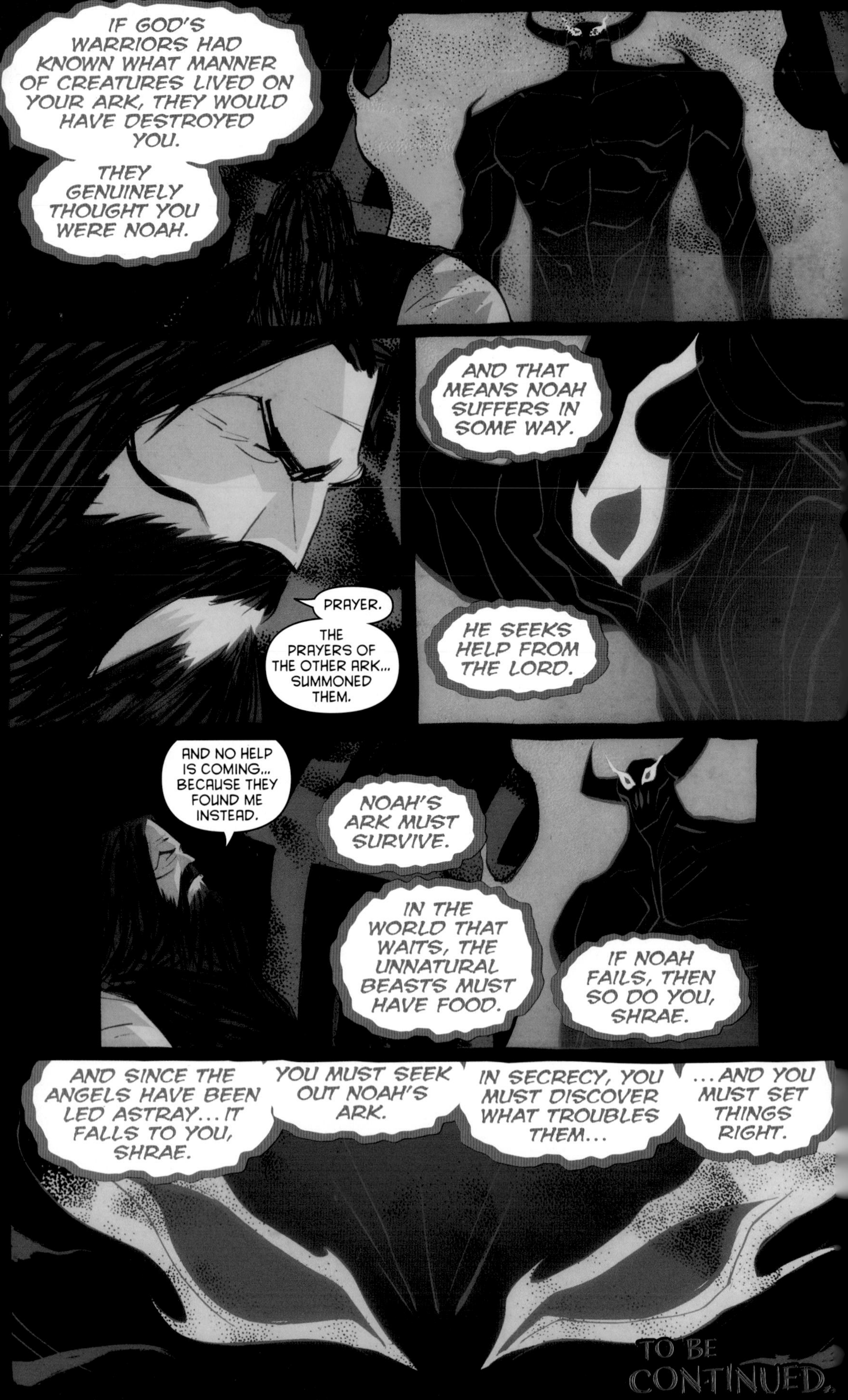
IF GOD'S WARRIORS HAD KNOWN WHAT MANNER OF CREATURES LIVED ON YOUR ARK, THEY WOULD HAVE DESTROYED YOU.
THEY GENUINELY THOUGHT YOU WERE NOAH.
PRAYER.
THE PRAYERS OF THE OTHER ARK... SUMMONED THEM.
AND THAT MEANS NOAH SUFFERS IN SOME WAY.
HE SEEKS HELP FROM THE LORD.
AND NO HELP IS COMING... BECAUSE THEY FOUND ME INSTEAD.
NOAH'S ARK MUST SURVIVE.
IN THE WORLD THAT WAITS, THE UNNATURAL BEASTS MUST HAVE FOOD.
IF NOAH FAILS, THEN SO DO YOU, SHRAE.
AND SINCE THE ANGELS HAVE BEEN LED ASTRAY... IT FALLS TO YOU, SHRAE.
YOU MUST SEEK OUT NOAH'S ARK.
IN SECRECY, YOU MUST DISCOVER WHAT TROUBLES THEM...
...AND YOU MUST SET THINGS RIGHT.
TO BE CONTINUED.

DARK ARK™

COVER GALLERY

AFTERSHOCK™

Issue 1
PHIL HESTER w/ ERIC GAPSTUR & MIKE SPICER
Variant Cover

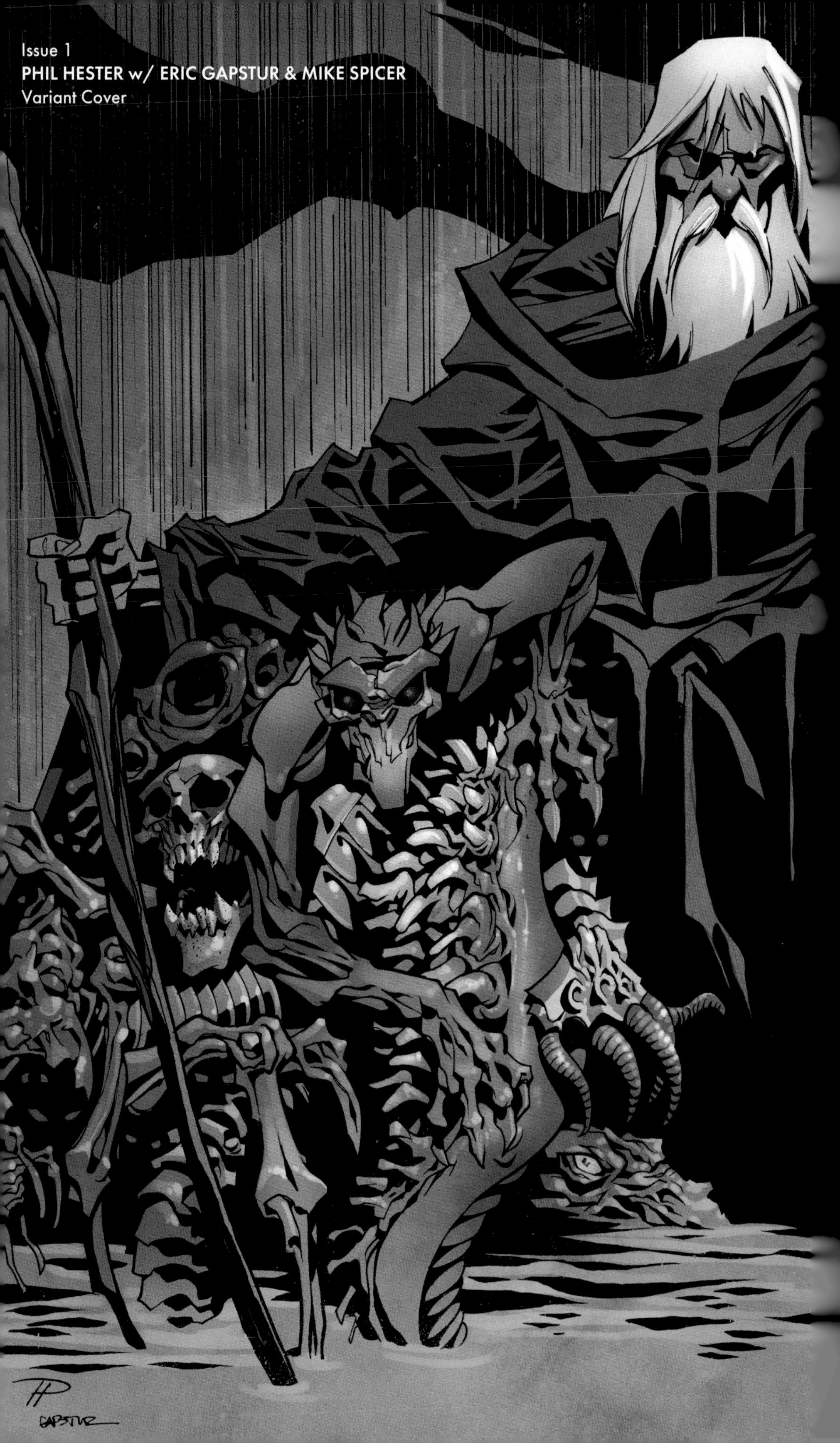

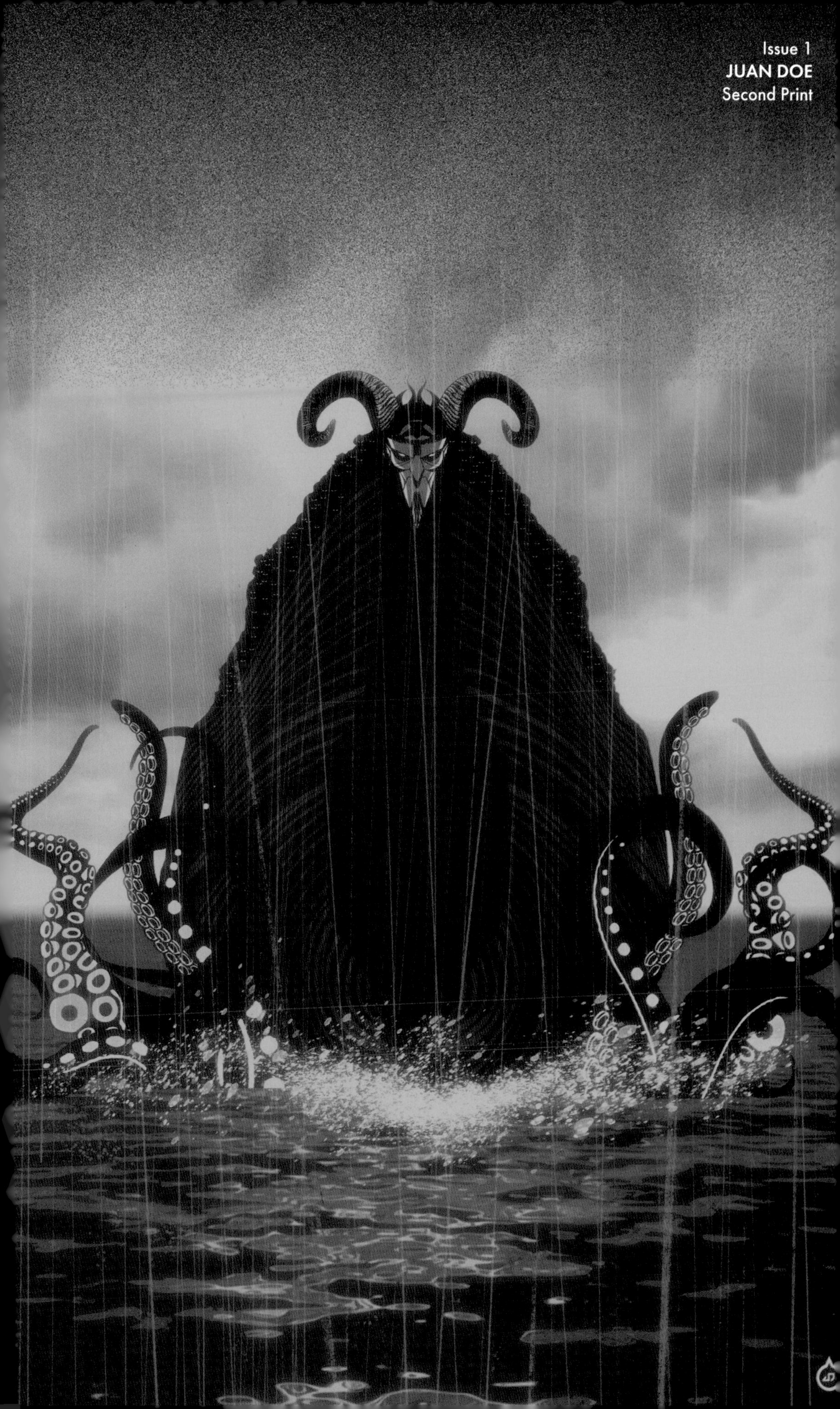
Issue 1
JUAN DOE
Second Print

Issue 1

PHIL HESTER w/ ERIC GAPSTUR & MIKE SPICER

Baltimore Comic Con AfterShock Exclusive Variant

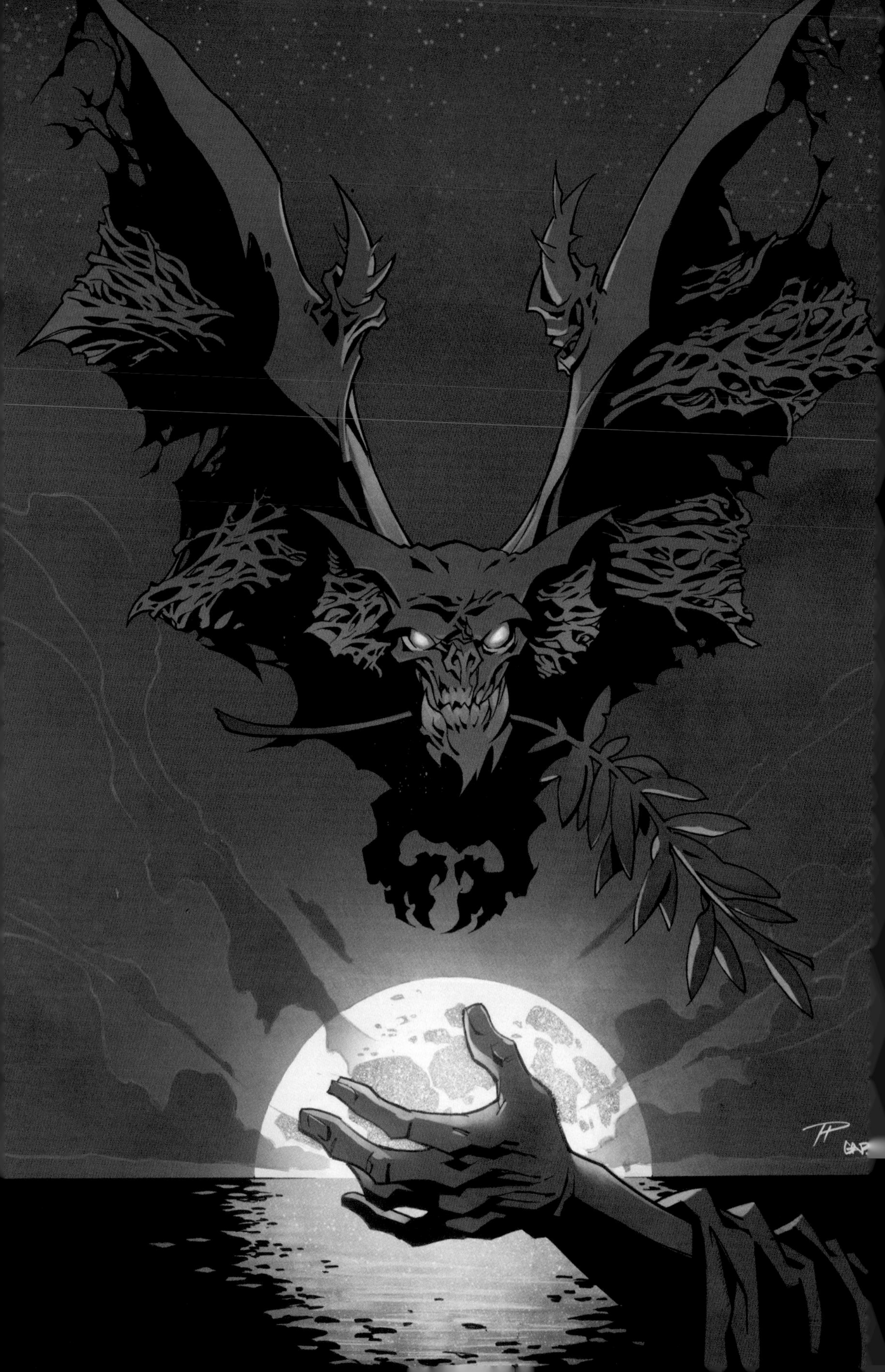

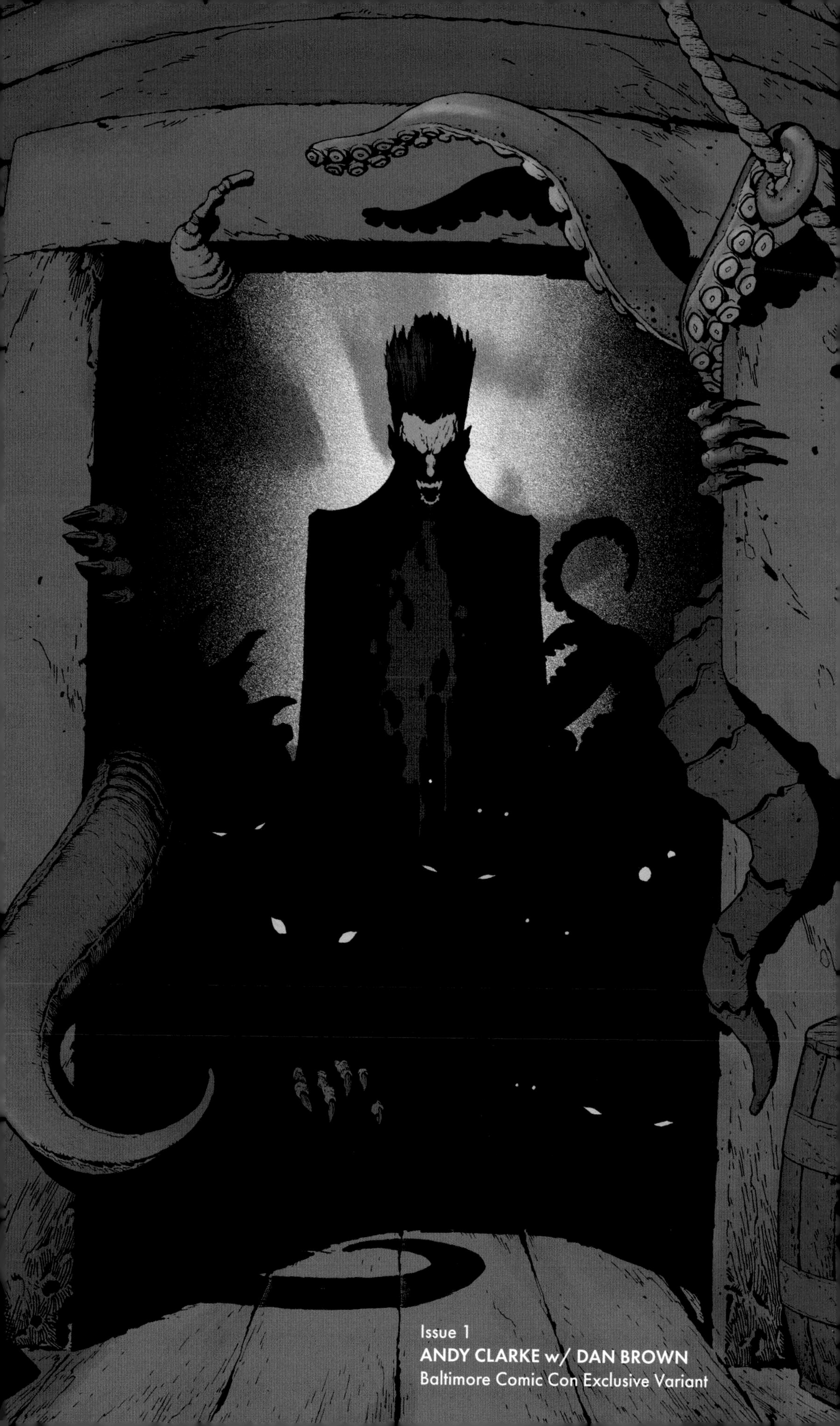

Issue 1
ANDY CLARKE w/ DAN BROWN
Baltimore Comic Con Exclusive Variant

Issue 1
PATRICK OLLIFFE
Retailer Bonus Variant

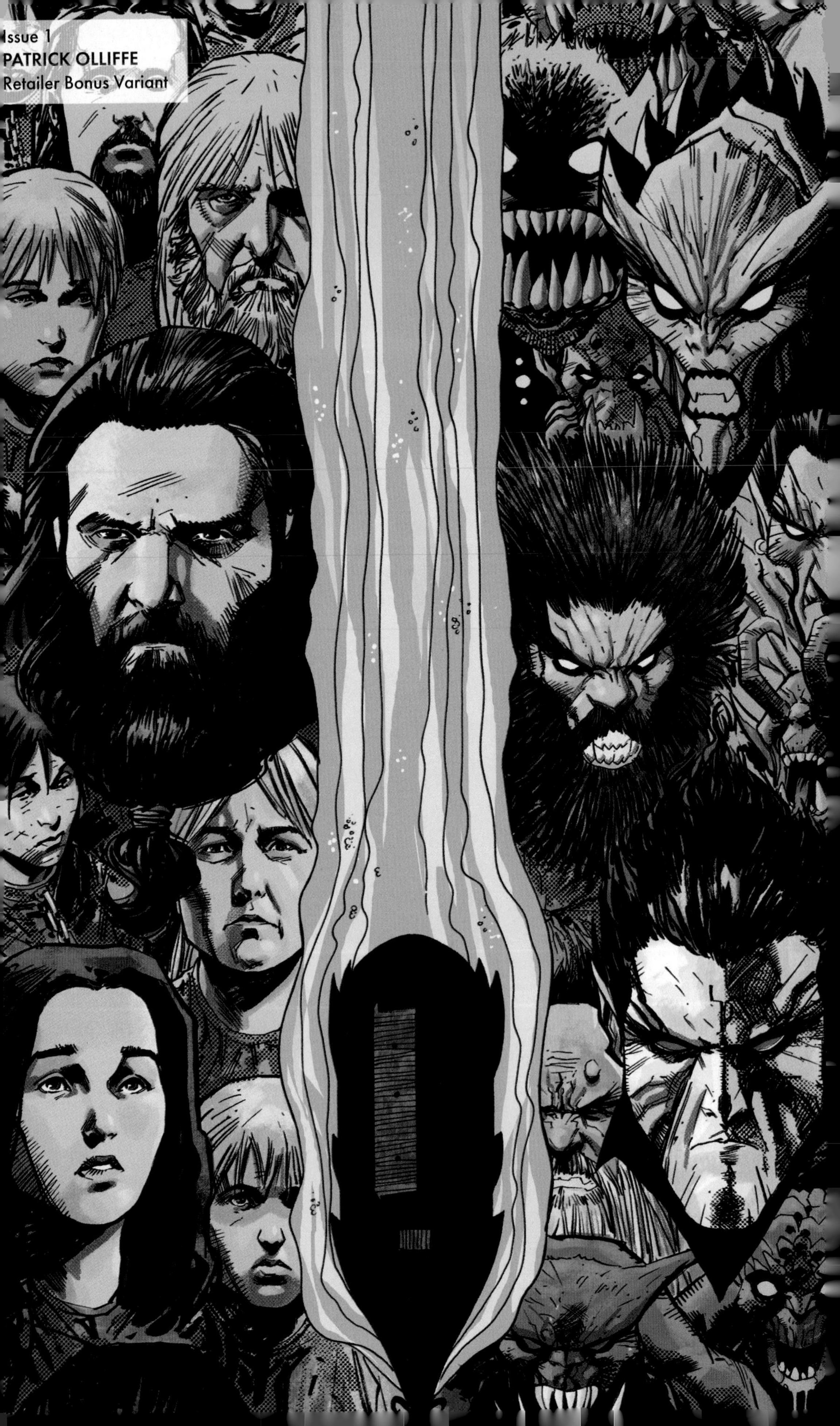

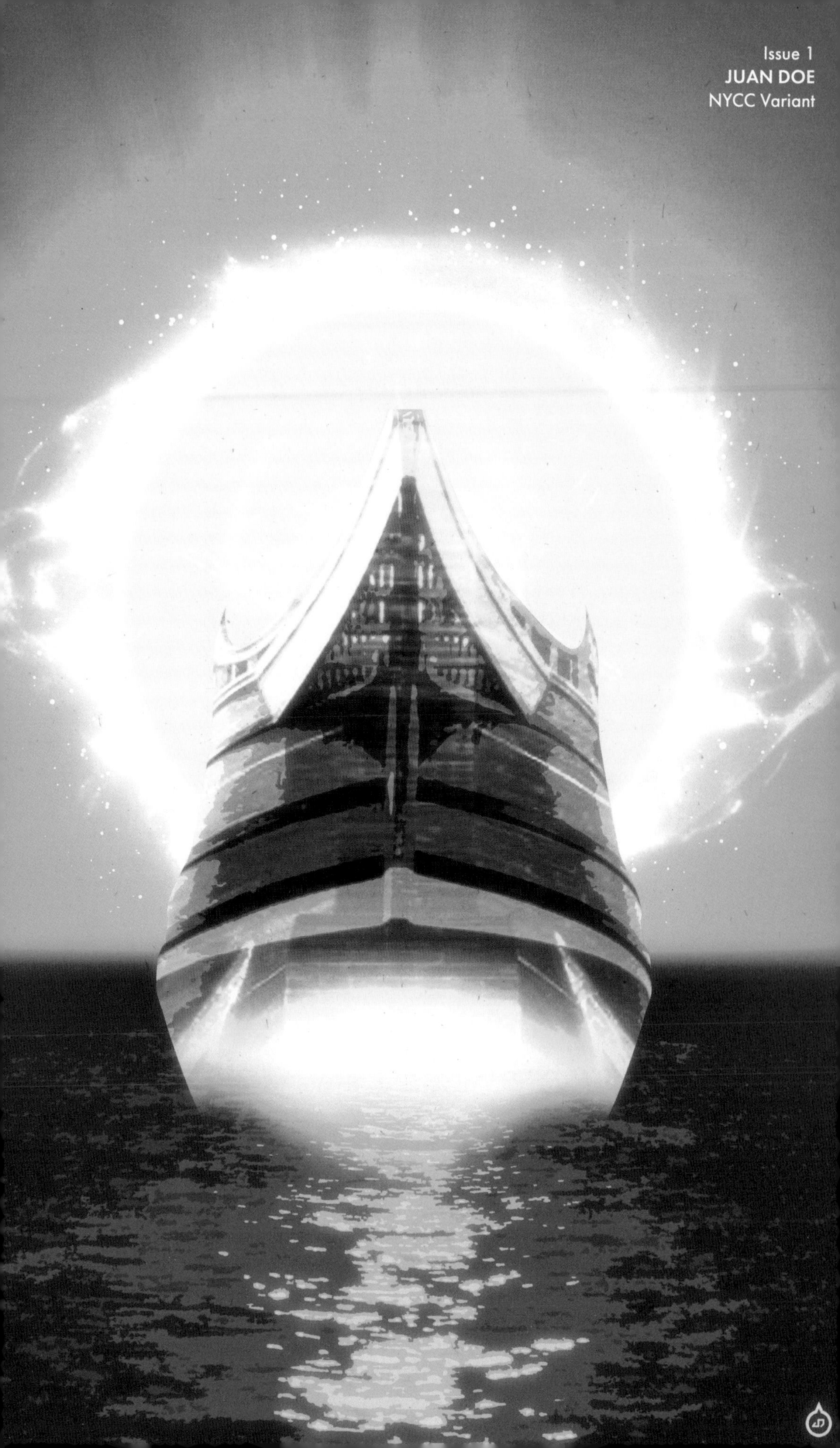

Issue 1
JUAN DOE
NYCC Variant

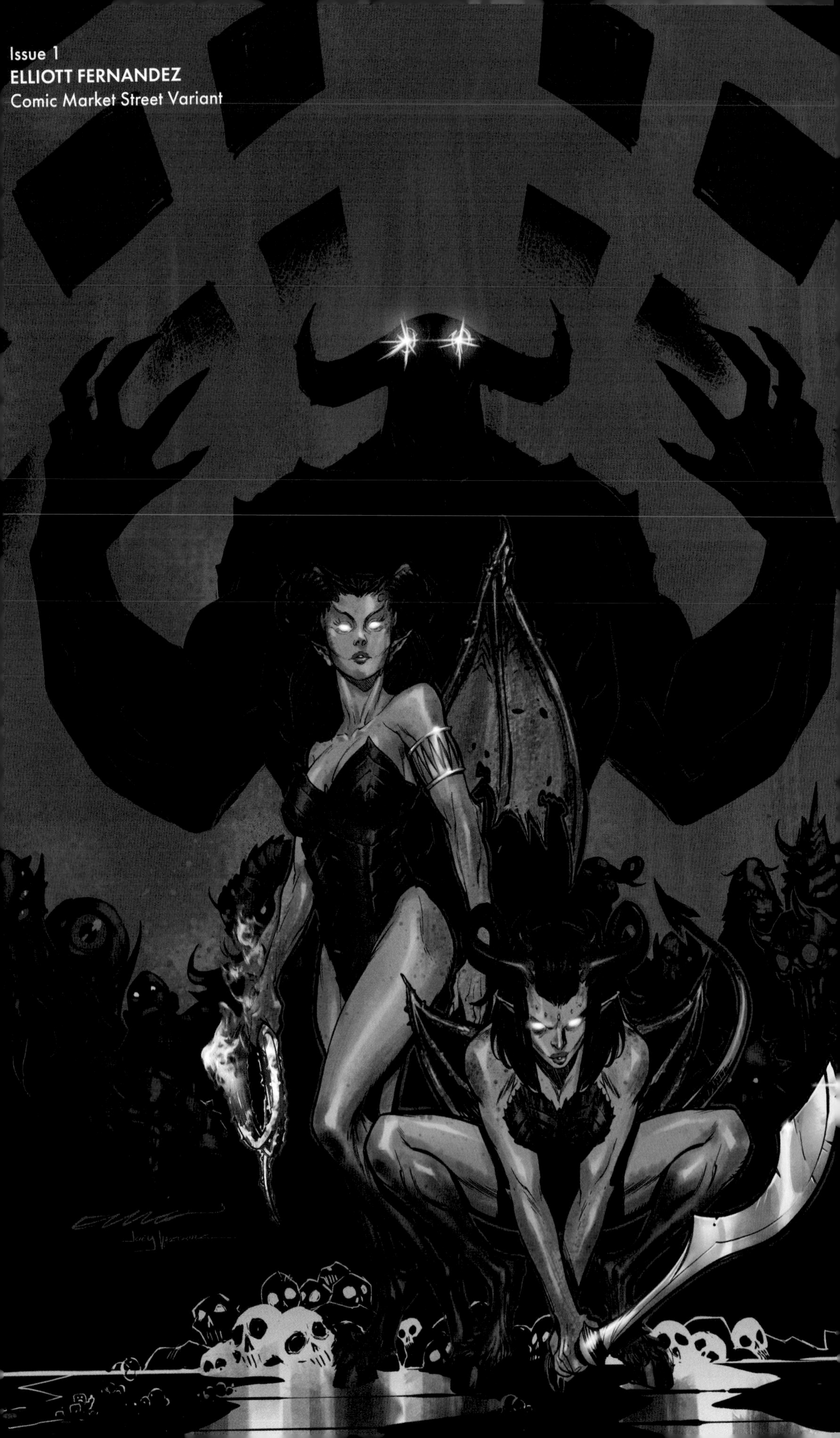
Issue 1
ELLIOTT FERNANDEZ
Comic Market Street Variant

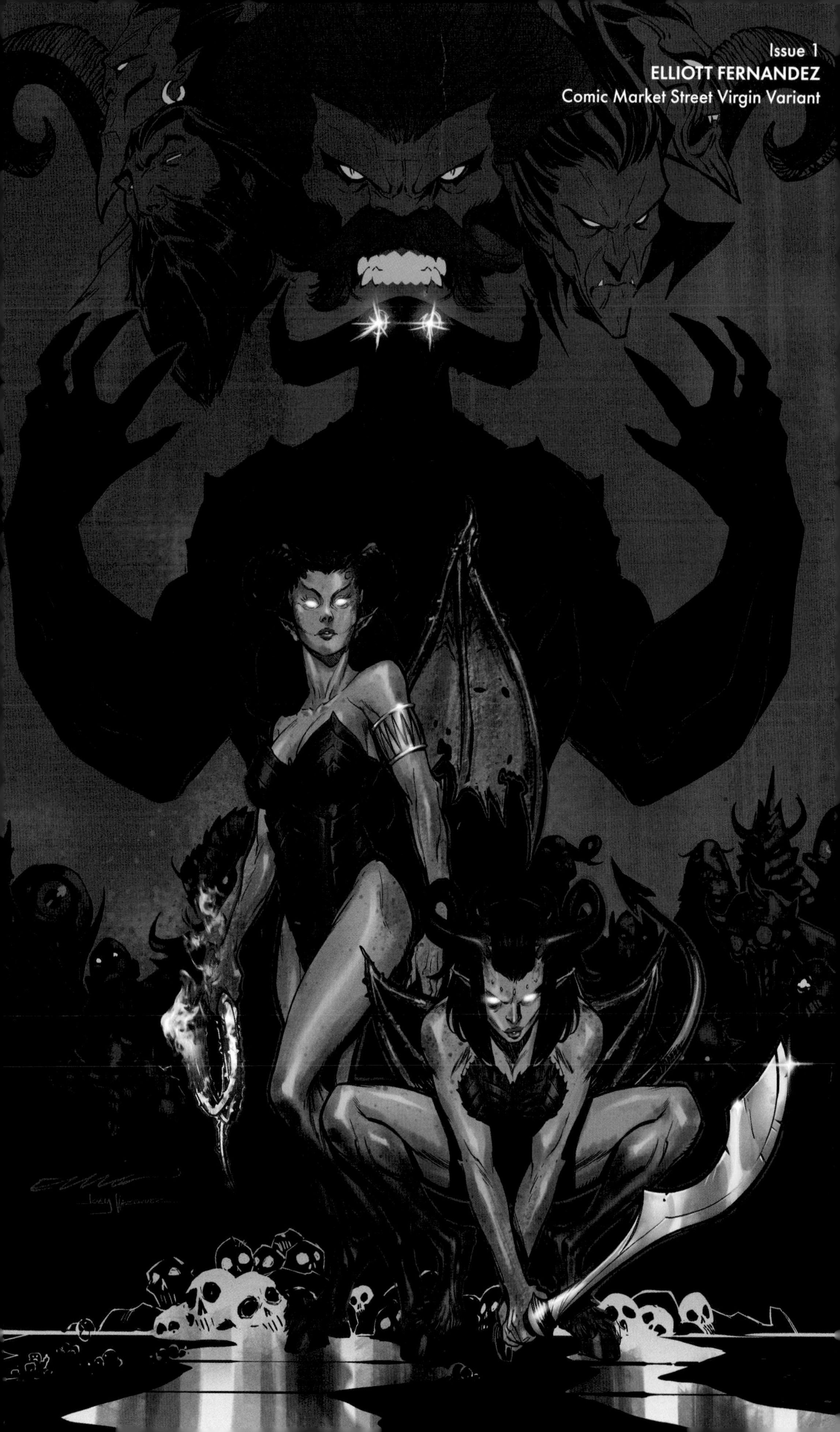
Issue 1
ELLIOTT FERNANDEZ
Comic Market Street Virgin Variant

Issue 1
NAT JONES
Gotham Central Variant

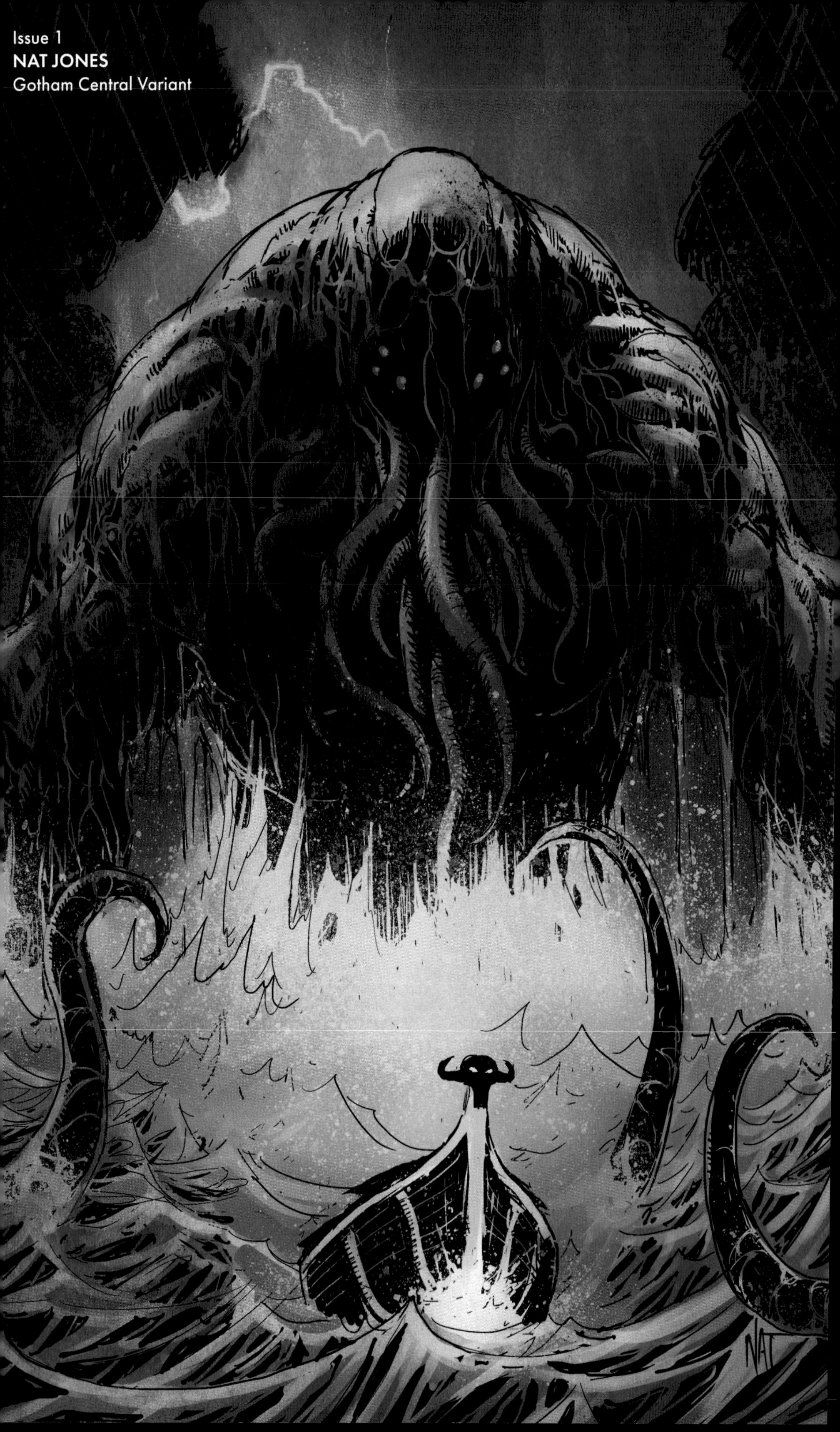
NAT

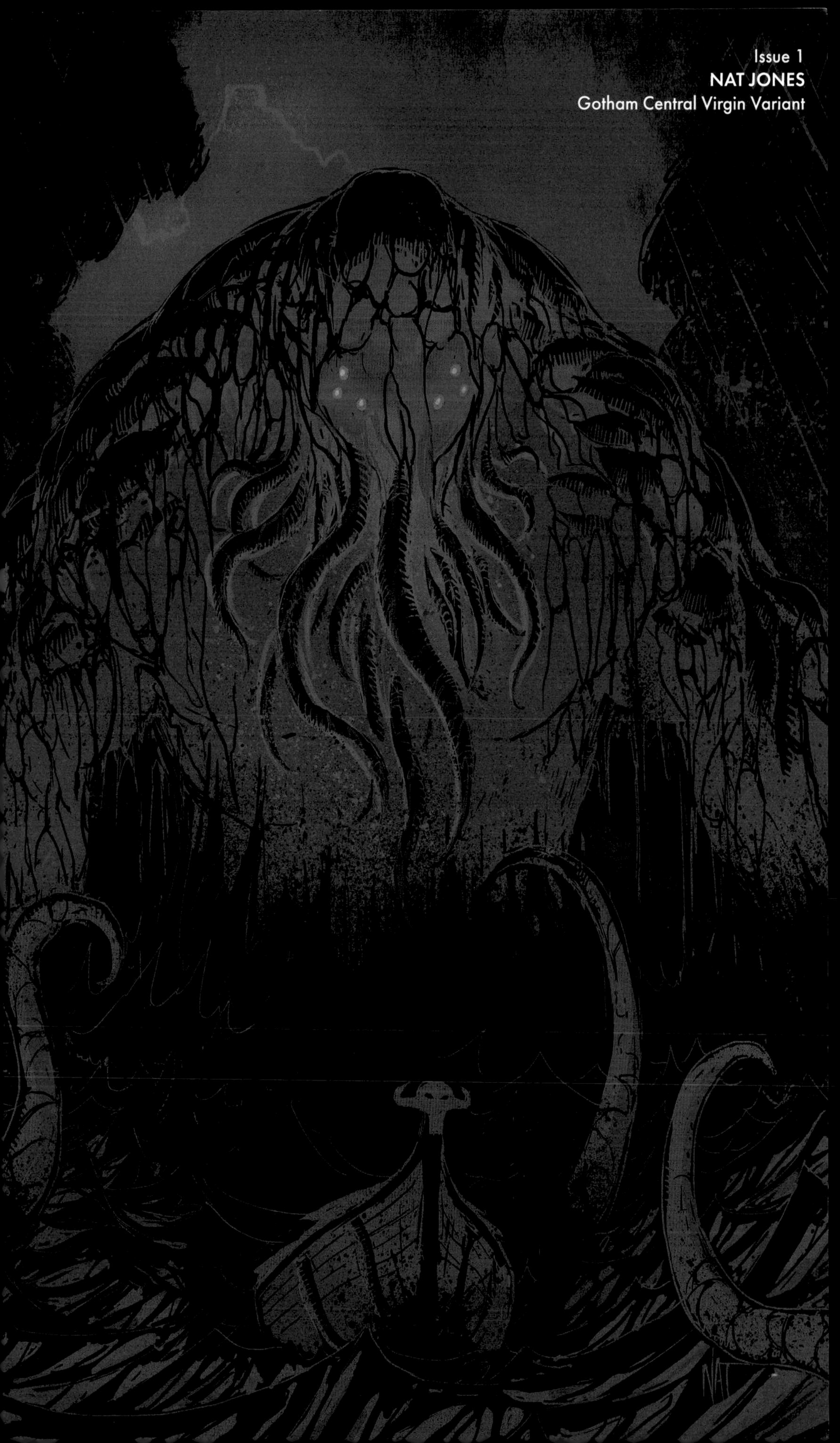

Issue 1
NAT JONES
Gotham Central Virgin Variant

Issue 1
MIKE ROOTH
More Great Art Variant

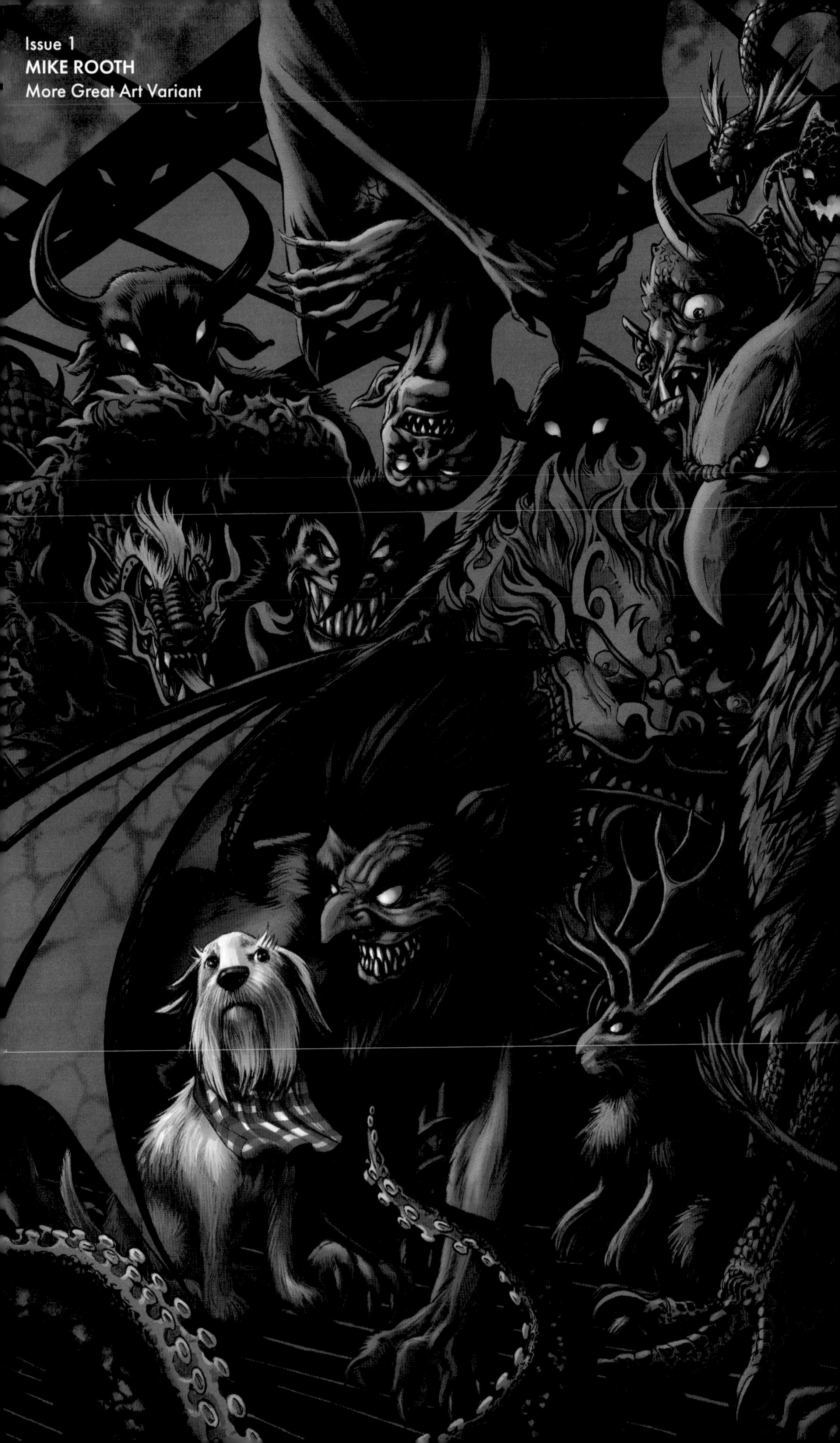

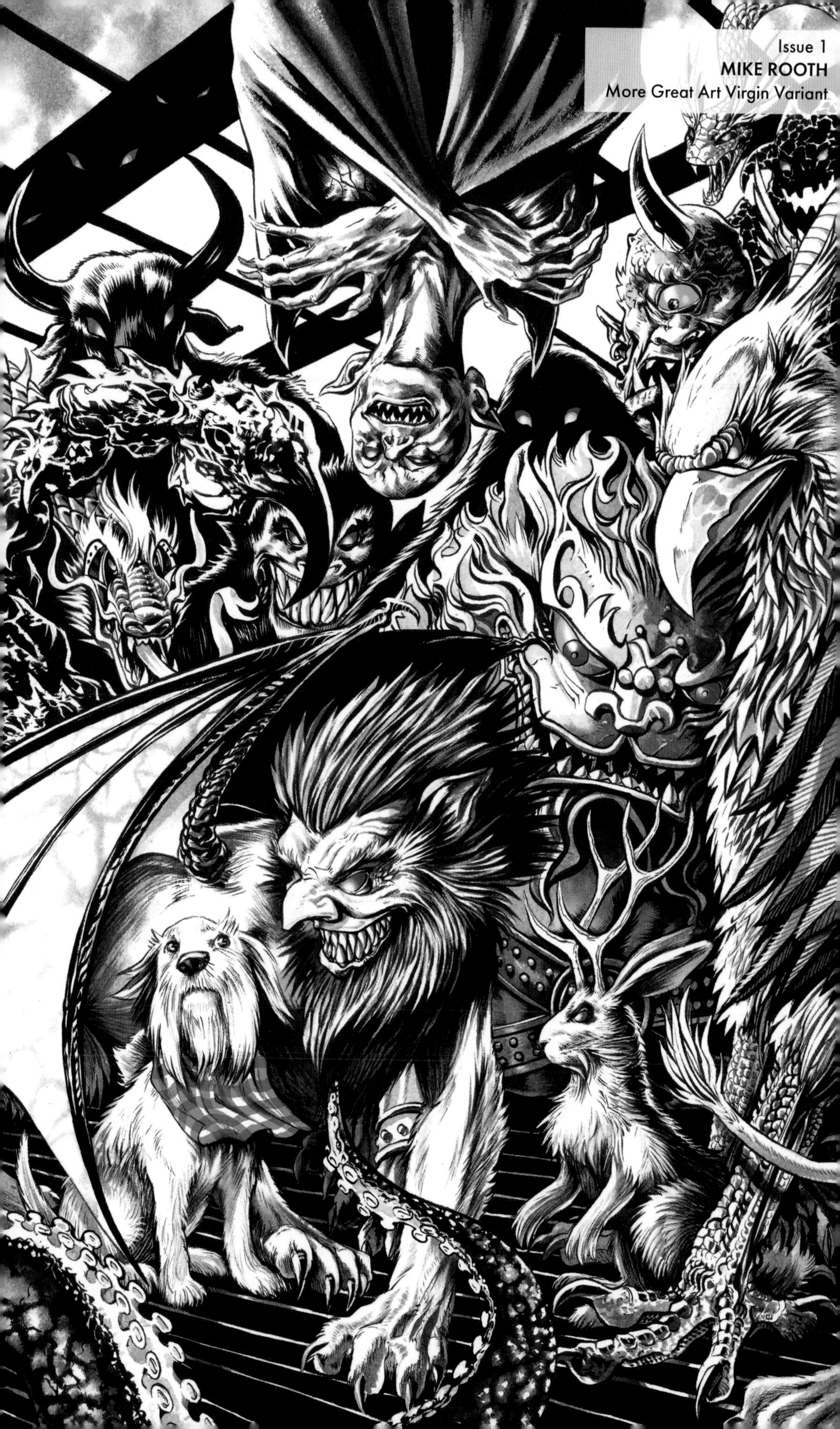

Issue 1
MIKE ROOTH
More Great Art Virgin Variant

Issue 1
BEN TEMPLESMITH
Sad Lemon Variant

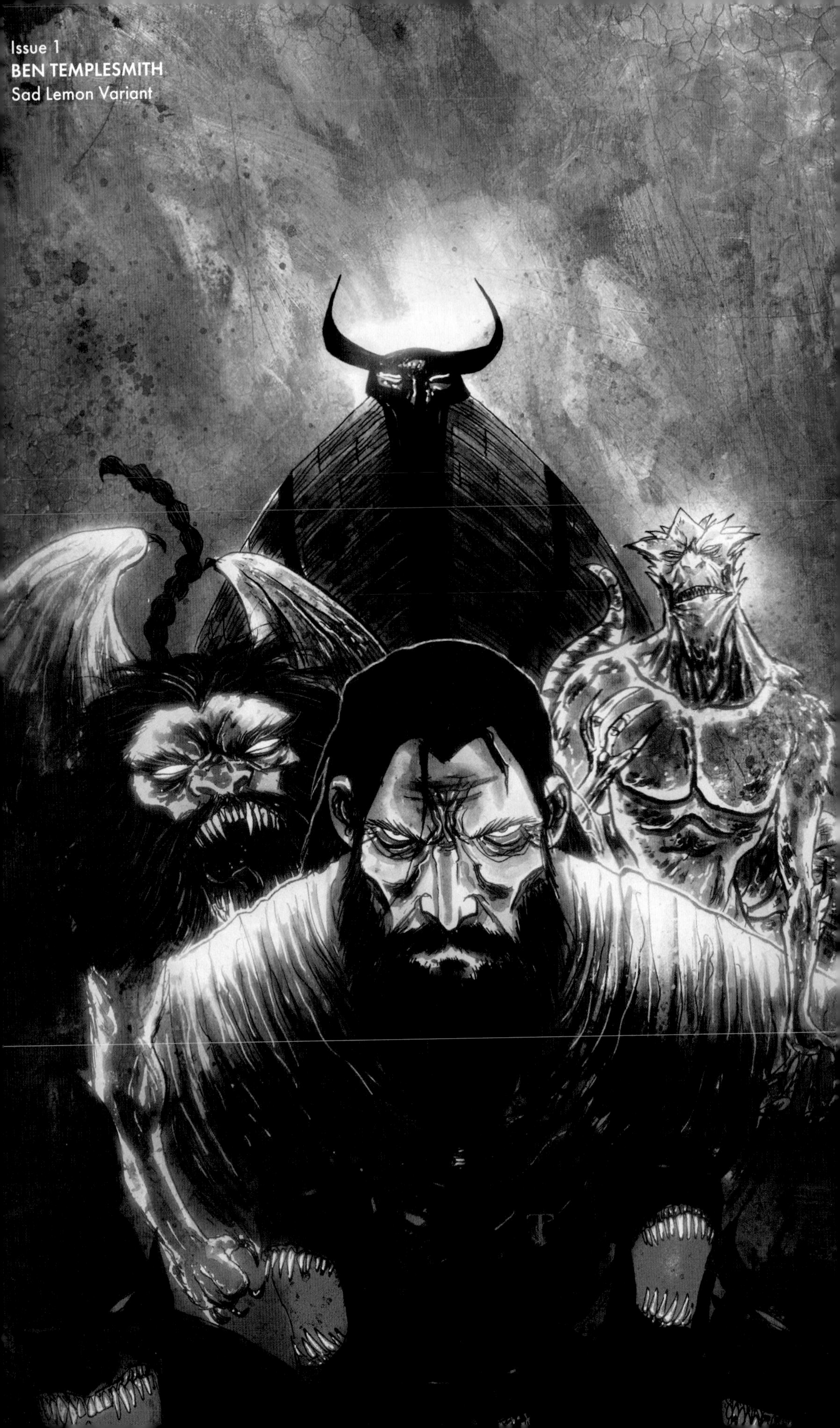

Issue 1
ALESSANDRO VITTI
Scott's Collectibles Variant

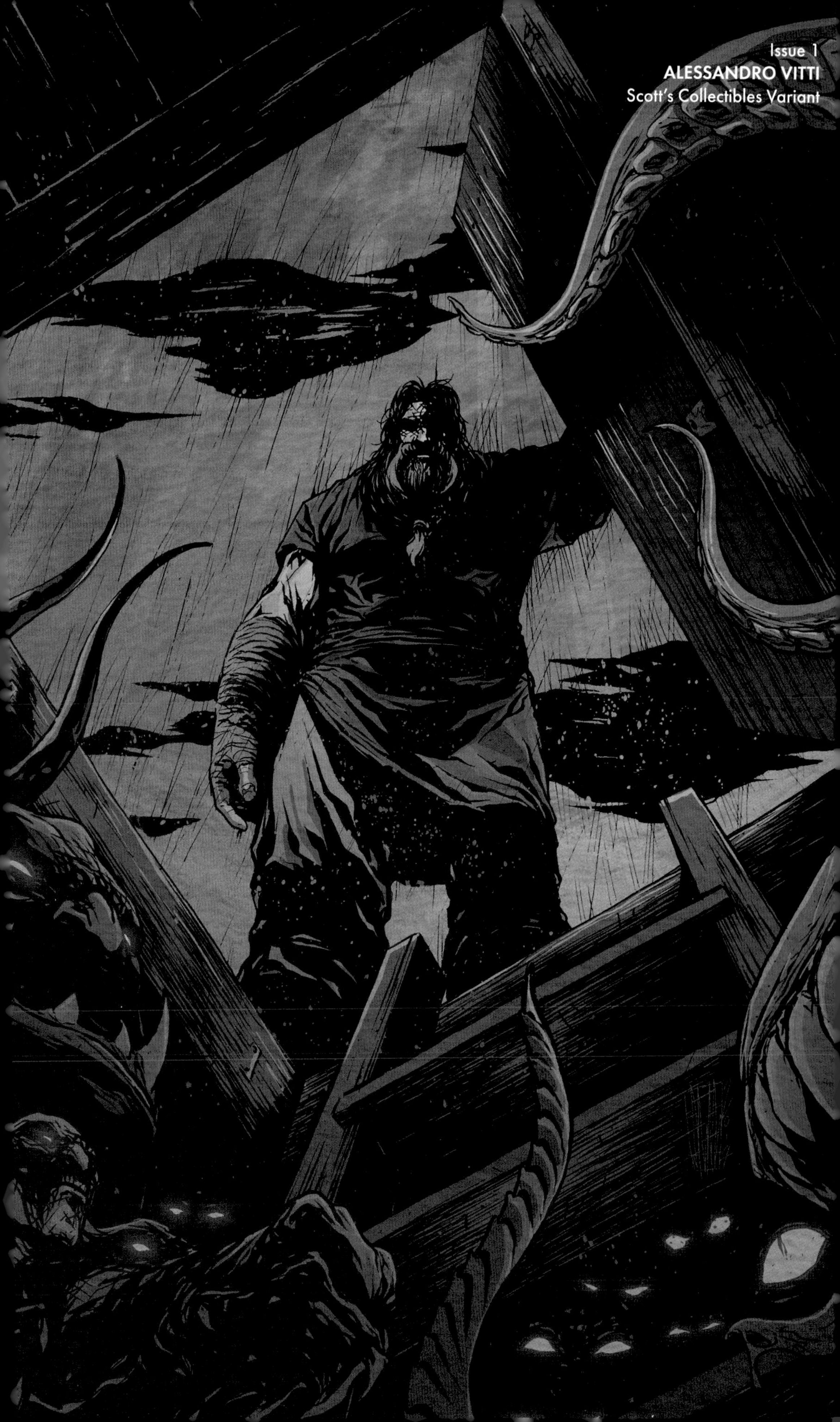

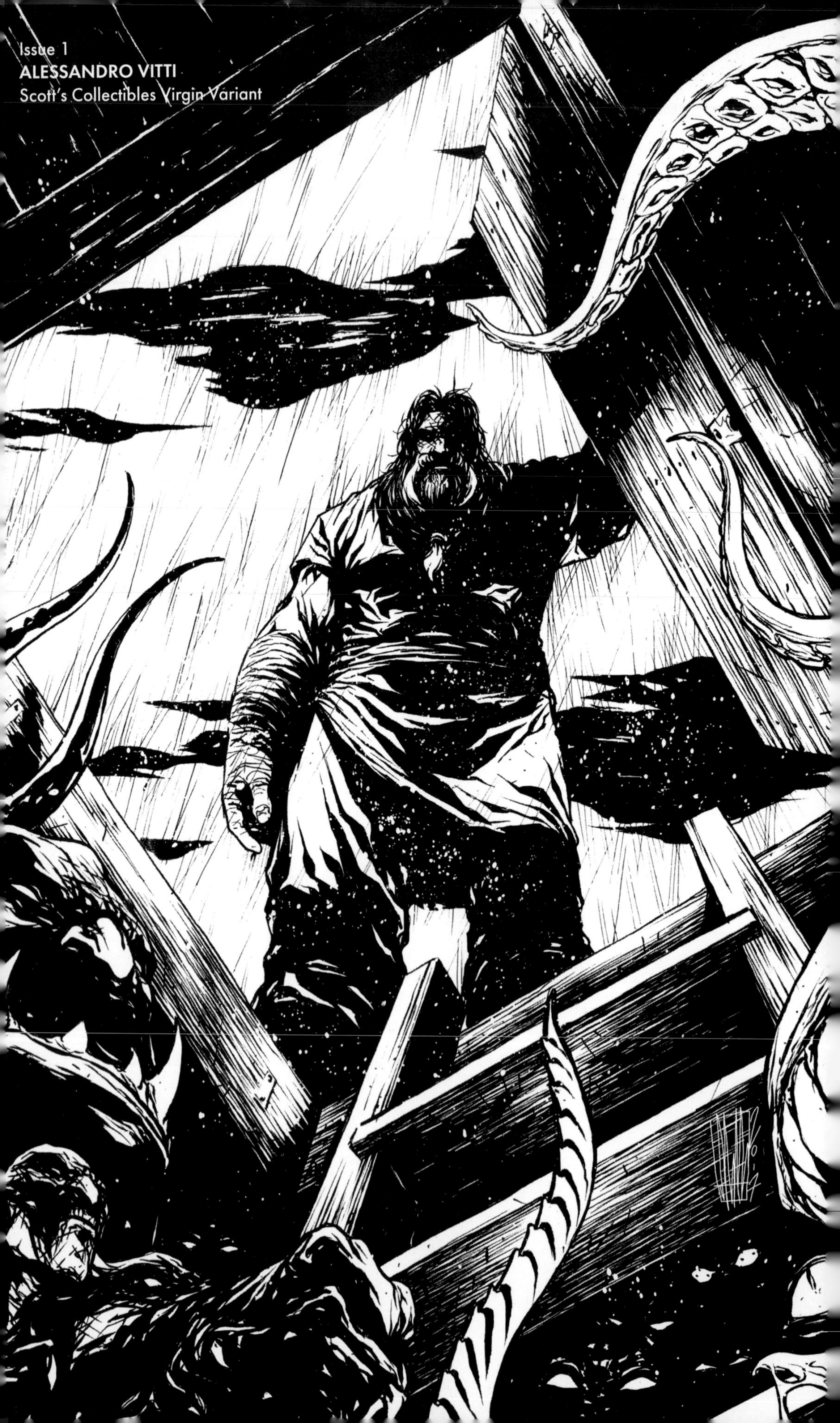

Issue 1
ALESSANDRO VITTI
Scott's Collectibles Virgin Variant

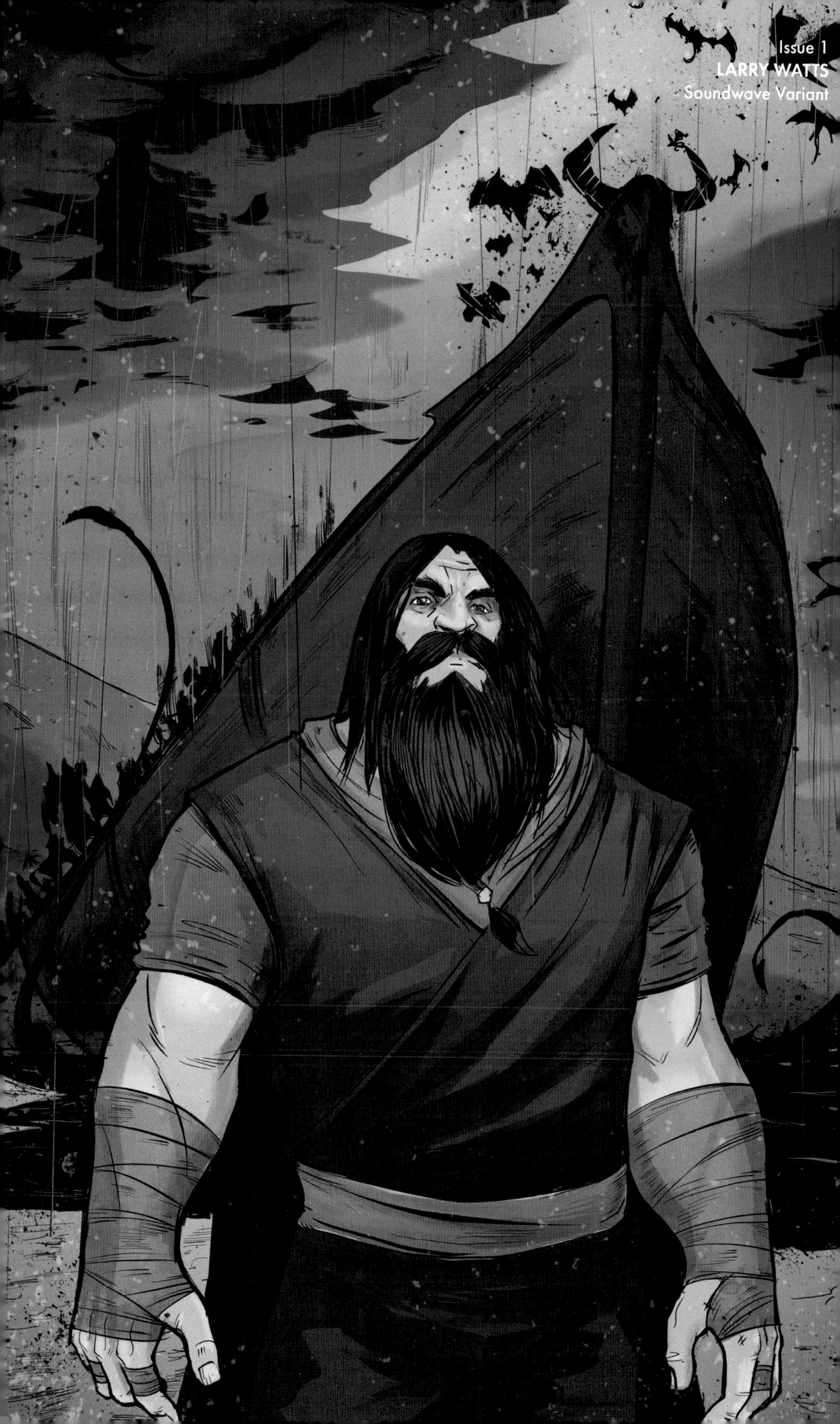
Issue 1
LARRY WATTS
Soundwave Variant

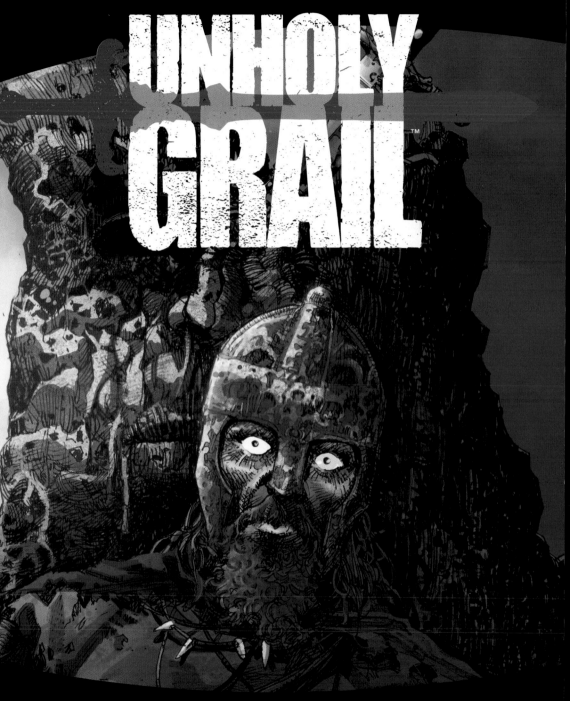

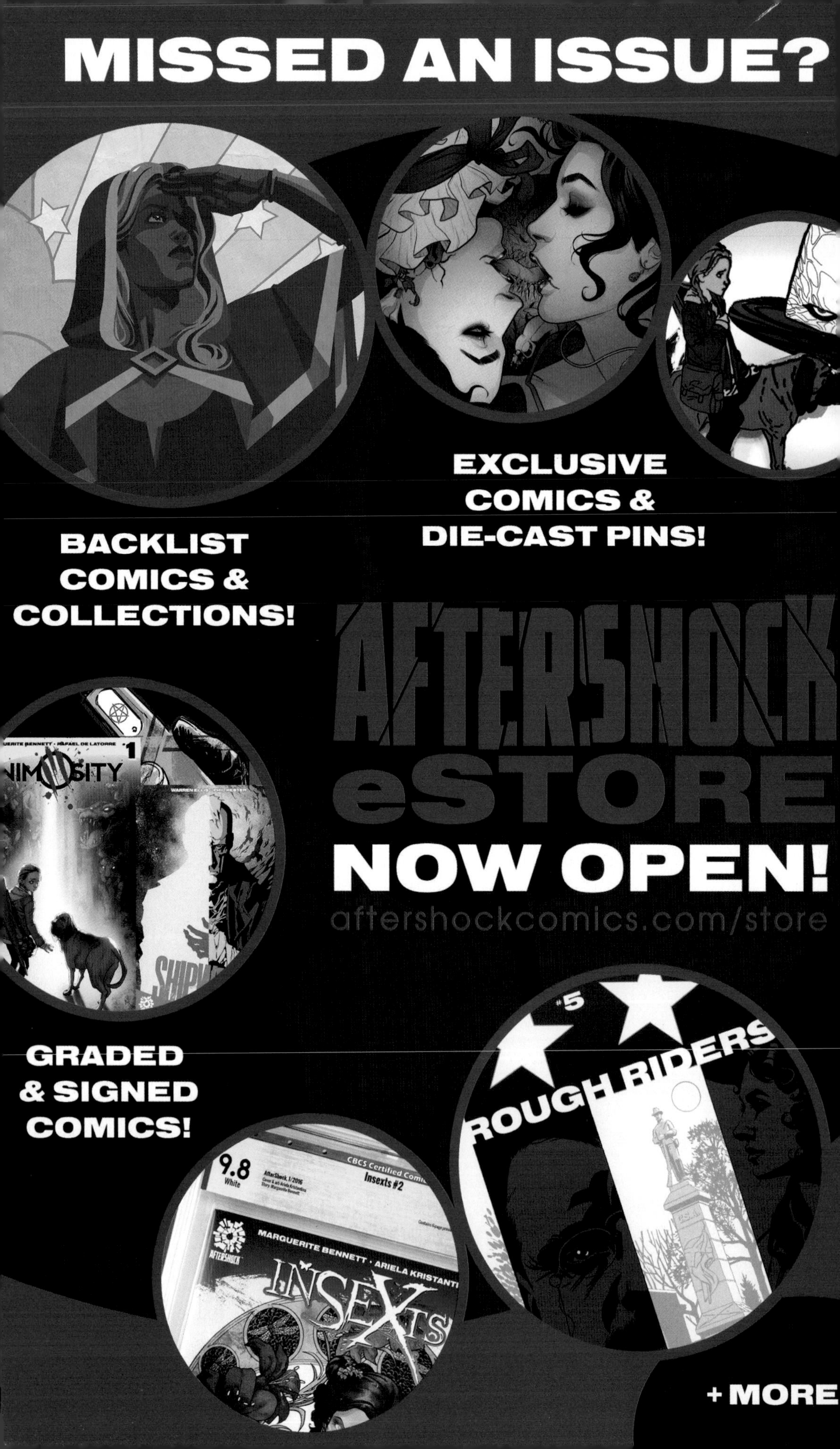
MISSED AN ISSUE?
BACKLIST COMICS & COLLECTIONS!
EXCLUSIVE COMICS & DIE-CAST PINS!
AFTERSHOCK eSTORE
NOW OPEN!
aftershockcomics.com/store
GRADED & SIGNED COMICS!
9.8
White
CBCS Certified Comic
Insexts #2
MARGUERITE BENNETT · ARIELA KRISTANTI
INSEXTS
#5
ROUGH RIDERS
+ MORE

CHECK OUT THESE GREAT AFTERSHOCK
COLLECTIONS!

ABOUT THE
CREATORS OF

DARK ARK

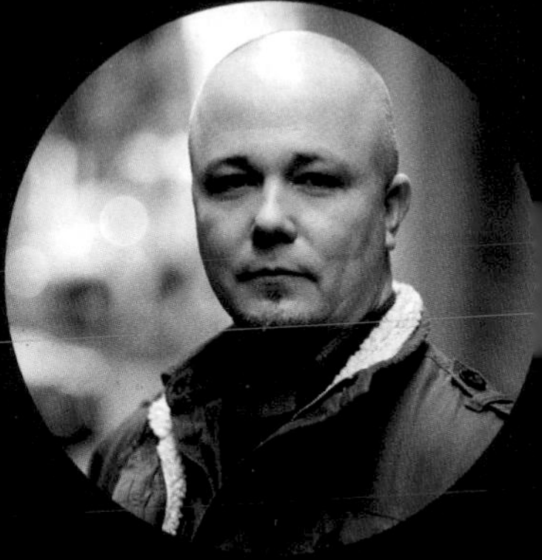

CULLEN BUNN writer

@CullenBunn

Cullen is the writer of such creator-owned comics as *The Sixth Gun, The Damned, Harrow County* and *Regression*. In addition, he writes *X-Men Blue, Monsters Unleashed* and numerous *Deadpool* comics for Marvel.

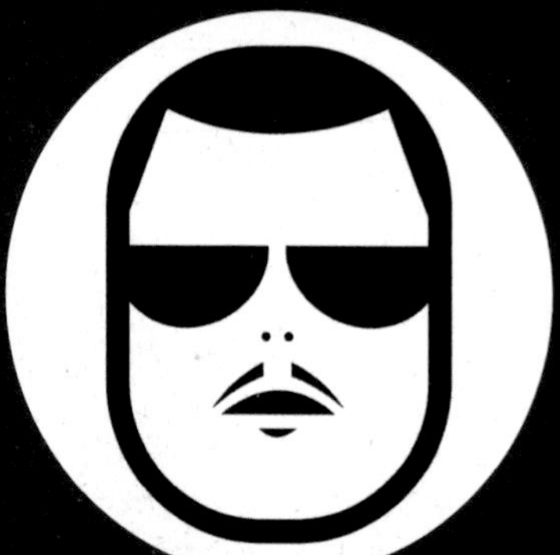

JUAN DOE artist

@juandoe

Juan Doe is a professional illustrator with over ten years experience in the comic book industry. He has produced over a hundred covers and his sequential highlights include the *Fantastic Four in Puerto Rico* trilogy, *The Legion of Monsters* mini-series for Marvel and *Joker's Asylum: Scarecrow* for DC. He has illustrated AMERICAN MONSTER, WORLD READER, ANIMOSITY: THE RISE and now DARK ARK for AfterShock Comics.

RYANE HILL letterer

@Ryane_Hill

Ryane Hill is a native Californian living with her husband and two French Bulldogs in the beautiful Pacific Northwest. After years of working in the background as a production assistant, and gaining experience with both lettering and design, she is extremely excited to have the opportunity to work with AfterShock Comics on ALTERS and DARK ARK.

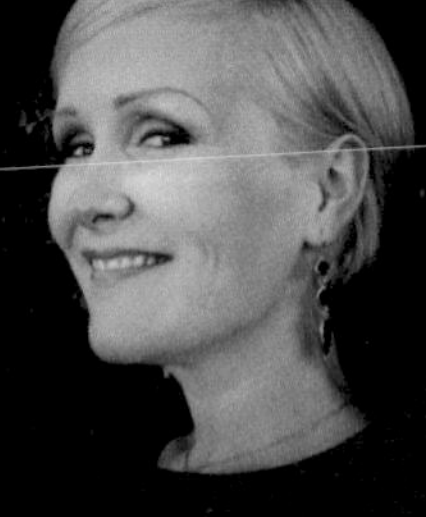

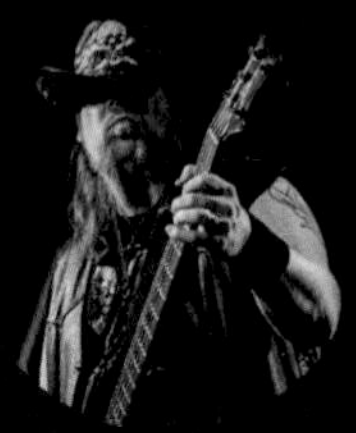

DAVE SHARPE letterer

@DaveLSharpe

Dave grew up a HUGE metalhead, living on Long Island, NY while spending summers in Tallahassee, FL. After reading *Micronauts* (and many other comics), Dave knew he had to have a career in the business. Upon graduating from the Joe Kubert School in 1990, he went on to work at Marvel Comics as an in-house letterer, eventually running their lettering department in the late 90s and early 00s. Over the years, Dave has lettered hundreds of comics, such as *Spider-Girl, Exiles, She-Hulk* and *The Defenders* for Marvel, and *Green Lantern, Harley Quinn, Sinestro* and *Batgirl* for DC Comics. Dave now works on both *X-O Manowar* and *Faith* for Valiant Comics in addition to his lettering duties on AfterShock's *The Revisionist*. Dave also plays bass and is way more approachable than he looks.